Contemporary Issues in Thematic Apperceptive Methods

Contemporary Issues in Thematic Apperceptive Methods

Edited by

JEROME KAGAN, Ph.D.
Chairman, Department of Psychology
Fels Research Institute
Antioch College
Yellow Springs, Ohio

and

GERALD S. LESSER, Ph.D.
Associate Professor, Educational Clinic
Hunter College of the City of New York
New York City

GREENWOOD PRESS, PUBLISHERS
WESTPORT, CONNECTICUT

Library of Congress Cataloging in Publication Data

Conference on Contemporary Issues in Thematic Apperceptive Methods, Fels Research Institute, 1959.
Contemporary issues in thematic apperceptive methods.

Reprint of the ed. published by Thomas, Springfield.
Includes bibliographies and indexes.
1. Thematic apperception test--Congresses.
I. Kagan, Jerome. II. Lesser, Gerald S.
III. Title.
[BF698.8.T5C66 1959a] 155.2'844 76-7536
ISBN 0-8371-8842-3

Originally published in 1961 by Charles C. Thomas, Publisher, Springfield, Ill.

Reprinted with the permission of Charles C. Thomas, Publisher

Reprinted in 1976 by Greenwood Press,
a division of Williamhouse-Regency Inc.

Library of Congress Catalog Card Number 76-7536

ISBN 0-8371-8842-3

Printed in the United States of America

MEMBERS OF THE CONFERENCE ON CONTEMPORARY ISSUES IN THEMATIC APPERCEPTIVE METHODS

JOHN W. ATKINSON, PH.D., *Associate Professor of Psychology, University of Michigan*

SEYMOUR FESHBACH, PH.D., *Associate Professor of Psychology, University of Pennsylvania*

WILLIAM E. HENRY, PH.D., *Professor of Psychology and Human Development, University of Chicago*

ROBERT R. HOLT, PH.D., *Professor of Psychology and Director, Research Center for Mental Health, New York University*

JEROME KAGAN, PH.D., *Chairman, Department of Psychology, Fels Research Institute, Yellow Springs, Ohio*

DOUGLAS T. KENNY, PH.D., *Associate Professor of Psychology, University of British Columbia, Vancouver, Canada*

RICHARD S. LAZARUS, PH.D., *Professor of Psychology, University of California, Berkeley*

GERALD S. LESSER, PH.D., *Associate Professor, Educational Clinic, Hunter College of the City of New York*

BERNARD I. MURSTEIN, PH.D., *Associate Professor of Psychology, and Coordinator of Research, University of Portland, Portland, Oregon*

PAUL H. MUSSEN, PH.D., *Associate Professor of Psychology, University of California, Berkeley*

KENNETH PURCELL, PH.D., *Senior Research Psychologist, Jewish National Home for Asthmatic Children at Denver*

JULIAN B. ROTTER, PH.D., *Professor of Psychology, The Ohio State University*

EDWIN S. SHNEIDMAN, PH.D., *Co-Principal Investigator, Central Research Unit, Veterans Administration Center, Los Angeles, California; and Research Associate, University of Southern California*

IRVING E. SIGEL, PH.D., *Chairman of Research, The Merrill-Palmer School, Detroit, Michigan*

SILVAN S. TOMKINS, PH.D., *Professor of Psychology, Princeton University*

JOSEPH VEROFF, PH.D., *Study Director, Survey Research Center, and Assistant Professor of Psychology, University of Michigan*

PREFACE

One of the major obstacles to systematic and substantial progress in the social sciences is the immaturity of our methods of measurement. This is especially true in the area of personality measurement. Psychologists have proliferated some plausible hypotheses about personality functioning from which relevant behavioral predictions have been deduced. However, when decisions are made about the type of instruments to be used in evaluating the hypothesis, we often must choose from three types of data-gathering devices — questionnaires, interviews, and projective methods. The first two techniques are ordinarily less suspect than projective measures because they contain a certain amount of content validity. If a large sample of subjects is asked, "Do you like your mother more than your father?" and significantly more yes's than no's are obtained, it is safe to conclude that, in general, people profess to like their mothers more than their fathers. Students of personality, however, are usually interested in processes which either are not available to conscious verbal report or are subject to both conscious and unconscious distortion under direct questioning. Thus, techniques which might evade the individual's watchful censor were bound to develop. In the last quarter century, a great many projective instruments have made their way into clinics and laboratories. Use of these techniques has characteristically involved the assumption that the subject's response to the task reflects wishes, conflicts, and preoccupations that represent unconscious material which many subjects may view as dangerous to reveal.

As with any new instrument, enthusiasm ran high. Anecdotal evidence supported the wish that these instruments provided some solution to the methodological dead end that characterized personality measurement in psychology. As more rigorous research evidence accumulated, it gradually became clear that we did not completely understand the inner workings of these instruments. It became obvious that unknown and unsuspected variables were playing a vital role in the individual's responses to these stimuli. We clearly needed a theory about how these instruments worked, in addition to theories about the personality that responded to the "projective" stimuli.

It was this conclusion that motivated the planning of the present conference. By convening a group of psychologists who were engaged in research on the problems associated with one technique, we hoped to gain some insight into the laws governing projective test behavior. We chose to concentrate on apperceptive methods rather than projective tests in general for several reasons. First, it seemed that the response processes required by different projective devices were not psychologically homogeneous. When an individual is given a TAT card he is asked to "Make up a story" about the card; when he is handed a Rorschach ink blot he is instructed to "Tell what it looks like." These different instructions (setting aside for the moment the differences in stimulus material) elicit markedly different cognitive sets in the individual. The request to "Make up a story" implies that the subject ignore the individual, discrete objects depicted in the stimulus. It obligates the individual to integrate the separate objects into an action sequence and to assign motives, emotions, and action to the perceived objects. The Rorschach instruction, "What does it look like?" engages a different cognitive set. It suggests to the subject that he describe what he sees rather than functionally interrelate the separate stimulus objects into a narrative. It is quite likely that much different verbal material would be obtained if the instructions to these two tests were reversed and the examiner asked for a TAT card, "Tell me what it looks like," and for the Rorschach, "Tell me what is happening on the ink blot."

Thus, it should not be surprising that apperceptive instruments have produced a specific vocabulary which has no analogue in other tests. The concepts of the hero, needs and presses, transcendence, motive ambiguous and motive nonambiguous stimuli are samples of the constructs that only have primary relevance for apperceptive methods and are not fundamental to the other projective methods. Thus, communication should be facilitated if a group of psychologists addressed itself to a homogeneous class of instruments that appeared to involve the same type of interpretive behavior.

A second reason for choosing the apperceptive method is its record of predictive and construct validity. Careful evaluation of published work leads to the conclusion that variables coded from "stories to pictures" have fared better in the validity arena than variables derived from any other projective test. Ignore, for the moment, differences in the theoretical rationales that authors have used to explain their results. Apperceptive variables have shown significant correlations with such disparate behaviors as changes in intelligence quotient, level of aspiration, overt aggression, conformity, leadership in a group, grades in school, and anxiety over sexuality.

These individual correlations are far from perfect and individual prediction from apperceptive stories is still a dangerous procedure. Moreover, in many cases we are not sure *why* these correlations occurred, because we are unable to specify the cognitive events that transpire between the presentation of the stimulus and the verbal production of the story. We have long since acknowledged that all stories are not projections of the individual and the term projective technique is an anachronism. Hopefully, the papers in this volume will shed some light on the nature of thematic behavior.

THE ISSUES

The Story as a Response. Despite the many years of work with apperceptive instruments, we still do not understand the nature of the psychological events occurring when a person tells a story to a picture. It was the hope of Murray and other early investigators that the story was somewhat isomorphic with a daydream or reverie and thus the term fantasy appeared to be an appropriate label to apply to this verbal product. In the first paper in this volume, Dr. Holt carefully analyzes the important differences between a reverie or fantasy, on the one hand, and a story to a picture. His analysis forces us to recognize that a story is not at all like a daydream and that it is fallacious to defend this premise.

Dr. Richard Lazarus offers two principles which he believes determine the content of a story — a principle of substitution and one of defense. Dr. Lazarus suggests that references to motives which are not gratified in overt behavior are more likely to occur in the story than motives which do find gratification in the environment. Hence the term substitution is used. The principle of defense suggests that if the motive intensity is too high, anxiety will be aroused and the motive content will not appear in the story. The presence of a motive in a story indicates that it is not being gratified and is not a source of intense anxiety.

Measurement of Motives through Stories. Initially, the major interest in apperceptive stories lay in their assumed link to motives. Murray's list of need variables was the almanac to which many clinicians and researchers turned when they interpreted story material. McClelland, Atkinson, Veroff, and their colleagues have continued to work within this motive framework. They do not assume that strength of motive and story content have a direct and simple relationship with each other. However, their work is guided by the implicit assumption that the content of a person's verbal products bears a lawful relation to the intensity of his motives and they hope to discover the exact nature of this relationship. Since a TAT story is one convenient way of obtaining a language sample under controlled stimulus conditions, the apperceptive method is frequently used by this group. Dr. Joseph Veroff's paper on the results of a nationwide survey of achievement motive measures is an example of this approach.

Dr. Seymour Feshbach raises a crucial issue for the understanding of an apperceptive story and its potential for the measurement of motive variables. Working from Dr. Neal Miller's model for approach and avoidance gradients, Feshbach emphasizes the role of conflict upon story production. An extreme view of the role of conflict would hold that if a motive is believed to be associated with a source of anxiety, then the anxiety may elicit inhibiting or defensive responses which may alter the content of the story. It is possible, therefore, to defend the statement that it is extremely difficult to measure motive intensity from any aspect of a person's contemporaneous behavior. This issue is of paramount importance. Contemporary psychology is very dependent upon the use of motivational variables and yet it has not developed a valid method for their assessment.

Stylistic Variables. Although the coding of motivational content has been the most popular approach to story material, there has always been a minority who concentrated on "how the story was told" as opposed to "what was told." During recent years there has been a rapidly accelerated interest in variables related to styles of perceiving and styles of language expression. The evidence strongly suggests that story material is a valuable clue to a person's style of thinking. Dr. Edwin Shneidman directs our attention to the logic of the story for indices of psychopathological processes.

Dr. Jerome Kagan concentrates on one specific stylistic variable — the tendency to ascribe affect states to TAT figures. He demonstrates that this response tendency is quite stable over time, shows intra-individual consistency over a variety of instruments, and is related to the tendency to verbalize motives and conflicts.

The Stimulus. An early error made by many clinicians involved the assumption that the TAT picture was sufficiently vague and ambiguous that its manifest perceptual meanings could be ignored in the evaluation of the story content. This is one of the more serious errors that has been made in the history of psychological methods. Study after study has demonstrated that the objective nature of the picture dictates much of the content and prediction can be improved if the ambiguity of the stimulus, for specific contents, is carefully assessed. Moreover, some contents, aggression for example, have different predictive significance if they occur to an ambiguous stimulus than if they are associated with a stimulus which does not suggest the content in question. Dr. Bernard Murstein reviews the array of existing research on the role of the stimulus and suggests the ways it may influence the story response. He proposes a method for conceptualizing the diverse empirical evidence regarding the role of the stimulus.

Dr. Douglas Kenny presents a provocative model for story analysis which places emphasis on the person's initial categorization of the stimulus. Dr. Kenny suggests that the individual first categorizes the stimulus. The rest of the story is primarily influenced by the schemata that are elicited by the initial categorization response. This approach has important theoretical and research implications which are elaborated by Dr. Kenny in his paper.

The discussions during the sessions were lively and pointed. Three issues repeatedly claimed the spotlight. The question of whether stories can indirectly or directly reflect motives was debated continually. The papers on stylistic variables directed the group's attention to the definition of a style and the relation between motives and styles. The role of stimulus pull, the scalability of motivational variables, and the role of conflict also provoked important discussion.

We decided, therefore, to present edited sections of the discussion following each formal presentation. The standard format included initial remarks by the primary discussant followed by general group discussion.

The primary discussant's comments are presented in full but only a small and edited fraction of the group discussion is included.

It is hoped that this volume helps to clarify some of the major issues associated with the use of apperceptive stimuli. Considering the paucity of sensitive techniques in psychology, any methodological advance is to be cherished.

The conference was supported by a research grant (M-2884) from the National Institutes of Mental Health, United States Public Health Service. The detailed arrangements for the meetings and the preparation of the manuscript were smoothly and skillfully handled by Leah Johnson to whom we owe a large debt of gratitude. Finally, we would like to express our appreciation to Drs. Lester W. Sontag, John I. Lacey, and Stanley M. Garn for their encouragement and advice during all phases of the conference.

J.K.
G.S.L.

Yellow Springs, Ohio

CONTENTS

Contemporary Issues
in
Thematic Apperceptive Methods

THE NATURE OF TAT STORIES AS COGNITIVE PRODUCTS: A PSYCHOANALYTIC APPROACH[1]

Robert R. Holt, Ph.D.
Research Center for Mental Health
New York University

RECENTLY reading a draft of Gardner Lindzey's forthcoming SSRC monograph on projective techniques, I was surprised at the grounds on which he criticized theoretical writings about the Rorschach and TAT, including Rapaport (43) and Schafer (44). No author to date, says Lindzey, has applied psychoanalytic theory to the understanding of such tests in more than a partial or fragmentary way. When I saw him not long ago, I challenged him on this point. "Why should or how could all of the great sprawling corpus of psychoanalytic theory be applied to the rationale of, for example, the TAT?" I asked him; "Isn't it reasonable and standard scientific procedure to take only those aspects of a theory that are directly relevant, when we conceptualize a kind of phenomenon?" Thus, I argued, we don't call on hydrodynamics nor quantum theory to conceptualize the stresses and strains in a bridge with a certain construction and a certain load. Dr. Lindzey didn't accept my analogy. A slice of behavior as big and rich as a TAT, he rejoined, is in no way as circumscribed as a problem in mechanics; it's more like taking a certain house and asking what physical concepts are needed to deal with all the physical phenomena contained in it. As we talked, he convinced me that any aspect of psychoanalysis I mentioned could be useful or involved somehow in the rationale of the TAT.

[1]I wish to express my gratitude to Drs. H. A. Murray, David Rapaport and Roy Schafer for careful reading of the manuscript and valuable suggestions. I also want to acknowledge my indebtedness to the parallel discussions of these issues by Dr. Leopold Bellak (3,4).

Therefore, my first and most grandiose conception of what I might talk about here was nothing less than a complete metapsychological treatment of TAT rationale, bringing to bear on the problem the five points of view that Rapaport and Gill have described. In a weak moment I sent our chairman the title: A metapsychological reconsideration of TAT rationale. Naturally, to live up to the title turned out to be entirely too ambitious; I discovered that I could either give it a quick five-minute rubdown or else work it for years, but nothing manageable in between. I still think the job should be done, and I hope someday to do it. Today, however, I'll content myself with a brief sketch of what a metapsychological treatment might include, and then concentrate on a small corner of the problem.

In a paper presented not long ago, although as yet unpublished, Rapaport and Gill (42) carefully reconsider the nature of metapsychology — the meta-theory of psychoanalysis. Freud had originally said that a complete (that is, metapsychological) theoretical treatment of a phenomenon from a psychoanalytic standpoint required its discussion from three points of view: dynamic, economic and topographic. Rapaport and Gill have expanded and revised this to include *five* metapsychological points of view, which are clearly implied by the development of psychoanalysis. They are the dynamic, economic, structural, genetic, and adaptive points of view.

"The dynamic point of view demands that the psychoanalytic explanation of any psychological phenomenon include propositions concerning the psychological forces involved in the phenomenon." This refers most generally to the fact that behavior is motivated, and more specifically to the proposition that specific motivational forces are largely responsible for the production of the kind of material that appears in a TAT story. The concept of wish-fulfillment is a dynamic concept: that dreams and fantasies, and to a limited extent TAT stories, are dynamically shaped so as to represent a state of affairs in which needs are gratified. Further discussion of the dynamic point of view would include categorization of the forces and their modes of action, as this bears upon story production.

"The economic point of view demands that the psychoanalytic

explanation of any psychological phenomenon include propositions concerning the psychological energy involved in the phenomenon." This entails the conception that cognitive processes consist of "ideas" that are cathected by quanta of drive energy, and which may be hypercathected — the theoretical operation corresponding to consciousness. The concepts of neutralization of energy and bound versus mobile cathexis are essentially economic ones; together with propositions dealing with transformations of psychological energy, these make up the theoretical core of the concepts of primary and secondary process, which comprise the basic psychoanalytic groundwork of a theory of thinking. The economic point of view applied to an understanding of TAT stories, then, would attempt to spell out in process terms the microdevelopment of the ideas and the energic considerations that determine the primary or secondary process nature of the finished thought product. This would amount to a rather long chapter in the metapsychological discussion.

"The structural point of view demands that the psychoanalytic explanation of any psychological phenomenon include propositions concerning the enduring psychological organizations involved in the phenomenon." Here would be probably the longest chapter, for a great variety of psychological structures must be hypothesized to account for cognitive functioning. Hartmann (22) has divided these into two great groups: the apparatuses of primary autonomy and the apparatuses of secondary autonomy. The former are the inborn structures that make possible perception, learning, memory, thinking, feeling, abilities, and action. The apparatuses of primary autonomy are developed by evolution, are inherited and develop largely through maturation. The apparatuses of secondary autonomy are developed by learning. They include defenses, memory traces, ego identity, habits, interests and adult motives. Besides such a catalog of types of structures involved in TAT stories, the structural point of view applied to this problem would modify and enrich the description of process begun from the economic point of view, showing how the developing thought is guided, molded, and steered by psychic structures, many of which leave their characteristic imprint on the finished product.

"The genetic point of view demands that the psychoanalytic explanation of any psychological phenomenon include propositions concerning its origin and history." Under this heading falls the entire psychoanalytic theory of development, which would have to be invoked to explain the emergence of much content (and also to explain the process of making genetic interpretations). The genetic point of view also calls for an understanding of TAT stories in terms of the development of thinking generally and the development specifically of fantasy and its expression in play and story telling.

Finally, "the adaptive point of view demands that the psychoanalytic explanation of any psychological phenomenon include propositions concerning its relationship to the environment." This is the last of the major developments of ego psychology, and was given its major expression in Hartmann's 1939 monograph (22), on ego psychology and the problem of adaptation. Under this heading we would have to consider the role of the society and culture within which the story telling is taking place, and specifically the influence of the immediate situation and setting. Taking a TAT is part of some adaptive pattern, such as getting help for mental illness, applying for a job or matriculation in a training program, earning money as a subject in an experiment, etc. All of these matters affect the stories and the way that they are told. The subject also has to adapt himself to the examiner and what he says, particularly the *instructions.* The latter, together with the picture, pose a specific adaptive task: the subject has to make up a story using the picture. The term "story" has meaning to him depending on his past participation in his culture, and his contact with all manner of tales, from nursery books and comic strips on up to novels and avant garde short stories. (This is of course bringing in partly genetic and partly structural considerations, since what the subject has learned in the course of his development, we assume, is recorded in structural trace organizations or schemata, which affect the on-going thought process.) The test situation, the instructions and the pictures are a reality which the subject must perceive. Psychoanalytic theory emphasizes the reality-concept aspect of this (the degree to which perception is veridical and complete) and the reality testing aspect (the extent to which reality is distinguished from fantasy, dream, or other internally produced ideas). These considerations of the adaptive point of view, we shall see, are crucial in distinguishing fantasies from TAT stories.

I realize that what I have said has been very general, but I hope it will give some idea of the range and complexity of contemporary psychoanalytic theory and the variety of considerations that theory brings to bear on the analysis of any particular phenomenon, like telling a TAT story. In the rest of this paper, I have concentrated my efforts on the question of just what kind of cognitive-affective product a TAT story is, and in particular, to what extent it may be said to be a fantasy.

The first publication on the TAT was a paper by Christiana D. Morgan and Henry A. Murray in 1935, boldly entitled: A Method for Investigating Fantasy (33). It would be easy to cite many passages in that paper and in later publications (35) where they used the terms interchangeably or spoke of "stories (fantasies)."[2] Since then, many others have written about the TAT and related techniques, and have very frequently referred to them as methods of studying fantasy (1, 2, 23, 28, 31, 49). I just looked through the indices of the last ten years of the Psychological Abstracts under the heading, *fantasy,* and have been surprised to find that a great majority of the American references — except for psychoanalytic, clinical contributions — have been papers on the TAT and related thematic tests.

[2]Today, Murray comments: " 'A method for investigating fantasy' meant, of course, a method of educing story constructions which are susceptible of interpretation in terms of fantasies (largely unconscious). In 1936 what we had in mind for the TAT was to reveal (through interpretation) the kind of material—semi-conscious and unconscious imaginations—that analysts were dealing with. Fantasy was the only available, generally-accepted, word. The stories, according to our hypothesis, were not fantasies themselves but were molded or shaped by fantasies, *to some extent. But even here* it is hard to draw a sharp line, since most story-composers are aware of more or less vivid images and *imagents* (imagined events) preceding or accompanying their spoken or written words. Fantasy, in my lingo, is an involuntary, undirected stream of images and imagents. Story composition is based on this, but involves direction (say, the intent to write a comic story and hence a little mental magnet attracting influxions of potentially comic elements), and evaluations of these influxions. rejections of some, acceptances of others, etc., etc." (Murray, 1959) I am most grateful to Dr. Murray for this clarifying statement and for his permission to quote it.

Should we assume, then, that the word *fantasy* means nothing more nor less than a TAT story? Usage would not really support that conclusion, and of course the idea of the TAT as a test of fantasy would be a complete tautology. Let's see what the excellent recent psychological dictionary of English and English has to say about fantasy: "imagining a complex object or event in concrete symbols or images, whether or not the object or event exists; or the symbols or images themselves: e.g., a daydream. — Fantasy is usually pleasant and represents a sort of wish fulfillment. Originally synonymous with imagination, it is now distinguished by the fact that, if it represents reality at all, it is whimsical or visionary, not primarily either constructive or reproductive. Yet it is not necessarily delusive or pathological. Freud made distinction between dreams of fantasy and those showing dream work." A fantasy, then, seems to be a daydream; let's look at the definition of that term: "a reverie while awake. — Usually the unfulfilled wishes of the dreamer are imagined as fulfilled. Wishes are not disguised and fulfillment is imagined as direct, without repression. Daydreaming is not inherently pathological." So a daydream seems to be a reverie! English and English define reverie as: "a state in which the train of thought or of images is little directed purposively, and in which one is relatively insensible to external happenings. — Reverie may have a single coherent object but does not have a theme: e.g., one may think about the old homestead, its discomforts, the joys one experienced there, how it has fared, etc. without these thoughts having a theme. In a daydream, there is said to be a theme, even when the objects change and even though the theme may be difficult to discern."

These definitions are not terribly enlightening (except perhaps for the fact that they say nothing about TAT stories!); they suggest that there is little clear distinction between these three concepts in general psychological use. Fantasy, however, seems to be the most inclusive term, and reverie differs from the other two in being restricted to wandering thinking that is not thematic and which moreover takes place in a less fully waking state of consciousness than a daydream.

When we turn to psychoanalytic literature, we don't find a

great deal more clarity about definitions. Fenichel (8) offers the following rather general one: "As long as thinking is not followed by action it is called fantasy. There are two types of fantasy: creative fantasy, which prepares for some later action and daydreaming fantasy, the refuge for wishes that cannot be fulfilled." Freud was not usually much concerned with precise and inclusive definitions, but in his introduction to Varendonck's book he goes into an interesting discussion of terminology. Bleuler (5) had proposed the term "autistic thinking" for fantasy, but Freud said that this was not happily chosen. Varendonck's own suggestion, "foreconscious thinking," Freud thought "misleading and unsatisfactory" as a designation for the subject matter of the book, since daydreaming was not much changed in its character when it went on consciously, as it certainly did some times, and since directed thinking might be preconscious as well as conscious.[3] So Freud proposed that the mode of thought-activity involved in daydreaming should be called "freely wandering or fantastic thinking, in opposition to intentionally directed reflection. At the same time it should be taken into consideration that even fantastic thinking is not invariably in want of an aim and end representations." Here, as he had done in an earlier paper (16), Freud refers to the fact that there are no clear-cut, dichotomous types but many intermediate states and transitional forms between fantasy and other types of thinking, ranging from dreams, on the one hand, to directed, secondary process thinking on the other.

It should be apparent that when we talk about fantasy we are dealing with a broad range of cognitive processes and products, a somewhat chaotic and neglected realm that could use some systematization. The only book devoted specifically to the topic is that of Varendonck (51), but as Rapaport points out, "he fails to distinguish among the varieties of fantasy-thinking, such as hypnagogic and hypnopompic reverie, daydream, etc."

Rapaport speaks with such conviction because he has made an intensive study of the phenomena in this realm, both as reported in the literature (38) and in a study of his own fantasy-

[3]Nevertheless, Fenichel preserved the usage, speaking of "preconscious fantasy thinking" (8, p. 46).

ing (39, 41). For a total of eight weeks, Rapaport worked at recording his own thought processes during the time from retiring until deep sleep; he learned to do this by a kind of automatic writing which he could carry on except in states of dimmest consciousness or closely approaching dreaming sleep. Rapaport says of these records: "They: *First* – contain thought fragments which do not seem to differ from waking thoughts; *Second* – they contain segments about which I noted while recording that they are just like the daydream into which I occasionally drift off, interrupting my regular work, in the daytime, and their character – as recorded – bears this out; *Third* – they contain material which is introduced by comments to the effect that I am unable to continue recording, sleepiness is catching up with me . . . reveries or some of them 'hypnagogic hallucinations.' They vary greatly in length, and in character, some of them are like dreams, some quite unlike the latter; *Fourth* – these records contain dreams, but these also vary greatly in character" (39) (cf. 3,4).

Despite the fact that he gives his experiences four names, Rapaport notes that there is a continuous series of phenomena, on which this four-fold scheme has been imposed. It gets to be very difficult, for example, to distinguish a hypnagogic hallucination and reverie from a dream. Let me cite a personal experience in support of this point. A few months ago, I was a subject for Dr. William Dement, in a trial of the technique he and Kleitman worked out of awakening people while they are dreaming, as ascertained by the presence of rapid coordinated eye movements (6). After a series of awakenings, in the middle of the night I started to fall asleep thinking of a forthcoming event about which I was a little apprehensive because it might disrupt my work. Suddenly I roused myself, realizing that I had begun to dream that the stack of out-boxes at my office in which I keep papers I am currently working on was toppling over. Here was apparently a perfect example of what Silberer (47) called the autosymbolic phenomenon: the representation of an abstract idea – here, that my work would be upset – by a concrete hypnagogic image depicting it. According to my EEG, I was asleep, and it was in the middle of the night, yet this was the same kind of brief pictorial reverie that Silberer had reported slipping into after working during the day or early evening. Perhaps it makes little sense to try to impose a categorical order on an essentially continuous set of phenomena.

Since classification can take us no further, let us turn to something more like a dimensional analysis. Rapaport (39) cites three major dimensions along which these fantastical phenomena vary, the last of which is subdivided into four.

1. *The amount of reflective awareness — the awareness not only of a content but of the awareness that one is aware (or the possibility of it).* This variable has a somewhat erratic relationship to the level of awareness; in some senses, I think we would agree that we are at the peak of conscious awareness when we are so deeply committed and fully absorbed in some cognitive activity that we have no self-consciousness, no immediate reflective awareness, though in such a state retroflection (as Troland called it) is of course always possible. And at the other extreme, in dreams, surely we lack this consciousness most of the time; and yet we are all familiar with dreams in which there occurs the comforting thought, "this is only a dream." Rapaport points out the fact that this last experience is not a complete example of reflective awareness, but is something close to it. In general, in states under the broad heading of fantasy there is less reflective awareness than in usual realistic or directed thinking.

2. *The ability to exert effort, to "will."* Rapaport says of this variable that it is "rather vague" yet it is useful. "The more closely the dream state is approximated, the less it is possible to exert voluntary effort." Varendonck (51) noted, as did Rapaport, during his recording of a daydream that as it started to approach true dreaming, the act of recording became more and more effortful and would be broken off.

3. *"The differences between these states show up in the formal characteristics of thought"* (39). This is the clearest respect in which these states vary, Rapaport says, and he goes on to subdivide these formal characteristics into the following four:

a. *Imagery vs. words.* Varendonck (51), Kris (27), and Rapaport (38), all agree that as one regresses from directed thought through reverie towards dreams, imagery (particularly the visual) becomes increasingly prominent and words much less so. McKellar (30) reports that most hypnagogic images are auditory, but in any event purely verbal imagery plays a small role. It is true, for many people imaging accompanies ordinary directed secondary process thought, yet somewhere down the line an important transition takes place: memory images or imagination images give way to a qualitatively very different hypnagogic or dream image, which is a great deal closer to a hallucination. Such hallucinatory images are very rarely found in states of full waking awareness, and then usually under states of considerable stress or deprivation (30), or in psychosis. A good deal of to-do has been made about the emergence of such "hallucinations" in so-called sensory deprivation, a condition in which subjects' reality contact is artificially disturbed. As I have argued elsewhere, these phenomena closely approximate hypnagogic images, which are appropriate to the altered state of consciousness (20).

b. *Implication versus explicitness.* A characteristic feature of waking thought, Rapaport says, is the explicitness with which representation takes place, whereas in dreams and dream-like forms of thought implication is common. For example, Rapaport cites a fragment of a dream, in which he is with his father and knows that his father is satisfied with him; the record adds, "I do not know how I knew that: there was no external expression on him to show that." A closely related point is the difference in continuity between waking and dream-like thought. In the latter, there is no need to make explicit the transitions from one image or concept to another, whereas in waking—especially in communicative—thought, a great deal needs to be spelled out that would otherwise be left unsaid.

c. *Rational versus autistic logic.* In dream thought, Rapaport says, the place of correct logic "is taken by forms like 'pars pro toto,' 'post hoc propter hoc,' 'what holds for the little, holds the more so for the big,' that is by participatory, syncretic, animistic forms; the so-called dream-mechanisms, or mechanisms of the primary process: condensation, displacement, substitution, prevail here." And of course symbolism too. As is true of the other variables, the difference is not absolute; waking thought is sometimes illogical and autistic, and dreams vary a great deal in this respect. Studies of dreams in our laboratory have consistently shown that the truly fantastically dream-like dream is not a very usual phenomenon (though of course the method of obtaining data may be partly responsible); many reported dreams are quite prosaic accounts of events that might really have happened, in which there is no disturbance of the logical straightforwardness of the events. Indeed, there are numerous famous examples of the solution of mathematical problems in sleep (21). In an unpublished study of the dreams of field-dependent and field-independent adolescents, Carol Johnson found frequent reports of dreams that differed in no respect from ordinary, simple wish-fulfilling fantasies, for example: "I dreamed that we had an examination and my paper had the highest mark in the class." The dream-work mechanisms that are so characteristic of dreams and reveries may also be seen in the conscious waking thought of normal subjects taking the Rorschach test[4] (26).

d. *Sophisticated versus primitive syntax.* The verbalization corresponding to or taking place in the various states studied by Rapaport in himself varied a great deal in its syntax. From the deepest levels, the language was primitive and incorrect.

Therefore, as Rapaport makes quite clear, there are no perfect correlations in this field between any of these characteristics and the level of awareness of type of fantastic thinking, yet there are strong general trends of the kinds pointed out above.

There are several other dimensions that may be implicit in the above but are worth making explicit. First, there is the degree to which thinking is *directed* as against "freely wandering." This may be conceptualized as the degree to which sets or anticipations, which usually guard thinking and keep it from straying away from the point, are operative. One of the striking characteristics of fantasy thinking is the chain-like way in which it wanders from the point at which it started, often proceeding by means of what Freud called "unessential" links or principles of

[4]This is not to say that they operate in the same ways; the differences between dreams and Rorschach responses are surely more impressive than the similarities. Yet one can observe condensations, symbolic responses, and even autistic logic in non-patients' Rorschachs.

association. This is perhaps the basic point underlying one of the two continua that Kris (27) saw in this kind of thinking, the one "reaching from problem-solving to dream-like fantasy." (The other was words vs. imagery.) That is, in order to solve problems, thinking has to be kept at the task by guiding sets.

Another obvious dimension of fantasy is the degree to which the images and events correspond to reality. The dream-work mechanisms of course play a large role in producing fantastic deviations from reality, but there also may be unrealistic conjunctions in fantasy, like anachronisms — imagining oneself to be present in a remote historical era — or unrealistic turns of events, in which condensation, displacement, and symbolization play no apparent role.

A third additional dimension is the degree of narrative structure. A usual concept of the daydream is that it is a kind of miniature drama or story, with some kind of at least minimal plot or sequence of events. Yet fantasies and related types of thinking vary all the way from long drawn-out, highly complicated narratives, to wandering thought without any plot or narrative connection, to single images unconnected to anything else by any sort of continuity.

Finally, an important dimension of variation is the *affective* involvement of fantasy-thinking. Some daydreams (especially in isolating persons) have a poverty of affect, being almost purely cognitive events; in most others, however, strong affects (e.g., anxiety, lust, hatred) suffuse the thoughts and images.[5]

If we pause and look at the above mentioned points about types of fantasy from the standpoint of the metapsychological points of view, most of them turn out to be economic and structural considerations. As yet unemphasized is the obvious *dynamic* one, that many fantasies tend to be obviously wish-fulfilling. Yet this is a dimension of difference too, for surely there are many kinds of fantasy in which no obvious or easily discernible wish-fulfillment takes place. Let me give another personal example: one night not long ago as I was lying in bed just about to go to sleep I had a hypnagogic image of a roof top with a dragon

[5]I am grateful to Dr. Roy Schafer for calling this point to my attention.

lying across it, the scales of the dragon being beautifully lacy, dark green ferns. This was a momentary presentation, like a lantern slide flashed on for a second or so and then taken away. I would accept it as a matter of assumption that this image was propelled into my awareness by some psychological force, and it is of course possible to make a symbolic sexual interpretation of it, which may be valid. The point, however, is that any wish-fulfillment that is involved is quite disguised and obscure, as compared to the "typical" daydream. As Smythies (48) says, hypnagogic images are often "without any *apparent* connection, emotional or volitional, with the aims, interests or feelings of the person concerned." (Italics mine.) Doubtless Smythies may be overlooking the role of defense and of the obscuring symbolic language of the primary process; nevertheless, the degree to which wish-fulfillment is *apparent* in the product is a clear dimension of variation.

There is a large category of fantasies in which wish-fulfillment is not evident, but in which the apparent opposite is very clear: daydreams in which anxiety or guilt play a large role. In such a fantasy, for example, a person may picture himself being subjected to all kinds of dangerous and harrowing experiences even including images of his own death by torture. The psychoanalytic explanation of these phenomena is essentially the same as the explanation of nightmares: they are defensive phenomena, in which an unconscious fantasy of some direct instinctual gratification is covered by a defensive presentation marked by anxiety and unpleasant events. The role of the superego and guilt over drive-gratification is clear in many such phenomena.

But defensive fantasies do not always take this nightmare-like form; they are quite various. It's interesting that in his first recorded discussions of fantasies,[6] Freud spoke of them as "defensive structures, sublimations and embellishments of the facts [which] at the same time serve the purpose of self-exoneration" (19, p. 196). In several of his later published papers (10, 14, 16) he described the defensive role of daydreams and other fantasies, and other analysts (8) have cited many examples of defensive

[6]Letter to Fliess of May 2, 1897.

fantasy: those involving or in the service of denial, identification, projection, etc.

Next, *genetic* considerations. Putting together pieces from various psychoanalytic sources (8, 9, 11, 12, 13, 14, 16, 17, 18, 39), I arrive at the following account: Fantasy begins with the first psychic activity, which according to the psychoanalytic primary model of thought is a hallucinatory experience of gratification following a frustration. Thus, fantasy is the oldest form of thought, one that continues throughout life. As Fenichel (8) says, fantasy "is merely the undifferentiated predecessor of thinking, in which all characteristics of the primitive ego [i.e., the primary process] are still to be seen." As childhood advances, it is increasingly displaced from consciousness by secondary process thinking and is driven into unconsciousness by the defenses as they develop. Except when the infant is in a state of what Wolff (52) calls alert inactivity, when he is able to respond realistically to his surroundings, we must assume that he is fantasying much of the time that he is awake.

As the infant matures into a toddler, gaining motor skills and ability to manipulate his surroundings, he also develops more specific desires, by canalization (Murphy, 34) of his originally diffuse urges. The more wishes, the more fantasies; for example, when the child's sexual desires are turned to the parent of the opposite sex he may try overtly to win her away from her spouse, but the Oedipus complex is basically, and largely remains, one big affect-laden fantasy. One of the most notable things about childhood is the emergence of play. Surely, in part, play is merely the pleasurable exercise of the sensory-motor apparatus, as Piaget (37) has pointed out. At the same time, however, the maturation of the effector apparatuses makes it possible for the child to act out his fantasies, which gives rise to dramatic play. Indeed, play may be looked on as a necessary consequence of the fact that both fantasy and motor skills develop before inhibitions and other defenses do. The child is not yet sophisticated enough to see through the transparent charades of his play nor have his defenses developed to the point where the acting out of his fantasies would be much hindered. So long as the child is not occupied with serious adaptive tasks, like going to school or being put to work, he is free to translate his inner fantasy into the external act of play. Freud (17) has specifically noted with respect to the alloplastic character of play, that "it is only this linking of it to reality that still distinguishes a child's 'play' from 'daydreaming.' . . . When the human being grows up and ceases to play he gives up only the connection with real objects; instead of playing he then begins to create fantasy. . . . I believe that the greater number of human beings create fantasies at times as long as they live."

Fantasy is thus originally preverbal, proceeding by means of images which are doubtless non-visual as well as visual. (Indeed, we often forget the extent to which a purely visual image is a symbolic shorthand for the full sensory reality of an experience; it is a first stage towards the development of concepts.) Ferenczi describes the preverbal stage of magic gestures, which are presumably part of the development of fantasy, but notes the great economy of effort that the learning of language introduces.

Adolescence is a time at which fantasies greatly burgeon, and many adolescents spend large amounts of time in daydreaming. Since the adolescent is adult in his sexual equipment, and has enough intelligence and knowledge to picture various possible roles in an adult world of work and amusement, yet is barred from participation in most of these activities, it is natural that he live them out in a trial or preparatory way by means of his daydreams.

A few *structural* considerations remain to be specified. Freud notes in a couple of places the fact that fantasies differ considerably in their esthetic pleasingness, and that the fantasies reported to him by some subjects are esthetically beautiful. This suggests the role of *abilities* in the genesis of fantasies, something that is not often mentioned because it plays a rather inconspicuous role. Since fantasies rarely involve much problem-solving, intelligence and resourcefulness need not obviously be drawn upon in their construction. Bleuler (5) wrote: "For the realistic function there is only *one* correct result, [but] autism has 'endless possibilities' (Jung) and its goals can be reached in the most varied ways. Thus the differences between good and poor functioning of the latter do not appear great even when they are most extreme. While there is a difference in principle between correct and false inferences or arithmetic calculations, the tale of a child and that of a genius are equivalent as far as autistic purpose and subjective fulfillment are concerned." Rapaport comments on this statement: "It would seem that there is a radical difference between the tale of the child and the genius. The latter, besides being subjective fulfillment, is deliberate action, planned for in character, and communicative in aim. The role which the ego plays in bringing it about and shaping it from an impulse or inspiration is different from that in the child's tale." Though Rapaport, in taking up the term "tale," seems to be talking more specifically about story-telling than Bleuler was, it still seems likely that his remarks would apply to some uncommunicated daydreams of highly intelligent persons. Certainly one is struck by the ingeniousness of some of the daydreams Varendonck and Rapaport report having had, and in the history of scientific discovery there are many instances of creative solutions to difficult problems during fantasy-thinking.

Freud points out another structural factor when he says that fantasies are "built up out of and over the childhood memories" (14). Speaking about the memory materials on which fantasies draw, he wrote (17): "We must not imagine that the various products of this impulse towards fantasy, castles in the air or daydreams, are stereotyped or unchangeable. On the contrary, they . . . fit themselves into the changing impressions of life. . . . The activity of fantasy in the mind is linked up with some current impression, occasioned by some event in the present, which had the power to rouse an intense desire. From there it wanders back to the memory of an early experience, generally belonging to infancy, in which this wish was fulfilled. Then it creates for itself a situation which is to emerge in the future, representing the fulfillment of the wish — this is daydream or fantasy, which now carries in it traces both of the occasion which engendered it and of some past memory" (17, p. 177).

I'll omit from this discussion any but the briefest mention of the role of fantasies in psychopathology. In order to understand hysterical fantasies and the patterns of acting out in character disorder, it's necessary to assume unconscious fantasy. Transformations of fantasies play important roles in the symptoms associated with a number of mental illnesses. For example, an obsession is an ego-alien fantasy (or fragment thereof) that insistently presents itself in awareness; a delusion is from one point of view a transformed fantasy that is accepted as a reality.

The *adaptive* point of view is perhaps represented to some extent by my remarks above about realism, but Hartmann (22) has attacked this issue much more directly. "What are the adaptive elements of fantasy life? Varendonck (51) . . . is of the opinion that the biological significance of fantasy-thinking, in sharp contrast to dream-work, lies in its attempts to solve problems of waking life . . . it is generally known that fantasy can be fruitful even in scientific thinking, which is the undisputed domain of rational thinking. . . . Another example in point is the auxiliary function of fantasy in the learning process. Though fantasy always implies an initial turning away from a real situation, it can also be a preparation for the reality. . . . It may fulfill a synthetic function by provisionally connecting our needs and goals with possibilities of their realization." Finally, Hartmann cites the adaptive function of some fantasies in increasing our insight into our own intra-psychic life, which may lead to increasingly effective mastery of the external world. Yet obviously this is another dimension of variation; it could hardly be maintained that all fantasies have equally adaptive implications.

I deliberately saved for last a point that belongs under the consideration of the adaptive aspects of fantasy: the relation of fantasies to literary products. In his paper on this topic, Freud (17) made the best case I know of for the parallels between fantasies and stories, and although he was talking about the popular products of published writers, his remarks apply almost equally well to TAT stories. I have summarized his points and added to them a little in Table 1. By way of discussion of that table, let me quote from this delightful little paper of Freud's.

First, stories of the kind he is talking about "all have a hero who is the center of interest, for whom the author tries to win our sympathy by every possible means, and whom he places under the protection of a special providence." The hero, we know as we read, cannot really come to a bad end no matter how severe

TABLE 1

SIMILARITIES BETWEEN FANTASIES AND TAT STORIES

1. Both tend to follow the general narrative format, with a central figure or *hero* who has various adventures.
2. In both there tends to be little characterization of persons other than the hero; they are just auxiliary and supplementary figures.
3. The goals and activities portrayed in both reflect S's personal goals and needs; likewise, abilities, personal memories, defenses, information, sentiments and attitudes, patterns of interpersonal relations, personal style and many other aspects of personality are used in the construction of both.
4. Both exist in a variety of forms, using various mixtures of primary process and secondary process.

his trials. "It seems to be, however," Freud adds, "that this significant mark of invulnerability very clearly betrays – His Majesty the Ego, the hero of all daydreams and all novels." In novels, all women fall in love with the hero, which is hardly realistic but quite usual in daydreams. (Incidentally, these last two qualities of invulnerability and irresistibility are not so prevalent in TAT stories.)

Second, in popular stories, there is little characterization, as in fantasies: people other than the hero are either 'good guys' or 'bad guys.'

Third, in this paper, Freud stresses the common element of wish-fulfillment in fantasies and in stories, though to apply the point to TAT stories one has to generalize it a little bit more, as I have in Table 1. This point really boils down to the fact that fantasies and stories are motivated quasi-creative products in the production of which most aspects of the total personality may play a role. This is not to deny, however, that all of these factors may not show themselves somewhat differently in fantasies than in TAT stories.

Freud was quite aware of this last fact: "We do not in any way fail to recognize that many imaginative productions have travelled far from the original naive daydreams, but I cannot suppress the surmise that even the most extreme variations could be brought into relationship with the model by an uninterrupted series of transitions." Note that Freud is only drawing parallels, while maintaining the distinction and recognizing important differences; he does not say that stories and similar products of creative imagination *are* fantasies. Later, he notes another difference: to hear another person's fantasies gives us no pleasure, "they repel us, or at least leave us cold." But the products of a man of literary talent give great pleasure, "arising probably from many sources." Specifically, the writer "softens the egotistical character of the daydream by changes and disguises [enabling us to obtain vicariously the deeper pleasure of daydreaming], and he bribes us by the offer of a purely formal, that is, esthetic, pleasure." Thus, Freud makes it quite clear that there are striking and essential differences between fantasies and stories, as well as similarities.

Nevertheless there is one more similarity I have listed in the table, in an attempt to put down every resemblance that seemed defensible: the fourth point. It is one, however, that could be made about almost any other cognitive product, and does not particularly differentiate the TAT and daydreams from anything else. It's worthwhile to notice, however, that TAT stories exist in quite a variety of forms and, in part, overlap with fantasies on the dimensions we have seen above on which fantasies differ one from another.

In the paper cited, Freud (17) goes on: "If our comparison of the imaginative writer with the daydreamer . . . is to be of any value, it must show itself fruitful in some way or other." He proposes, therefore, that the works of authors may be studied in ways learned from the analysis of fantasies. Specifically, he suggests that in a creative work, "some actual experience which made a strong impression on the writer had stirred up a memory of an earlier experience, generally belonging to childhood, which then arouses a wish that finds a fulfillment in the work in question, and in which elements of the recent event and the old memory should be discernible. Do not be alarmed at the complexity of this formula," he adds, "I myself expect that in reality it will prove itself to be too schematic, but that possibly it may contain a first means of approach to the true state of affairs."

With reference to the other kind of writing, which uses readymade material, Freud makes the canny suggestion that the writer's individuality "can express itself in the choice of material and in changes in the material chosen, which are often considerable." Much of such material — for example, myth — is itself to be considered "distorted vestiges of the wish-fantasies of whole nations."

This was an idea that had appealed to Freud ever since 1897, and he had used published works as a source of inferences about the personality of their authors several times earlier (11,15). Many other analysts, notably Hitschmann (24), took up the suggestion and applied it with great eagerness to the works of many famous writers. Because of this psychoanalytic tradition, therefore, it's easy to see why Morgan and Murray decided to elicit stories from their subjects and to try to learn from such material about the subjects' fantasy life.

On the whole, the similarities between TAT stories and fantasies or daydreams are not particularly far-reaching or impressive. How about the differences? Let us see what they are and what their implications are for an understanding of TAT stories.

TABLE 2

Differences Between Fantasies and TAT Stories

FANTASY	TAT STORY
1. *Quality of consciousness:*	
Produced in a dreamy or abstracted state of consciousness; little reflective awareness.	Produced in full waking state of consciousness, with reflective awareness.
2. *Spontaneity vs. effortfulness:*	
A passive cognitive product: arises spontaneously, with a feeling of drifting rather than one of responsible effort; self-imposed.	An active cognitive product: produced by an act of conscious 'will' or deliberation, in response to an externally imposed task.
3. *Imagery vs. verbalization:*	
May be non-verbal, in whole or part, made up of sensory images.	Always verbal in nature (though imagery may at times play a subordinate, ancillary role).
4. *Implication vs. explicitness:*	
Continuity and transitions often implicit, also connotations or attributes of persons.	Continuity, transitions, etc., usually explicit; less use of implicit connotations.
5. *Primary vs. secondary process (formal aspects):*	
May use formal properties of primary process openly in the finished product.	Product rarely shows evidence of primary process, or does so only under shelter of various conventions.

FANTASY	TAT STORY
6. *Memorability:* Often unhypercathected, repressed, or otherwise unavailable to recall.	Typically receives full hypercathexis and is easily remembered; seldom fully repressed.
7. *Narrative structure:* Little plot, loose structure; little modelling after literary forms.	Externally imposed narrative structure, with plot, suspense and other literary devices copied from culturally given models.
8. *Dynamic aspect: role of drives and defenses:* Content generally dictated by rather direct wish-fulfillment or by anxiety and defense; drives expressed may be un-neutralized.	Content much less obviously dictated by these aims; drives expressed are generally more neutralized.
9. *Involvement of affect:* Usually accompanied by strong affects, which are often crude.	Affects involved are rarely strong, usually more differentiated and mature.
10. *Role of external reality (stimulus):* Sometimes set off by an external stimulus, but latter may play no real role in the product, which need not be responsible to it.	Always set off by a complex external stimulus pattern (picture, setting, etc.); S is under pressure to respect and use reality of picture.
11. *Role of abilities:* Since there is little adaptive challenge or relevance, abilities often play little role.	Abilities play a large role in shaping the product; adaptive challenge is always present.
12. *Relation to action:* Merges into planning; may be followed or accompanied by acting out (or living out).	Has little relation to planning; does not lead to acting out (or living out); only minor acting out accompanies.
13. *Self-relevance:* Egocentric and obviously self-relevant; S typically appears as main figure (hero).	S rarely appears in story; self-relevance often not obvious to S; less egocentric.
14. *Role of communication:* Rarely communicated; if so, usually to an intimate; considered highly private.	Always communicated, to a distant, professional person; relatively public.
15. *Range of subject-matter:* May be repetitive, stereotyped, dealing with a narrow range of problems, situations, persons, needs.	The TAT pictures force S to deal with a substantial variety of basically important situations, types of persons, needs, problems.

The list in Table 2 is much longer than in Table 1, and indeed it could have been extended. Notice that the dimensions of fantasy cited above are mostly included in Table 2.

The first difference, in the quality of consciousness, is based on the first dimension mentioned by Rapaport. Even though there is some range, daydreams (the type of fantasy that is closest to the TAT story, and therefore the fairest subject for comparison) typically take place in a special state of consciousness. Miller (32) calls daydreaming unconscious in the special sense of being "unresponsive to stimulation" and says: "subjective report puts it midway between waking and dreaming, and it can easily shade off into either one."

It is fairly obvious that, except under the most exceptional conditions, TAT stories are told in a state of full waking awareness. The level undoubtedly fluctuates somewhat from moment to moment during story-production, but still within rather narrow limits. If, as Rapaport contends (41), the level of consciousness has a marked effect on the organization of thinking that goes on, this may be the most crucial and fundamental difference between fantasies and TAT stories, one from which a number of the others proceed. The state of our knowledge about states of consciousness and accompanying modes of thought-organization is as yet too scanty and unbuttressed by research to permit definite causal statements. But it seems quite likely that the state of consciousness heavily determines the role of imagery (#3 in Table 2), memorability (#6), and the roles of external reality (#10) and of communication (#14).

Second, spontaneity vs. effortfulness, or passivity vs. activity (40): one of the most strikingly characteristic things about typical daydreaming is that it is not done deliberately, but rather one feels that he has been "drifting" when he suddenly comes to his senses and realizes that he has been deep in a fantasy. Fantasy has an almost ego-alien characteristic in this way; occasionally, of course, we deliberately lose ourselves in daydreams, but for the most part they come upon us unwittingly — often even at times of such high seriousness as listening to a paper in a scientific conference! If you were wool-gathering during the past few minutes, for once you may be comforted by the fact that you were only illustrating the point made in the paper. — Thus, we can call a fantasy a *passive* cognitive product, one in which the deliberating ego plays a small role. Very occasionally, one may encounter a subject who tells TAT stories in an almost equally effortless and spontaneous way, though even here the spontaneity is not complete since the examiner has, after all, asked for a story. Most characteristically, however, it is an *effort* to tell a story; one must search about for materials; the effort takes some time and is punctuated by gaps while the subject tries to think of something to say. Surely a daydreamer never had to pause and think up something to say to himself! The very fact that a reaction time of anywhere from a few seconds to several minutes intervenes between the presentation of the picture and the beginning of the story is in itself impressive evidence of the effortful, active character of story telling as a cognitive act. A slightly different aspect of the same point is the fact that no one tells you to daydream — you do it if your own non-volition; whereas a TAT story canot by definition arise spontaneously but must be eliciated by an externally imposed obligation.

Third, the role of imagery and of verbalization: fantasies may be partly or entirely non-verbal, whereas TAT stories by definition are made up of words.[7] Especially as daydreams verge on hypnagogic reveries, as we have seen, they may become more and more entirely pictorial, like dreams, words appearing only as speeches of the pictured figures; or they may be made up of vivid auditory imagery rather than visual. Of course, a daydream may be as purely verbal (especially in people who have predominantly non-visual, but verbal imagery) as a TAT story, and in some stories the influence of imagery can at times be divined. After a particularly vivid bit of description of a scene other than the card, I have sometimes inquired and found that the S had developed the story partly in terms of visual imagery. And of course, when Card 16 is handled properly, the S is *asked* to create a visual image and then make up a story about it. This point is closely

[7]For this reason, I have not attempted to make use of Rapaport's interesting point about syntax. There may well be important differences between the linguistic usages of fantasies and stories, but the situation is confused by the fact that fantasies must be verbalized to be studied, and they are usually put into words in a state of consciousness different from the one in which they were produced.

related to the next one, since a reverie may be made up entirely of images without any connective tissue for continuity.

Fourth, the issue of implication vs. explicitness in the finished daydream or story. As we have seen, fantasy needs no explication of transitions, personal connotations, or the bases of associative chaining; this is closely related to the thirteenth point, the role of communication. Since the daydream is for strictly personal consumption, much that would need elaboration and explanation can merely be stated. In addition, however, images or thoughts may have the property Rapaport described, as in dreams, so that you *know* something about a person or thing without its being spelled out.

This last property is strange to the TAT story, which must live up to social standards of intelligibility. Therefore, unexplained transitions and gaps in continuity are rare in stories.

The fifth difference bears on the role of the primary process in the reported product. The daydreams we have to study (and perhaps even more so, the ones we don't get our hands on!) are often marked by contradictions, sudden unrealistic transitions in time and space, condensations, displacements, symbols, and other formal characteristics of the primary process. Since the daydream is responsible to no one, is usually unreported and perhaps even is usually unavailable to conscious memory, it has little need for secondary revision and the conventions of the secondary process. Nevertheless, most reveries that we know about are somewhat more orderly than dreams, probably due to the fact that they are produced in a state of consciousness marked by greater vigilance (which in turn may be a function of the greater availability of hypercathexis).

TAT stories, however, rarely show much evidence of the primary process in the reported product. Even though the primary process may have played a great role in the silent development of the story, the finished product is generally orderly, with no obvious, tolerated contradiction, autistic logic, or blatant unrealism. Rarely, I should add, *unless* we ask the subject to regress in the service of the ego by telling us a fairy story, dream, or the like, and then only certain flexible and well-controlled subjects are able to introduce much primary process. When the primary process obviously shows itself in the TAT story of a normal person, it is usually under the shelter of the "once upon a time" convention of fairy story, science fiction thriller, or the like.

The sixth difference listed in Table 2, the memorability of the product, is closely related to the first point, the quality of consciousness. The fact is that a daydream is fragmentary, fleeting, and generally unreportable. Taking place as it does in a special state of consciousness, it may receive relatively little hypercathexis and thus may not be available to deliberate recall. Since I have started writing this paper, I've been paying a great deal more attention to my own daydreams, and – possibly for this very reason – I have found them annoyingly wispy. There is rarely any kind of story development, sometimes only a single image of gratification or a wished-for state of affairs. One is often uncertain whether this fragmentary recall is due to the fact that much of the fantasy has taken place unconsciously and only a bit of it has appeared above the surface, available to reflection.

Parenthetically, at this point, I'd like to remark that Dr. Leo Goldberger and I are currently carrying on an experiment in reality deprivation, in which we cause our subjects to lie upon a comfortable bed and to do nothing for eight hours, their eyes and ears being prevented from taking in meaningful stimuli by means of experimental devices that produce a homogeneous, monotonous field.[8] What better invitation to daydream? We systematically inquire about fantasies at the end of the eight hour period, and the remarkable fact is that most subjects deny having had any. Although they sleep a good deal of the time, they *are* aware of having been awake, of not having been thinking about anything in a directed or rational way, yet they cannot report what their "freely wandering thoughts" have been. This is in spite of the fact that by the time subjects have gone into this situation we know them fairly well, they have written intimate autobiographies for us and have been subjected to many hours of testing and interviewing, so that one would hardly expect a great deal of ordinary reticence. We doubt that the lack of

---

[8]This work is being carried out under Contract No. AF33 (616) -6103) . It is quite possible that the conclusion reached here is specific to the kinds of young male subjects we have used.

reported daydreams is due to conscious withholding, therefore; it seems more a matter of the intrinsic difficulty of catching hold of a fantasy and recalling it.

TAT stories are of course sometimes rather fragmentary, but in a different sense. The brevity of a TAT story is usually the inability of the story teller to get started at all; he almost never gives you only a bit of the beginning or a single scene from the end of a possible story; instead, he simply describes the picture and stays very close to the pictured scene. Whether long or short, the TAT story (being produced in full conscious awareness) is fully hypercathected and is available to direct recall. When doing the Self-Interpretation, one very rarely finds it necessary to read back the story to the subject. He usually has it in mind and if requested can repeat it substantially unchanged. (I'm aware of the fact that there *are* changes and occasional loss of an entire story, and that a whole technique may be made out of getting a subject to recall his TAT stories some time later and noticing the discrepancies. That does not destroy the basic point.) If it were not for this memorability, the valuable technique of Self-Interpretation would be impossible (cf. 29).

The seventh point of difference deals with the degree of narrative structure. Daydreams are characteristically loose and fluid in organization (hence, incidentally, less memorable than stories). They do not follow a set model such as the one suggested by the TAT instructions; there may be no clear-cut beginning nor end; and the fantasy may dwell upon the situation of gratification much longer than is characteristic of stories. Many fantasies have little suspense and little plot. An unstudied but potentially very interesting question would be the extent to which fantasies of different persons incorporate delay or simply plunge directly into gratification. Casually, it would appear that as people become older and more sophisticated, up to a point, their conscious fantasies are less infantile and direct, incorporating more story-like properties. With plenty of precedent and its own history to draw upon, the fantasy does not need to be much affected by literary models, though as a person steeps himself in literature his own daydreams *may* take on somewhat more of a literary cast.

When we turn to TAT stories, we find that the instructions,

in whatever variation, always incorporate a demand for a description of the scene depicted in the picture, events leading up to it, thoughts and feelings of the characters, and an outcome. Most examiners also ask for a plot, a dramatic and interesting story. In doing so, they are implicitly or explicitly telling the subject that he is to follow the model of the short story, a literary form that is characteristic of our own era. Hardly anyone can help but draw on schemata that have been laid down by the many stories he has first had read to him and then later on read himself. One of the main features of plotting is suspense. In the Broadway model, a plot means "boy meets girl, boy loses girl, boy gets girl." In the daydream, the middle part is generally dispensed with, and often enough even "boy meets girl" falls by the wayside; "boy gets girl — right into bed" may be the principal scene. Then too, many subjects give their characters fictional names or introduce dialogue, descriptions, trick endings, and other literary devices that are little found in daydreams.

The eighth difference, the dynamic aspect, has to do with the nature of the motivation expressed. Despite the fact that the same subject may at one time daydream and at another time tell TAT stories, and remain the same person with the same basic needs and interests, still the way that those needs are expressed will differ in the two media. The fact that the daydream is private and uncommunicated, that it is a regressive and often not recalled kind of thinking, makes it possible for the fulfillment of wishes to be relatively direct and for the wishes themselves to be unsublimated and close to the hypothetical state of original drives. If someone has annoyed us, we can easily imagine killing him, or inflicting on him tortures we would not even consider witnessing in reality, much less carrying them out ourselves. This is not to say that all daydreams deal exclusively with raw sex and aggression; many of the examples Varendonck gives in his book deal with such relatively sublimated matters as his anxieties about his doctoral thesis.

The drives expressed in TAT stories, by contrast, are generally less blatant and less obviously related to direct instinctual aims. The exigencies of communicating the story to an examiner cause most subjects to stick to what is "decent" or "reasonable" or "socially acceptable." Their own needs, which may indeed be mirrored in the stories, are much more indirectly and inferentially involved than in the case of daydreams. A man may express his heart's desire in his fantasies, but keep such precious thoughts to himself while taking the TAT.

The ninth difference is closely related to the preceding one. Perhaps because of the un-neutralized nature of the drives implicated in fantasies, the latter tend to incorporate more affect than TAT stories do. Again, there is a good deal of overlap; as was noted above, some fantastical thinking involves little emotion, and many tellers of TAT stories put a good deal of affect into their productions. Yet there remains a difference in central tendency, so that we note it as a significant loss of distance when the subject gets appreciably angry, sexually excited, or anxious while telling a tale, even one in which such emotions are appropriate — but to the characters, not to the author. As this last distinction is much more blurred in fantasy, intense and less differentiated affects are appropriate and typically occur to a greater extent than in story-telling.

The tenth difference bears on the role of external reality. Quite often it is possible to find an external stimulus that has set off a train of fantasy thought. Varendonck reports a number of such in his book. On the other hand, a good deal of fantasy thinking takes place at night when we are in bed in a state of relative stimuluslessness; at such times, and at others, a fantasy may take off from any chain of thoughts. Thus, at the end of the day we may reflect on a number of the impressive events that have happened to us and perhaps have delayed reactions to them in the form of daydreams. One could argue that, in such an instance, the fantasy is in fact a delayed reaction to an external stimulus; indeed, it's hard to imagine a fantasy without *some* reference to external stimuli. The point, however, is that a fantasy need not take off directly from an externally presented stimulus, nor need it include any particular representation of the stimulus if one does incite it. Daydreaming is under no pressure to include or pay attention to anything external at all. A TAT story, on the other hand, is directly constrained to include in a responsible way a description of the picture, the immediate external stimulus that has evoked it. The instructions, the general attitude of the examiner (that this is a serious business) and the setting, all conspire to impress this requirement on the subject.

By way of a slight digression, I find it interesting to note that the old tradition at the Harvard Psychological Clinic, where the emphasis was so heavily on motivation, was to pay little attention to perceptual distortion or stories in which the subject took liberties with the reality of the picture. If he asked what the object was on the floor in 3BM, for example; S would be encouraged to interpret it any way he wished; "It can be anything you'd like." In this setting, perceptual distortions are not mentioned by Murray (35) except as indicators of the strength of needs. It is only fair to point out, however, that in a relatively non-pathological population of college men, such formal features were relatively unimportant (cf. 53,25). By contrast, Rapaport, Gill, and Schafer (43), working with a variety of psychiatric patients, explicitly recognize the role of stimulus and instructions in constituting an adaptive requirement and thus a situation in which reality testing can be studied.

The eleventh point follows from the last one: if there is an adaptive challenge, then abilities play more of a role in the product than where there is none. In reveries, except those that verge on planning, the principal moving force is wish rather than reality: hence, adaptation plays very little part, if any, in many fantasies. In the productive daydreams of inventors or of people who develop scientific theories or solve mathematical problems, the fantasy may deal with an internalized reality, but this is the exception rather than the rule. The ordinary garden variety wool-gathering reverie pays precious little attention to reality, and abilities have little relevance to the task of producing a satisfying imaginary gratification of some wish. If the wish is forbidden by defenses and if direct gratification cannot be allowed even in fantasy, then abilities may join hands with defenses in devising ingenious by-passes. And in the more sophisticated fantasies of people who characteristically think in terms of reality, and who may pose themselves problems that must be solved in accordance with a definite internalized set of rules, abilities will play an increasing role in the final product.

In TAT stories, which are produced in response to an external request and which involve accommodation to a usually highly structured stimulus card, abilities typically play a considerable role. William E. Henry (23) has shown that intelligence can be estimated from TAT stories with a significant and rather high degree of accuracy ($r = .85$), and surely we are not entirely disingenuous when we tell the subject, "this is a test of imagination." The *ability* to be imaginative, to express one's thoughts in vivid and well-structured language, the ability to enter imaginatively and emphatically into the inner lives of other people and thus to create convincing characters in one's stories, the ability to take hold of a rather complicated set of instructions and to hold together a coherent train of thought over a period of quite some minutes without external prodding — all of these are abilities in the true sense, and such abilities are displayed, to a larger or a smaller extent, in all TAT stories.

The twelfth difference bears on the relation to action. A consequence of the relative lack of control and defense accompanying drive expression in some people's fantasies is that they sometimes lead to a direct acting out of the need in question. To take a prosaic example, if I get thirsty working at my desk on a June afternoon, I may have a fantasy about drinking a delicious bottle of wine, and may thereupon stop by at a liquor store on the way home to dinner. In this respect, fantasy shades off into planning. Another kind of fantasy — generally unconscious — accompanies acting out. For example, typical displacements, in which we take out our anger on persons who are safely below us in a social hierarchy, are usually accompanied by a fantasy (perhaps unconscious) of getting even with the person who is really bothering us.

TAT stories are very rarely accompanied or followed by any obvious acting out. Despite the fact that my focus so far has been entirely on the stories themselves, I agree with Schafer (44) that *test behavior* is an integral and equally important aspect of the TAT. When a story containing themes of succorance — dependence on older and wiser persons to bail the hero out of his difficulties — is accompanied by requests to repeat the instructions, and followed by the subject's asking if it wasn't a good story, we see the same need that is expressed thematically being acted out in the relationship to the examiner. Indeed, such congruences between interpretations based on behavior and on content (and on formal aspects of the stories, too) are among our best ways of checking and verifying our inferences. Yet this kind of acting out remains rather pale and insignificant compared to clinical examples from the histories of character disorders. For instance, in a recent paper Ehrenreich (7) describes the hypnotherapy of a man who had committed a bizarre, impulsive murder in a dissociated state. The reconstruction makes it very plausible that he was acting out a fantasy of retaliation against a woman who had traumatically seduced him in his childhood (and against several other women), and then in his cutting the lungs out of the body and trying to blow them up, he was enacting an unconscious fantasy of bringing back to life his dead sweetheart. Of course this is an extreme case in all respects, but I trust it makes the point.

The thirteenth point has to do with self-relevance. To be sure, it is true as Murray has pointed out that both TAT stories and fantasies are anthropocentric and have a figure of dominant interest, a hero. But fantasies are typically egocentric, imaginary events in which the daydreamer himself takes the leading role. It is an unusual TAT story in which the teller is presented as the hero. Because of this self-involvement, it is plain enough to anyone that his own daydreams are relevant to an understanding of his personality, that they express something important about him. One of the central points of Murray's rationale for the TAT is that the process of projection enables a subject to express a great deal about himself in a TAT story without any awareness of this fact. The point is easily verified in routine clinical practice with the TAT, if one follows Murray's original practice of inquiring into the sources of stories, or if following Luborsky (29) one asks for a self-interpretation. Using either method, one quickly discovers that a large proportion of patients have great difficulty in seeing much if any self-relevance to the great majority of their stories.

The fourteenth difference in Table 2 is in the role of communication. As Freud (16) remarked, "daydreams are invested with great interest, carefully cherished and usually concealed with some shame, as though they belonged to the person's most intimate possessions." Because a daydream is such a regressive kind of cognitive-affective product, it may seem childish, silly, or nonsensical, the feelings too strong and the wishes expressed too self-indulgent or embarrassingly direct to be told — except to someone to whom one is very close. The fact is that psychoanalysts are the ones who hear the most reports of fantasies, and then often at the cost of much struggle with resistances. Outside of analysis, we're more likely to tell our daydreams to our closest friends or our wives than we are to casual acquaintances.

TAT stories, on the other hand, are typically told to an examiner who does not in reality have a very intimate relationship to the subject; they are quasi-public utterances. This fact, and all of the other attendant circumstances under which testing takes place, may have a very considerable effect on what is communicated to the examiner; the effect may take place partly in conscious censorship and to a large extent through a less conscious molding of the response process itself. The point needs a little qualification, for "in many circumstances under which testing is carried out a relatively strong fantasy relationship may also be present — the tester as therapist, as parental figure, etc." (46).

The fifteenth and final point of difference between daydreams and TAT stories deals with the range of subject-matter touched on. Since fantasies are spontaneous, indulged in due to an inner urge, there is nothing to stop them from being monotonously stereotyped and repetitive, while the variety of situations presented in the TAT cards tends to stimulate discussion of different subject matter. It takes a powerful preoccupation indeed to produce a set of stories with identical themes told to a set of cards as varied as the TAT, though in profound emotional states like a depression even this effect can be achieved, as Tomkins (50) has pointed out. Theoretically, we could dispense with pictures entirely, and simply ask the subject to tell stories. Aside from the advantage of standardization that the pictures introduce, and the fact that they make it easier for people who are not particularly creative to get started, the pictures have the distinct advantage of presenting the S with a series of situations of varied emotional significance with which he must deal; the pictures confront him with persons of both sexes and various ages, in given configurations, and strongly suggesting types of problems – any part of which a given S might prefer to avoid, and could fail to touch on in his spontaneous fantasies. In this way, the TAT enables us to take stock of many departments of personality, which might otherwise be locked to us.

You may have noticed, by now, that most of the differentiating characteristics of fantasies listed in Table 2 *may* be true of TAT stories, too. We have all encountered stories in which the S himself appeared, or loosely structured ones, or fragmentary, or bizarre stories rich with formal indications of the primary process. Stories sometimes do contain "raw" instinctual themes – and so forth. Certainly a TAT story *may* be and sometimes is very much like a fantasy, far down the continuum towards the dream, just as some dreams are quite reasonable, prosaic and pedestrian.

Why aren't stories more often like daydreams?

We get a hint at the answer by noting that when they are, the teller is usually quite a sick person. Fantasy is a regressive kind of thinking, and a good deal of our mature ego-structure has been set up to enable us to think in a more effective, orderly and realistic way. The emergence of regressive thinking indicates a decompensation of these controlling structures and thus a loss of ego autonomy from drives – or else a controlled, playful relaxation of defenses by a person who signals his intention by saying, "This is going to be a ghost story," or who has been asked to tell a fairy story. The whole point is that the nature of the TAT calls for secondary process thinking with only a little, well-controlled admixture of primary process for life and color. For this reason, we can easily recognize the uncontrolled emergence of primitive thinking and make diagnostic use of the fact.

Now that we have gone through all these differences and have agreed – I hope! – that a TAT story is *not* a fantasy, it is fair to ask, Was this trip necessary? Is all of this distinction-making more than a terminological quibble? I think it amounts to a good deal more, and this is the reason I concentrated at such length on the differences. There would be little harm in simply defining the word "fantasy" as meaning "TAT (or other thematic test) story" if it were not for the fact that the term has its own meaning, in general as well as in psychological usage: that is, a product of uncontrolled imagination, a daydream or reverie. This last is unwanted semantic baggage you must carry if you stick to the familiar misusage; you must constantly make it clear that when you speak about fantasy you don't mean it in the sense most people will assume.

The other danger is that if we call stories fantasies, we will overlook or forget all the important aspects of TAT stories that make them what they are. This is the implication of the tradition that says the TAT is a test of motivation, while the Rorschach tells us about personality structure. Of course, the first approaches to TAT interpretation were focussed entirely on content analysis, and for many people this is still the whole story. Such a narrow conception may lead to missing the boat diagnostically and to an impoverishment of what the TAT can give us generally. As you will recall from the Englishs' definitions (quoted above), the general concept of both fantasy and daydreams is that they represent "a sort of wish fulfillment" and that "wishes are not disguised and fulfillment is imagined as direct, without repression." This view stated in these definitions is an extreme one, of course, but it highlights the traps one can fall into by considering stories as fantasies. Parenthetically, I'd like to observe that this tendency — to consider the TAT as a test of fantasy and to look at the stories from a primarily motivational point of view — looks very much like a hangover from the early days of psychoanalysis, before the days of ego psychology. Before 1923 was the heyday of id-analysis, in which defenses and other ego-structural factors, and adaptive considerations of all kinds were ignored. Psychoanalytic theory and practice have come a long way since then, and since the work of Sigmund and Anna Freud, Hartmann, Rapaport, Kris and several others. Must TAT workers lag, and confuse themselves with anachronisms? Certainly we don't *have* to.

I propose, however, that one of the TAT's *strengths* is the fact that it elicits the kind of material it does, with some aspects or elements of fantasy, but many differences. Mostly the differences are related to its being a set task with adaptive requirements, and mostly one sees the effects of these features through the formal aspects of the performance. They indicate not only gross pathology, as already indicated, but also various specific types of disorder. For example, one sometimes picks up paranoid trends through fantasy-like content, such as themes of persecution; much more often, however, they may be seen in stories with ordinary content but the characteristically litigious formal feature of deriving everything by tortured reasoning from the picture itself. Here is a useful diagnostic indicator that we would not have had if the TAT really opened up a door into the unconscious through which fantasies might pour out.

The example is not an isolated one. Most of the inferences about personality structure that we can draw from the TAT depend on these non-fantasy aspects, as I have tried to argue in a recent paper (25) and as Schafer has so beautifully shown (45).

The similarities between TAT stories and daydreams that exist enabled Murray and Morgan to treat stories much as if they *were* fantasies, and to analyze them in the same way, with considerable validity. Two factors may be distinguished in their (perhaps misleading) success: first, they were dealing with Harvard undergraduates who were normal in the sense that they weren't seeking help, and lacked the kind of psychopathology that produces the most dramatic formal features of stories, but who were highly non-normative in their verbal creativity and flexibility. These boys could really make up stories, imaginative ones that had much of the feel of a fantasy; I still recall my shock when after some years at the Harvard Psychological Clinic I started using the TAT clinically — the meagreness, the flatness of the stories I got contrasted sharply with the ideational riches of the Harvard student. The other factor was Murray's and his co-workers' great interest in *dynamics* to the virtual overshadowing of other aspects of personality. Despite the fact that

Explorations contains scores of non-dynamic variables (i.e., structural, genetic, adaptational, even economic ones) covering most of personality, the principal concept of the book is the *need,* and the need-press combination or thema seems to be a close second. Now we have seen that even dynamically, TAT stories differ from fantasies, but the differences in this respect are not too great: after all, the stories *do* contain goal-strivings, just as fantasies do, and even if they are not the same goals, it is not easy to tell the difference.

Let us take it for granted that a thematic test story is quite a different cognitive product from a typical daydream. What *is* the relation between the two? We have already spoken of one relation, a formal one: at their extremes, these two types of thought products are adjacent and even overlap somewhat with respect to a number of continua (such as that from primary to secondary process).

A more substantial and intimate relation was originally suggested by Morgan and Murray (33) before myself: that TAT stories draw on fantasies for their material. It fairly often happens that to Card 16 Ss tell obviously wish-fulfilling stories, sometimes in the first person. In the Self-Interpretation, such Ss frequently say, "This is a favorite daydream of mine," or the like. Any person's repertory of fantasies is likely to contain a fairly innocuous candidate for this kind of display, for example, themes of occupational success or of a pleasant vacation in beautiful surroundings. Yet the blank card is a special case in several respects; it offers the S no reality to cling to but forces him to fall back entirely on his own resources. Thus, it fails to have a number of the characteristics listed in Table 2 as typical for the TAT, and *ought* to stimulate the most fantasy-like stories. But how about stories told to the other cards? It probably happens quite rarely that the story-teller, when given one of the typical pictures, produces a ready-made daydream and offers it as a story after making a few elementary changes, as from the first to the third person.

Nevertheless, Ss may draw on ready-made material from fantasy when dealing with structured pictures too, under certain conditions. *First,* there must be a pre-existing fantasy relevant enough to the picture to be brought to mind by it (not necessarily consciously). *Second,* the S must have a flexible enough defensive structure so that he is allowed access to such material, which in many persons is kept under strict repression. *Third,* the S may draw on fantasy for a story if some other, non-fantasy material (such as personal memory) is not even more relevant, ready, and suitable for partial drive-discharge. The story is a product of many forces and conditions, in addition to and in interaction with the fantasies that are touched off. The latter must ordinarily undergo many changes, therefore; requirements of social communication may expurgate them, requirements of fitting the picture may truncate them, the whole apparatus of anticipations, abilities and models may take bits of several fantasies, remold, transform, revise and elaborate them — and all of this silently — so that the teller himself does not recognize much similarity between his own fantasies and the finished product. It is easy to see how many circumstances can change the role played by each of these non-fantasy sources: the relation between E and S, the nature of the situation, increase in inner need or conflict, decompensation of defenses, and so forth — all could change so as to let fantasy play a larger role. They may also, in other variants, keep it out entirely. Thus, if the fantasy material suggested by 13MF is so strongly repressed in a very inhibited young man that any hint of it is ruthlessly deleted by his defenses, he may block completely, merely describe the picture, or draw on some extra-personal material such as newspaper stories, novels, friends' adventures, or the like, none of which may give more than an indirect hint about his own sexual fantasies.

If the relation is so uncertain, how have we gotten away with calling TAT stories "fantasies" for so many years? I have talked glibly in my own test reports about "the characteristics of the patient's fantasy life," meaning nothing but what his TAT was like. Why could we? Because *nobody checks.* The resident on the case is going to assume automatically that when the psychologist talks about fantasy the latter knows more than he does; the analyst who does know about the patient's fantasies just skims through the jargon in the report looking for what he can use; and the personality researcher, if he is interested in fantasy at all, accepts the TAT as a measure of it and never thinks to *test* this assumption. Is it not remarkable that in twenty-five years of work with the TAT, no one has published a comparative study of the daydreams and TAT stories of the same Ss? (I hope I will be corrected from the floor if I have missed such an experiment.) It is high time someone did it.

REFERENCES

1. Beier, E. G., Gorlow, L., and Stacey, C. L.: The fantasy life of the mental defective. *Am. J. Ment. Deficiency, 55*:582-589, 1951.
2. Bell, J. E.: *Projective Techniques: A Dynamic Approach to the Study of the Personality*. New York, Longmans, 1948.
3. Bellak, L.: A study of limitations and 'failures': Toward an ego psychology of projective techniques. *J. Proj. Tech., 18*:279-293, 1954.
4. Bellak, L.: *The Thematic Apperception Test and the Children's Apperception Test in Clinical Use*. New York, Grune & Stratton, 1954.
5. Bleuler, E.: Autistic thinking. In D. Rapaport, *Organization and Pathology of Thought*. New York, Columbia Univ. Press, 1951.
6. Dement, W., and Kleitman, N.: The relation of eye movements during sleep to dream activity; an objective method for the study of dreaming. *J. Exp. Psychol., 53*:339, 1957.
7. Ehrenreich, G.A.: Headache, necrophilia, and murder; a brief hypnotherapeutic investigation of a single case. Paper presented at the joint meeting of the Southwest Psychological Association and Kansas Psychological Association, Topeka, Kansas, 1959.
8. Fenichel, O.: *The Psychoanalytic Theory of Neurosis*. New York, Norton, 1945.
9. Ferenczi, S.: Stages in the development of the sense of reality. *Sex in Psychoanalysis*. New York, Basic Books, 1950.
10. Freud, S.: Screen memories. In *Collected Papers*. Vol. V, London, Hogarth Press, 1950.
11. Freud, S.: *The Interpretation of Dreams. Standard Edition*. Vols. IV & V, London, Hogarth Press, 1953.
12. Freud, S.: Fragment of an analysis of a case of hysteria. *Standard Edition*. Vol. VII, London, Hogarth Press, 1953. Pp. 3-122.
13. Freud, S.: Three essays on the theory of sexuality. *Standard Edition*. Vol. VII, London, Hogarth Press, 1953. Pp. 125-244.
14. Freud, S.: My views on the part played by sexuality in the aetiology

of the neuroses. *Standard Edition.* Vol. VII, London, Hogarth Press, 1953. Pp. 271-279.

15. Freud, S.: *Delusion and Dreams in Jensen's 'Gradiva.'* London. Allen & Unwin, 1921.
16. Freud, S.: Hysterical phantasies and their relation to bisexuality. *Collected Papers.* Vol. II, London, Hogarth Press, 1953. Pp. 51-58.
17. Freud, S.: The relation of the poet to day-dreaming. *Collected Papers.* Vol. IV, London, Hogarth Press, 1953. Pp. 173-183.
18. Freud, S.: *A Child is Being Beaten.* A contribution to the study of the origin of sexual perversions. In *Collected Papers.* Vol. II, London, Hogarth Press, 1953.
19. Freud, S.: *The Origins of Psychoanalysis.* New York, Basic Books, 1954.
20. Goldberger, L., and Holt, R. R.: Experimental interference with reality contact (perceptual isolation): method and group results. *J. Nerv. & Ment. Dis., 127*:99-112, 1958.
21. Hadamard, J.: *The Psychology of Invention in the Mathematical Field.* Princeton, N. J., Princeton Univ. Press, 1945.
22. Hartmann, H.: *Ego Psychology and the Problem of Adaptation.* New York, Internat. Univ. Press, 1958.
23. Henry, W. E.: *The Analysis of Fantasy: The Thematic Apperception Technique in the Study of Personality.* New York, Wiley, 1956.
24. Hitschmann, E.: *Great Men.* New York, Internat. Univ. Press, 1956.
25. Holt, R. R.: Formal aspects of the TAT: A neglected resource. *J. Proj. Tech., 22*:163-172, 1958.
26. Holt, R. R.: Manual for the scoring of primary process manifestations in Rorschach responses. Draft 7. New York. Research Center for Mental Health, 1959. (Dittoed).
27. Kris, E.: On preconscious mental processes. *Psychoanal. Quart., 19*:540-560. 1950.
28. Leary, T.: A theory and methodology for measuring fantasy and imaginative expression. *J. Pers. 25:*159-175. 1956.
29. Luborsky, L.: Self-interpretation of the TAT as a clinical technique. *J. Proj. Tech., 17*:217-223. 1953.
30. McKellar, P.: *Imagination and Thinking: A Psychological Analysis.* New York, Basic Books, 1957.
31. Masserman, J. H. and Balken, Eva R.: The clinical application of fantasy studies. *J. Psychol., 6*:81-88. 1938.
32. Miller, J. G.: *Unconsciousness.* New York, Wiley, 1942.
33. Morgan, Christiana D., and Murray, H. A.: A method for investi-

gating fantasy. The Thematic Apperception Test. *Arch. Neurol. & Psychiat., 34*:289-306. 1935.

34. Murphy, G.: *Personality; a Bisocial Approach to Origins and Structure.* New York, Harper, 1947.
35. Murray, H. A. and other workers of the Harvard Psychological Clinic: *Explorations in Personality.* A clinical and experimental study of fifty men of college age. New York, Oxford Univ. Press, 1938.
36. Murray, H. A.: *Personal Communication.* 1959.
37. Piaget, J.: *The Origins of Intelligence in Children.* New York, Internat. Univ. Press, 1952.
38. Rapaport, D.: *Organization and Pathology of Thought.* New York, Columbia Univ. Press, 1951.
39. Rapaport, D.: States of consciousness, a psychopathological and psychodynamic view. In H. A. Abramson (Ed.), *Problems of Consciousness; Transactions of the Second Conference.* New York, Macy, 1951.
40. Rapaport, D.: Some metapsychological considerations concerning activity and passivity. Two seminars given at Austen Riggs Center. June 16 and August 11, 1953. Unpublished.
41. Rapaport, D.: Cognitive structures. In *Contemporary Approaches to Cognition.* Cambridge, Harvard Univ. Press, 1958.
42. Rapaport, D. and Gill, M. M.: *On Psychoanalytic Metapsychology.* Paper presented to the New York Psychoanalytic Society, March 11, 1958.
43. Rapaport, D., Gill, M. M., and Schafer, R.: *Diagnostic Psychological Testing.* Vol. II. Chicago Yr. Bk. Pub., 1946.
44. Schafer, R.: *Psychoanalytic Interpretation in Rorschach Testing.* New York, Grune & Stratton, 1954.
45. Schafer, R.: How was this story told? *J. Proj. Tech., 22*:181-210. 1958.
46. Schafer, R.: *Personal Communication,* 1959.
47. Silberer, H.: Report on a method of eliciting and observing certain symbolic hallucination phenomena. In D. Rapaport (Ed.), *Organization and Pathology of Thought.* New York, Columbia Univ. Press, 1951, pp. 195-207.
48. Smythies, J. R.: The 'base line' of schizophrenia. Part 1. The visual phenomena. *Am. J. Psychiat., 110*:200-204. 1953.
49. Symonds, P. M.: *Adolescent Fantasy.* New York, Columbia Univ. Press, 1949.

50. Tomkins, S. S.: *The Thematic Apperception Test; The Theory and Technique of Interpretation.* New York, Grune & Stratton, 1947.
51. Varendonck, J.: *The Psychology of Daydreams.* New York, Macmillan, 1921.
52. Wolff, P. H.: Observations on newborn infants. *Psychosom. Med., 21*:110-118. 1959.
53. Wyatt, F.: The scoring and analysis of the Thematic Apperception Test. *J. Psychol., 24*:319-330. 1947.

DISCUSSION OF DR. HOLT'S PAPER

Silvan S. Tomkins, Ph.D.
Primary Discussant

D*r. Tomkins:* I guess the best thing I can say about the paper is that I will probably never again use the word "fantasy" loosely. I think the distinction was clearly and well made. I think it can no longer be a question that there are a number of differences between a TAT story and a fantasy. I am not altogether clear that I understand what a fantasy is. There are many varieties of fantasies, as Dr. Holt spelled them out. The distinction seemed to be a distinction between primitive and organized thinking. The distinction between primitive thinking and secondary thinking, is, as I see it, indifferent with respect to the question of the motives involved in thinking. We could conceive of these being somewhat independent variables with the same motive being represented in a primitive way of thinking or in an organized mode of thought. To some extent the distinction is indifferent with respect to the problem of motivation. I detected in this distinction a springboard for reducing the significance of motivation in TAT material. You maintained that since the TAT represented organized thinking, it was a mistake to simply assume that a TAT story *directly* expressed motivation, that there were structural features, cognitive styles, and so on. This second point can be made and defended, but it does not derive from the distinction between the primary and the secondary process, or between primitive thinking and organized thinking.

Secondly, if we distinguish primitive thinking and fantasy from TAT stories, we must also distinguish these from certain aspects of what Freud called the primary process. A fantasy, if it is not a TAT story, is also not pure sexual excitement or pure hostility. As I understand your distinction, it is essentially thinking which is influenced by motives but where the thinking is not tightly controlled or not controlled by some external criterion. So it is a distinction *within thinking* rather than a distinction between motivation and thinking.

So I would argue that both fantasy and TAT stories are thought products and can and do reflect motivation equally well. In one sense, Dr. Holt's theme represents the keynote of this conference. It is perfectly clear that many people have assumed a straw man. There are some people who maintained that the TAT represented in a very simple, if not simple-minded fashion, a few simple motives and that the TAT could be used easily and directly, without very many problems for the diagnosis of these motives.

Dr. Holt is saying that the human being is more complicated than this, that he doesn't just say what he feels, he doesn't just act on what he feels, that he has conflicting feelings. He is concerned with reality constraints; he is sensitive to environmental pressures, sensitive to a whole lot of things, and the final product is a resultant of a very complex set of processes. I don't think anybody in his right mind could argue about this general orientation.

In a way I think it is interesting that psychoanalysis has moved with the emphasis on ego-psychology. If I were to label this movement I would call it the return of the repressed, where the repressed is reality.

It seems to me this conference will make more headway if we put our cards on the table at the outset with respect to our value judgments about motives and man. There are two basic issues. One, what do you think a human being is like? What is your theory of motivation, of how a human learns, and so on? That is a long story. We all undoubtedly have somewhat different views on this. It would take me quite a few hours to say what I think, and I won't burden you. It is different from a great deal of what is said in these papers.

The second thing is perhaps more important, and that is, not only what do you think a human being is like but what do you think he *ought* to be like? And I submit that what you think he *ought* to be like will determine in very great measure what you think he *is* like.

I have spent some years studying ideologies over a wide range, from the foundations of mathematics through theology, theories of education, theories of socialization, theories of art, theories of government, jurisprudence, regarding them as projections, and I find in all of these dimensions there emerges a polarity on a few fairly simple issues.

One is, that the human being is and should be an end in himself, who in satisfying his own wishes can and should take enjoyment out of life. The other is that the human being is a neutral entity who achieves his status, either achievement status or moral status, by a struggle toward and conformity to a norm.

There is also a middle position, and I take it most of us are in the middle position or we wouldn't be here. We have one foot among the tender-minded, one foot among the tough-minded. We are, I think, in general, conflicted people, facing a little bit more one way than the other. What I am saying is that the emphasis is more in the direction of the normative, more in the direction of the tough-minded, in our affirmations. Let us be sure of the stimulus; let us be sure of the cognitive style.

To take just a few options here, we have the option, in defining motive, of stressing, as Atkinson has, the *aim* of the behavior. We can also define motive in terms of *arousal* conditions, which, I think, is quite a separate way of defining motives. We can also define motive in terms of just plain *affects*. That is to say, I have defined a motive as any object of any affect, meaning by object either the affect itself, that is, fear about fear or some other affect, fear about shame or shame about fear, or some percept, behavior, or thought. There is no limit, as I see it, to the objects of affects, and I take affects to be the primary motives.

I have laid my cards somewhat on the table. My feeling is that what Dr. Holt is saying is certainly true. It is true that TATs are influenced by everything under the sun. The question is, what is the magnitude of each influence; how seriously are we to take each one; what is the evidence for giving one influence a high weight and another influence a low weight?

In closing, may I say that Dr. Holt left himself vulnerable

in his concluding page when he said it was about high time somebody did a study on the relation between fantasy and TAT themes. I did a study on it. He had read it, as a matter of fact, but repressed it. The study simply was an examination of a small number of cases where people had fantasies that didn't get into the TAT. One case I reported was of a young graduate student in mathematics at Princeton, who spent almost six hours a day repeating a fantasy which took from an hour to an hour and a half to go through because it was so complicated. In the TAT, there was no evidence for it as far as I could see. Here is a case where fantasy and the TAT are completely divergent.

In one very specific case where I knew the problem, (the child was a kleptomaniac) there was no reference to stealing in the TAT. When he came to Card 3 he said, "This boy has a problem on his mind but we won't go into it." Anyone who knows something that he wants to withhold from you has no problem at all in withholding it from his story. The TAT is no royal road to information the individual has clearly in mind and doesn't want to communicate.

Dr. Kagan: Most of us are interested in assessing both wishes and defenses. These are some of the units we would like to code from fantasy material. On the basis of current research it seems easier to measure defenses. The paradigm seems to be: Present a stimulus which unambiguously illustrates a conflictful act and look for distortions in the interpretation. The distortion is a measure of defense. However, we also want to measure a unit or variable that has to do with wish. The wishes that many of us are interested in — achievement, aggression, sexuality — usually have attendant anxiety, and, therefore, defenses will be called into play. One might defend the statement, therefore, that we can never evaluate motive intensity by using contemporaneous behavior.

What then is the merit of using a fantasy technique to measure a hostile wish when we could ask a person "Do you hate people?" We assume that TAT stimuli allow us to assess wishes that are repressed or suppressed. However, we often overlook the fact that there are individual differences in the degree to which repression is present. There are individuals who are quite aware of their strong hostile impulses and produce blatantly hostile story material. Another group of individuals may have an equally strong hostile wish but no hostile story material appears. Our task in these cases is to discover the laws of distortion. At present we do not possess those laws which will allow us to decode the fantasy response, and assess the wish. The production of hostile content, therefore, can not be taken as a measure of hostile motivation since we have no independent measure of the individual's anxiety in this motive area nor his tendency to repress hostile thought content.

Dr. Lazarus: I can give you one instance where you might postulate the presence of the wish. The individual gives you no overt evidence of preoccupation with hostility, but if you present hostile stimuli you get huge autonomic changes. In other words, the answer lies in finding independent information related to the motive. It is a pattern analysis we are essentially looking for, finding independent evidence that the negative information we have, the absence of wish material, is simply a manifestation of a disguise, an evasive tactic, or a defense.

Dr. Holt: It might be clarifying, as a preliminary to the conference, for me to express my conviction that the TAT, like the Rorschach, is not a test of anything except in the general sense of personality. The TAT is, in Lee Cronbach's sense, "a wide-band instrument" which offers the opportunity of tapping many aspects of personality. It doesn't offer a guarantee in any particular case of giving you information on any one variable. It may be, in some cases, an excellent instrument to get at motivation. But for a given person you may have trouble in making any valid conclusions about motives. However, for that subject you may get excellent information about defenses. We go at it playing by ear essentially, using the material appropriate to the person.

Dr. Atkinson: There seems to be a presumption around the table that I don't share; i.e. that we know all about motivation; that we have a theory of motivation that is tenable and the task is to find an instrument that does the thing that the theory says it should do. If you look hard at all the available evidence about motivation theory today, I think you find that the standard theories are untenable.

One way of looking at the thematic apperception theory is that this is a very interesting method of collecting data in a fairly standardized way from human subjects. It is much superior to simply looking at the vigor of their movements as a way of measuring motivation variables. The task is to exploit this method, which can be standardized to a certain extent in order to develop a theory of motivation.

We can lean heavily on the best insights that have come out of fifty years of work both in the clinic and in the animal laboratory, concerning so-called motivation variables. We can lean heavily on the insight that the person is more likely to reveal something important about himself when you ask him indirectly rather than directly. I think beginning with that fact, we can begin to see what this instrument does, how it behaves, whether or not thought content does reflect anything about the person that we might control experimentally.

In brief, what I am trying to say is that part of the trouble that we have in evaluating whether or not thematic content is doing the same job as spontaneously produced fantasy, as a measure of motivation, is that we find the results from thematic apperception don't fit our preconception of the motivation process.

Dr. Lazarus: Taking the TAT or some variation of this instrument do you think the storytelling technique will help us understand the concept of motive?

Dr. Atkinson: I think we can go pretty far toward developing a meaningful conception of motive structure. Moreover, we will discover the fallibilities of this technique in the process and the need for subsidiary information. This conclusion is based on ten years' experience with the TAT in connection with achievement motives.

Dr. Mussen: How does this differ from what Murray was trying to do originally?

Dr. Atkinson: I don't think it does at all. I have looked at Murray's contribution and those who worked with him in the early days as finding a neat way of pouring a lot of thought content into the same mold to make possible some meaningful connections from which we could proceed to build theory. I don't mean to disclaim the importance of the psychoanalytic ideas we have. We ought to pump them for all they are worth. I think there is a difference between that and being preconvinced that the theory is correct and being disturbed when the instrument doesn't somehow reveal what the theory said it should.

There are human thought content documents that can be exploited if we ever learn how to read the content of the thought in psychologically meaningful ways. That is one of Freud's contributions; the idea that we can read the meaning of thought content in very subtle ways.

Dr. Murstein: Dr. Holt said that the TAT is a broad-band instrument. It may be a broad-band instrument for very rough dichotomies, say, between normals and psychotics, but when we get down to intra-class distinctions I think it becomes an extremely narrow-band instrument.

I have a hard time differentiating among normal college students on the basis of the TAT records, and the reason for this has something to do with the fact that these cards are so strongly structured that it is very difficult for any broad-band to emerge from these ends.

Dr. Holt: I will comment briefly on this point about broad-narrow band. Certainly the TAT is not everybody's cup of tea, and if it is not, there is no reason that you should struggle with it. If you can't get much out of it, I don't think that necessarily means that the data aren't there. It is a difficult instrument with which to work. I think it is a wide-band instrument in the sense that it offers a rich body of material on which to make a large range of inferences.

A SUBSTITUTIVE-DEFENSIVE CONCEPTION OF APPERCEPTIVE FANTASY

Richard S. Lazarus, Ph.D.
University of California, Berkeley

THE VOGUES and trends in psychological research and thought are constantly changing, and one of the victims of this change seems to be the old "New Look" in perception. There was great excitement in the late 1940's over the capacity of perceptual and apperceptive processes to reflect need states. While Freud had said that dreams were "the royal road to the unconscious," many psychologists interested in personality were suggesting that perception and certainly apperception were the "royal road to motivation." A great amount of research with apperceptive fantasy, particularly in the form of variations of the Thematic Apperception Test, was one of the substantial results of this conviction. It was performed not only for theoretical reasons but also to support the use of apperceptive fantasy to infer motivational dynamics in individual clinic cases.

The current trend only ten years later seems to be away from the notion that needs are reflected directly in perception and apperception. While there are notable exceptions, the emphasis has turned to structural variables related both to the external stimulus and to ego-control characteristics of the personality. If the directing qualities of needs have not been completely eschewed, then they have been sharply minimized in favor of these structural factors. This is occurring at the same time as the emphasis in psychoanalytic theory is turning away from the id and toward the ego and its adaptive functions.

There is no doubt that a number of theorists and research workers are still interested in the capacity of apperceptive fantasy to reflect needs. The predominant point of view of these psychologists is that, in the main, needs are directly reflected in apperceptive fantasy, at least under certain conditions. They appear as a kind of planning and problem solving (instrumental) activity with respect to the ultimate gratification of the most pressing needs. This orientation seems to have been the basis for the experimental work of McClelland and his colleagues (20) and its recent extensions (1). For the purposes of exposition I shall refer to this point of view as the *direct-expression* theory of apperceptive fantasy.

There are two propositions about needs and apperceptive fantasy which I should like to take up. One has to do with when and why it should be that needs might be reflected in apperceptive fantasy. I shall quarrel with the sufficiency of the direct-expression point of view, suggesting as more adequate a *substitutive* notion. The second concerns the importance of ego-control processes in guiding and even transforming (sometimes into its opposite) the expression of a need in apperceptive fantasy. I refer to this as the *defensive* conception of apperceptive fantasy. Let us consider these two aspects of the problem separately.

DIRECT VERSUS SUBSTITUTIVE EXPRESSION

I suppose the idea that needs would directly appear in the content of apperceptive fantasy is as old as the notion of wish-fulfillment in dreams and the concept of autism propounded by Bleuler (3). But experimental research along these lines by psychologists can be readily traced to the pioneer experiments of Sanford (24, 25) on degree of hunger and its effects on imagery and association. These studies, as well as later ones by Atkinson and McClelland (2), McClelland and Atkinson (19), Levine, Chein and Murphy (17) and Lazarus *et al.* (16) are so well known as to require no elaboration. The full list would be too long to present here. While there were rare negative findings (for example, 5), the evidence suggested that, in the main, there is a positive relationship between degree of hunger and the amount of hunger-related imagery in perceptual and apperceptive tasks.

However, one of the nagging features of this research was that very commonly the curve representing the relationship between degree of need and hunger-related imagery was either negatively accelerated or shaped like an inverted "U"; that is, the association was positive at lower degrees of food-deprivation, but often negative when food deprivation was extended beyond several hours. This "U" shaped curve has since become infamous in the field of need and apperceptive fantasy, and, in fact, there is abundant evidence that it also applies in the field of learning as well (viz., 8, 18). Sanford (24, 25), laid this "U" shape to the cyclical nature of hunger in response to habitual patterns of eating. Levine, Chein and Murphy (17) suggested the operation of two types of mechanisms, one related to primary process seeking of a satisfying object (food), the other, second leg of the curve to a more reality oriented process. This ego-process-oriented argument was never as telling as it might have been, not only because it was made after the fact, but also because hunger seemed less similar to the conflict-producing drives the Freudians emphasized and the food habit concept seemed so applicable. As we shall see, later research has increased the acceptability of the two-process interpretation.

The direct-expression point of view with respect to the operation of needs in apperceptive fantasy appeared to be supported by the data of these above studies if one looked only at the first part of the curve of association between hunger and food-related imagery, although the Brozek *et al.* (5) study is a notable exception. Further confirmatory evidence was produced by the work of McClelland and his associates (20) on the need for achievement. These experimenters produced a large variety of data which suggested a direct association between the inferred need for achievement and achievement-related imagery on a version of the Thematic Apperception Test.

If the McClelland type of data relating need for achievement and apperceptive fantasy were all that were available in the literature, one would have to admit that, at least for mild or moderate degrees of need arousal (the first part of the "U" shaped curve), there is a direct expression of this need in the content of apperceptive fantasy, and that TAT thematic content did, indeed, permit valid inferences about the strength and patterning of intrinsic needs.

But then there is the Brozek *et al.* finding that a group of men under semi-starvation conditions for months (and who not only talked incessantly about food but revised vocational plans toward becoming cooks and restauranteurs) showed no evidence of significantly greater hunger associations when formally tested. Moreover, a few years ago, some of us were attempting to explore the motivational antecedents of stress and also obtained data which did not fit the direct expression assumptions. Since threatening a subject with failure is a common laboratory procedure for inducing stress, we sought measures of achievement motivation in order to predict which subjects would be most threatened by the failure stressor condition. One of the measures we tried to employ was developed and used by McClelland. We began reporting (15, 27, 28) negative or sometimes insignificant relationships between the apperceptive fantasy measure of achievement motivation and other behaviors which should have directly reflected it, for example, task performance and behavioral evidence of achievement striving. At this time our misgivings about the sufficiency of the direct expression point of view were sharply increased. The data involved are readily available in the literature and need not be elaborated here. Moreover, they are not absolutely definitive with respect to the issue. But they did lead to what I consider a very forceful, as yet unpublished, experiment which I would like to summarize here.

Broverman, Jordan and Phillips (4) working with thirty-seven males of diverse ages and socioeconomic status, developed some behavioral life history indices of achievement motivation based on the Worcester Scale of Social Attainment. These could be characterized in terms of striving for occupational advancement (with job level controlled) as evidenced by such behaviors as letters written about jobs, interviews applied for, and seeking contacts for better positions. A fantasy measure of achievement motivation was derived from a Role Taking Test devised by Feffer (9). These measures, while based on a somewhat different approach to apperceptive fantasy, have some comparability to McClelland's categories of achievement imagery. No significant relationship was found between actual achievement (job level) and either achievement fantasy or achievement striving. However, and here is the interesting thing, *an inverse relationship was found between striving for achievement and the fantasy measure of achievement motivation.*

I would like to quote from these above researchers at this point because they attempt to offer a very interesting integration of their findings with those of other investigations:

> The results of this study demonstrate an inverse relationship between behavioral striving and achievement fantasy. This study thus supports an alternative-channels view of the expression of achievement motivation and appears incompatible with the general expression model advanced by McClelland and his co-workers.
>
> Interpretation of the present results, however, cannot proceed without cognizance of the numerous studies which support the general expression model by demonstrating positive relationships between achievement fantasy and striving. The alternate-channels view, which is supported by this study, can no more account for these instances of positive relationships than the general-expression model can account for the present results. Clearly an extension of thought is necessary to resolve this conflict of results. We are inclined to attempt such a resolution via an extension of the alternative-channels model.
>
> We would approach this problem by observing that many individuals do not seem to express their achievement needs in overt life behavior. Clinical literature is replete with descriptions of individuals who are blocked from striving towards intensely desired life goals, because of such factors as physical incapacities, anxiety about an environment that is perceived as threatening, or simply lack of the experience necessary to know how to approach these goals. One might say that the subtleties and complexities of society are too great for these individuals to master. Such individuals are frequently described as being under great pressure due to inability to express their needs in overt life behavior.
>
> We would suggest that such pressure impels the individual to seek alternative modes of need expression, not only in fantasy as suggested by Lazarus *et al.,* but also in behavioral striving when a task is simpler and less ambiguous than life problems.
>
> The experimental tasks used to assess behavioral striving usually have been precisely such simpler and less ambiguous situations. These tasks are safer and/or better structured than the situations

> in which most life goals are embedded, and they are made easy for the *S*s involved, so that intelligence can be said to play little, if any, part in achievement of them. Therefore, individuals who are blocked in expressing achievement motivation in real life might be expected to show a great deal of striving on these tasks.
>
> On the other hand, individuals who are able to activate achievement needs in life should have no need to exert themselves on tasks so distant from usual real-life concerns. In other words, individuals who are able to strive in real life should find such experimental tasks irrelevant to their achievement goals and hence show little striving in the laboratory, while individuals less able to strive in real life should react to the experimental task as a substitutive goal and show high striving in the laboratory. It would then follow from the present findings of a negative relationship between life striving and achievement fantasy that low laboratory strivers would be the low achievement fantasizers, while high laboratory strivers would be the high achievement fantasizers. Thus, a reversal of striving patterns from life to the laboratory may account for the positive relationships previously observed between striving and achievement fantasy. Such a reversal occurs, according to this argument, because performance of laboratory tasks, like fantasy, may serve as a substitute expression of blocked achievement motivation.

There appears to be something wrong or at least inadequate with the direct-expression point of view of apperceptive fantasy, even if we ignore, for the moment, the downward deflection of the "U" shaped curve (at high levels of need). I would argue that there are times when direct-expression applies and occasions where this principle is inadequate and requires invoking a substitutive principle similar to that described by Broverman *et al.* above.

It might be worthwhile pondering why needs should be reflected in apperceptive fantasy in the first place. The direct-expression viewpoint seems to assume that subjects engage in problem solving in their apperceptive fantasy. In other words, they are symbolically working out ways of gratifying the need state as in the anticipatory responses of association-learning theory (viz., 7). If this is so, I fear that the scoring system developed for evaluating need for achievement, for example, is not adequate to reflect this problem solving. It does not provide differentiation of subjects who simply fantasize the goal attainment from those who recognize a series of steps on the way to accomplish it. The distinction is similar to the case of two students who want to be doctors. One thinks only about the future accomplishment, the prestige and income; the other organizes his thoughts along a series of instrumental steps, getting to medical school, financing the education, taking alternative routes, etc. This latter type of anticipatory behavior is real problem solving. The apperceptive fantasies of achievement of some subjects reflect this reality oriented type of approach, while those of others appear to be merely wish-fulfillments.

I am suggesting that, in some cases, needs may be directly reflected in apperceptive fantasy in the fashion indicated above, but this is more like the ego-oriented fantasy which Holt (11) has just very wisely distinguished from the more undirected reverie or daydream in which the organizing, reality directed ego-processes are less involved. The substitutive principle fits much better the latter type of fantasy, some of which may also appear in TAT stories under certain conditions. From the psychoanalytic point of view (as, for example, presented by Rapaport, 23), when an impulse is not directly and immediately discharged motorically, the person (still operating under the primary process) hallucinates or fantasizes the satisfying object. The substitutive conception argues that only when a need is not being expressed in motor striving does it appear as wish-fulfillment in fantasy. Thus, when it does appear in apperceptive fantasy, there should be an absence of striving behavior with respect to that need. This is what Broverman *et al.* find. The subjects who show high evidence of achievement imagery on the Role Taking Test give less evidence in their life situation of striving for achievement. From one point of view, this is also what Brozek *et al.* find. The subjects are reported as already discharging the tension associated with hunger in talking and thinking about food and food occupations (motoric expression of the need) so that, in the formal associative and apperceptive tests, there is no reason to expect any increase of food related material. But this case is complicated because there is another possible explanation. This is that the degree of need was so great as to arouse the subjects to defensive activity, an aspect of the problem I am not yet ready to discuss. Anyway, I do not think that this latter explanation is a good one here because the subjects give no evidence of ego-defensive activity with respect to hunger in their normal day-to-day behavior (they talk of hunger freely). Nonetheless, the Brozek data must be explained. They are, I believe, terribly embarrassing to the direct-expression point of view.

Not only does the substitutive principle fit well into the psychoanalytic concepts of primary and secondary process thinking and the developmental theories of Werner (29) and Piaget (22) who refer to sensori-motor and conceptual stages of thought, but it also can handle the data on the vicarious relation between motoric expression and fantasy (for example, the work of Singer *et al.* (26), showing inhibited body movement positively related to increases in Rorschach M; and the older studies of Jones (12) on internalization and externalization in children). I propose that the substitutive conception of apperceptive fantasy is more fundamental than the direct-expression model the closer one comes to wish-fulfillment fantasy. While wish-fulfillment may become modified, as we shall see, by all sorts of ego-control processes, it is nonetheless basic to the relationship between need states and apperceptive fantasy.

THE OPERATION OF EGO-DEFENSIVE PROCESSES

The other major limitation of the direct-expression theory began to be pointed up strikingly by a now well-known study dealing with sexual arousal and apperceptive fantasy by R. A. Clark (6). This study deals essentially with the second half of the "U" shaped curve, and stimulated the reintroduction of ego-defensive conceptions into the apperceptive fantasy field. This ego-defensive conception seems now to be widely accepted as a modification of the direct-expression model.

You are undoubtedly aware of Clark's findings that stimulation of sexual impulses was associated with a significant *reduction of overt erotic imagery* on the TAT, although this negative relationship was changed by having the subjects drink alcohol before the procedure. Clark reasonably interpreted the negative association between sexual arousal and the amount of erotic apperceptive fantasy in a straightforward secondary process fashion. He argued that, in the social circumstances of the experiment (which produced conflict), the sexual stimulation was accompanied by anxiety and guilt. This, in turn, led to inhibition of anxiety-toned sexual imagery. In plain language, the subjects didn't dare to express their sexual feelings in direct imagery because these feelings (being socially or perhaps even personally taboo) yielded strong anxieties.

Clark's data are reminiscent of the clinical dilemma of having to infer strong urges from the absence of relevant ideational material as well as from its presence. This kind of dilemma led to the postulation of ego-defense in the first place. Of course, in the clinical setting, the practical problem is to differentiate between genuine disinterest or lack of conflict and the repression of, denial of, or reaction formation to strong, conflictful urges.

The Clark type of experimental observation still left us with lack of closure concerning under what conditions the ego-control processes would be operative to produce the inhibition of an impulse in fantasy. Many people guessed that his findings were relevant only in a relatively limited number of need areas, that is, whenever we were dealing with a need which ran seriously afoul of social taboos so that strong conflicts about its expression would often be generated. Thus, one could maintain that, in the great majority of cases, there should be a positive relationship between strength of motive and its expression in apperceptive fantasy, while in areas like sex and aggression the interposition of ego processes would transform the need expression.

I believe that this argument is made more difficult to maintain as a result of a recent study by E. J. Murray (21), who studied the relationship between sleep deprivation and apperceptive fantasy. He found that after about eighty-six hours of enforced sleeplessness, there were fewer TAT themes suggesting sleep compared with a non-deprived control group. Murray suggests that since the subjects wished to appear adequate and to conform to the demands of the experiment by staying awake, yet were terribly in need of sleep, any ideation about sleep would make their task of staying awake still more difficult and anxiety producing. It was therefore adaptive for the subjects to suppress any stimulus (thinking about sleep) which would enhance the strength of the already excessively powerful drive.

In recent years there has been increasing interest in ego-control processes in contrast with needs as they determine all manner of cognitive functioning. The research of George Klein (13) is pertinent here. He showed that the perceptual accentuation or diminution of apparent size of discs on which were printed thirst satisfying objects depended primarily upon what appear to be fairly stable cognitive characteristics of subjects rather than upon the presence of the thirst need. The thirst condition merely accentuated the already present cognitive tendency to overestimate or underestimate the size of objects. Thus, the need did not directly organize perceptual behavior, but operated through existing cognitive structures. There is a great deal of current effort to tie down the relevant cognitive system principles and to relate them not only to ego-defensive processes (the work of Gardner (10), for example) but to a theoretical context such as psychoanalysis. In fact, a fundamental and insistent theme of later papers in this conference is built around stimulus and structural factors rather than need as bases of apperceptive fantasy.

I would like to mention some of our own recent experiences with ego-control processes in apperceptive fantasy. We employed the TAT in order to determine potential stress sensitivity in subjects who were to be exposed via tape recordings to a series of threatening passages of differing psychological content. In addition to a neutral passage, one dealt with an erotic theme and the other with hostility. Since we were interested in determining in advance to what extent subjects had strong conflicts in either of these two areas, they were given a modified TAT type of procedure. First they were asked to tell a dramatic story to one of the cards (card 5 of Murray's TAT), following which they told "the most erotic story they could" to the same card, and finally, "the most hostile." Thus we were able to "test the limits" of their fantasy, so to speak, in the various content areas. You will recognize in this procedure a conviction about the importance of facing subjects with non-ambiguous stimuli as well as ambiguous ones, a point of view I mentioned in a brief paper some years ago (14). During the experiment proper, the subjects listened to an erotic and a hostile passage, after which, by means of rating scales, check lists and interviews, we sought information about the degree of arousal of the subjects and the manner in which they coped with the stimulus-induced disturbance. During each taped passage, continuous recordings were made of GSR and Heart Rate.

What must interest us at the moment is what we could learn from the test of apperceptive fantasy as it reflected either level of need and conflict with respect to sexual and hostile content, or ego-control factors which might determine need expression. I have selected two case examples to illustrate (rather than prove) the point that under conditions of great arousal apperceptive fantasy reflects ego-processes more than straight need representations.

One subject could not really enter into the task of expressing, in his reported fantasy, erotic feelings and impulses. The story is stilted and undetailed. There is little erotic imagery. From a content analysis we might regard him as weakly motivated in the sexual sphere. When faced, however, with the highly erotic tape recorded passage, he became exceedingly disturbed (large GSR changes compared with the neutral passage), and expressed this in his ratings of tension. In the interview statement after the erotic passage one also gets very little erotic imagery, some stilted references to sexual intercourse, and evidence of great tension.

This same subject was given a more detailed interview a week later (which this subject himself sought because the material was still on his mind). It developed that, at twenty-nine years of age, he had never had any sexual intimacy with a woman. He had been brought up under conditions of severe sexual taboo, and was planning to enter the ministry. Recently, he had begun to date a woman and was in considerable conflict over the sexual feelings she aroused. In fact, he expressed fears that he might not be able to control himself sexually. As he had listened to the erotic passage, he had become sexually aroused and extremely anxious about it. The sexual feelings were frightening to him and he regarded them as a sign of personal defect.

It might be noted that this same subject freely gave very vivid imagery related to aggression, and responded with little arousal to the aggressive passage. We had tapped in our experiment an area of special conflict for him. But the strong sexual needs never did get reflected in fantasy; it was the anxiety and inhibition which appeared in the constricted, almost imageless story. His TAT story (with instructions to tell the most erotic story possible) is presented below, followed by the written interview data.

TAT STORY

The woman has come home earlier than usual and has opened the door to see her young son with one of his girl friends on the divan in the living room. Both are completely nude and are completely absorbed in their activity. Each is not concerned with the prospect of interruption, knowing that the parents are both supposed to be away for a while and have yielded to the forces of their mutual desires. Though each has been dating others occasionally they will become a steady pair eventually raising a family.

Below are given his written answers to a series of questions directly following the period during which he listened to the erotic sound tape recording. The passage to which he refers is too lengthy to reproduce here.

Written Interview Following Erotic Sound Tape Recording

1. *What were your reactions to this passage?*
   It was disturbing to listen to. It seemed strange that the boy should go to a tent. The episode was annoying in the extent to which it was descriptive.
2. *What are the things in the passage that stand out in your mind?*
   The secrecy which compelled his slipping away after hours. The indications of the uncertainty by the boy while at the same time he felt assurance. The intensity of their sexual experience to the point of complete involvement.
3. *Write down as much as you can of what went on in the passage.*
   The boy waited until it seemed that everyone was asleep and slipped out of his dorm to a meeting with a girl in a tent. He tried to stay in the trees to avoid possible discovery. He stopped at the tent, went in. The girl said "So you came."

She moved quickly to him, grabbing him. He carried her to a rug and they engaged in sexual activity.

4. Check one or more of the following statements that come closest to expressing the way you felt during the presentation. Look over all the statements before you decide.

   A. I felt pleasantly excited.
   B. I felt little if any emotion.
   X C. I felt anxious or uneasy.
   D. I felt annoyed at myself.
   E. I felt annoyed at the experimenter.
   F. I felt annoyed at the people in the passage.

   If you would like to comment further on your feelings, please do so.

5. On the following scale, check *how you felt during the presentation.*

   Number 1 represents complete calm and relaxation; number 5 represents complete tension and upset; numbers 2, 3 and 4 are points between the two extremes.

calm,			X	tense,
relaxed 1	2	3	4	5 upset

6. On the following scale, check *how you typically feel.*

calm,	X			tense,
relaxed 1	2	3	4	5 upset

A contrasting subject reacted to the erotic passage with relatively little autonomic arousal. He gave a much more free (though not florid) erotic fantasy in his TAT story, and followed through in his interview with a rather detailed, more expressive reaction to the pleasurable excitement generated by the passage. His material is presented below.

TAT STORY

In the past, mother had told her daughter many important things about sex. Her repeated phrase to her daughter was, "Above all, keep your knees together at all times." The daughter knew that the mother was definitely against love making before marriage, but what the daughter didn't know was that she was conceived before her mother's marriage. For some time now her daughter had been going with a man who was so good looking (so the mother thought) that she wished she could go to bed with him herself. So one evening, before the boyfriend came to call on the daughter, the mother spoke softly to the daughter encouraging her to let the boy find his mark tonight. The daughter agreed that it would be a very satisfying idea and told her mother that she was just itching to have a little. So the poor young man innocently sits on the couch with the pretty young miss and is rewarded sexually the whole evening. When the mother opens the door to the room in which the two are making passionate love, she finds them both nude, "in position" and then very satisfied. She meditates, sighs, and returns to the kitchen.

Written Interview Following Erotic Sound Tape Recording

1. *What were your reactions to this passage?*
   I envied the boy no end. I loved and respected the girl for her recognition of a boy's desires and her willingness to comply. It seemed to be a very idealistic, much desired and satisfying event.
2. *What are the things in the passage that stand out in your mind?*
   Boy-girl; images of the naked girl (anima); vigorous activity; secluded place; secrecy; lack of resistance to temptation; satisfaction; thrusting motion; closeness-togetherness (ha!).
3. *Write down as much as you can of what went on in the passage.*
   Boy sneaks out of dormitory and meets girl in a tent. She is smoking in the tent and puts the cigarette out when boy arrives. Boy grabs her and kisses her. They go to floor of tent and boy seduces her. Clothes are removed skillfully by each and exploration of female by male proceeds which is accompanied by renewed sexual excitement culminating with an orgasm.
4. Check one or more of the following statements that come closest to expressing the way you felt during the presentation. Look over all the statements before you decide.
   X A. I felt pleasantly excited.
   B. I felt little if any emotion.
   C. I felt anxious or uneasy.
   D. I felt annoyed at myself.
   E. I felt annoyed at the experimenter.
   F. I felt annoyed at the people in the passage.
   If you would like to comment further on your feelings, please do so.
5. On the following scale, check *how you felt during the presentation.*
   Number 1 represents complete calm and relaxation; number

5 represents complete tension and upset; numbers 2, 3 and 4 are points between the two extremes.

calm,				X tense,
relaxed 1	2	3	4	5 upset [anxious]

6. On the following scale, check *how you typically feel.*

calm,			X	tense,
relaxed 1	2	3	4	5 upset

The point of these illustrations is that, at least in the first case, the TAT material reflects the ego-defensive processes elicited by sexual content far more clearly than sexual needs. The autonomic reactivity in the presence of the erotic story which was played to him on a tape recorder suggested strong arousal. The interview which he solicited gave further evidence of the potency of sexual conflicts in him, and how close to the surface this material was. Yet, when he was asked to tell the most erotic story he could to card 5 of the TAT, there is scarcely any evidence of direct sexual imagery. This feeble sexual content was still more than he could muster when he was asked to tell a story to the same card with usual TAT instructions which do not specify any required theme. Clearly, it was the inhibited, defensive aspects of his personality which came through rather than the impulses or needs themselves. The second subject, in contrast, who shows little arousal autonomically and little other evidence of disturbance from listening to the erotic passage, is more able to directly express a sexual fantasy on the TAT. These kinds of data continually point up the importance of ego-defensive processes in disguising need characteristics in apperceptive fantasy.

What then emerges as the generalized relationship between need-states and apperceptive fantasy, and how is the pattern to be understood? Empirically, there is evidence for a positive relationship, for a negative relationship, and for a curvilinear relationship (the "U" shaped curve). Surely the nature of the relationship depends upon a wide range of conditions, including the stimulus, the particular fantasy measure employed, the point on the dimension of arousal at which the observations are made, and the opportunity for various ego-control processes to occur and to be detected. In conceptualizing the underlying processes which determine the observed outcomes, I believe a number of principles are required. I wish to campaign for two of them as I suggested earlier, although many others may be necessary.

As I have already implied, the *first principle is a substitutive one. This maintains that there will be a positive relationship between need states and fantasy only when the need has been blocked from motoric discharge.* This is the condition of primary process fantasying. If a need is being adequately expressed in actual life striving, it will not be expressed in apperceptive fantasy except under special circumstances which are not yet clear. Thus, high levels of apperceptive fantasy imply moderate need levels in the absence of motoric expression; while low levels of apperceptive fantasy could reflect either low need or moderate need in the face of substantial motoric expression.

Notice that I have related high levels of apperceptive fantasy to only "moderate" degrees of need level. This is because of the *second principle, which states that as the need reaches excessively high levels (because of environmental blockage or internal conflict), the organism is under stress, and various ego-control processes to reduce the disturbance will be brought into play.* These (including ego-defenses) serve to alter or eliminate the cognitive expression of the need (in fantasy the associations and images related to the need and its objects are inhibited) because they only serve to intensify the already too strong need state and its attendant effects. Thus, Murray's subjects find it less disturbing to avoid thoughts of sleep than to permit such stimuli to further enhance the already aroused state.

The term "excessive" in the above statement is, of course, difficult to define, and may well depend on subject thresholds and other pressures to which the person is exposed. But we can readily assume that degree of need tension or arousal is a continuous dimension, and that beyond some point, new processes (ego-defenses, for example) emerge which have their own secondary consequences in behavior. This kind of notion is identical to the traditional concept of psychopathology which asserts that conflict-produced anxiety results in the elicitation of defenses which, in turn, are associated with distortions of reality and other symptomatic conditions.

One may wonder whether there is any difference in the consequences for apperceptive fantasy between needs which are blocked from expression because of an environmental obstacle (thwarting) or because of internal conflict resulting from the internalization of some environmental pressure (frustration). In some ways this is like the Freudian distinction between neurotic anxiety and objective anxiety. The need involved is blocked (e.g., repression), but in one case because of an internal struggle (usually unconscious) while in the other, it is inhibited or suppressed. I think that there may be a way of operationalizing this distinction. In the case of internal unconscious struggle, the defensive consequences in fantasy are not only inaccessible to the person, but they are rigid and refractory to any external manipulation. The need cannot be directly expressed under any circumstances (except, perhaps, under drugs, hypnosis or long term therapy). However, in the case of suppression because of inhibiting environmental circumstances, the alteration of these circumstances could well "unblock" the expression of the need. Our use of the "forced" TAT procedure is interesting in this regard. Often a subject, who under the usual TAT conditions gives very little, say erotic apperceptive fantasy material, can be encouraged to do so when told to tell the "most erotic story he can." However, I believe that in the case of the subject who manifests a neurotic internal struggle about erotic needs, he will still be unable to express these, even when the experimental conditions either require or encourage it. But this is a digression from our main theme.

It should be clear that the two principles, substitutive and defensive, deal with different aspects of the relationship between needs and apperceptive fantasy. The substitutive principle must apply only when the level of need is weak or moderate. Even here, its expression is probably contaminated by ego-control processes, for example, cognitive styles or attitudes which determine the formal ways in which the environment is apprehended. The defensive principle of apperceptive fantasy applies when the level of need is high enough to arouse considerable anxiety, blocked from direct motoric discharge either by environmental obstacles or by equally powerful, internal, conflicting needs.

There seems to be more agreement among current researchers

about the defensive principle than about the substitutive one. But the net impact of these notions for the evaluation of apperceptive fantasy is the implication that need states cannot easily be disentangled, from an assessment point of view, from ego-control processes. In other words, if a psychologist approaches a TAT record, he should find it impossible without additional information to make clear inferences about either needs or ego-control processes. The thematic material will be an end result of the dynamic interaction of both, and there is no clear way to separate their mutual influence from the apperceptive record alone.

This dilemma, I believe, can only be solved in one way, in the same way, logically, as the clinical psychologist makes inferences about psychodynamics from the behavioral evidence confronting him. This involves the use of behavioral patterns. It is reflected in the data I presented earlier to illustrate the problem of inferring sexual needs from the TAT in the face of ego-control processes which disguise them. In that illustration, I had access not only to the TAT content, but also to physiological reactions to similar types of stimulus material. Evidence that the subject was, indeed, aroused by it could be checked against the relative lack of sexual imagery on his TAT story. In the same way, we know that a subject is under stress, even when he denies it or appears bland and intellectualizing about an experience, because he evidences marked autonomic nervous system arousal at the same time.

There is nothing new or dramatic about this solution. It simply recognizes that one segment of behavior, no matter how rich it seems to be (as is often remarked about the TAT) can be terribly misleading concerning the total, complex, organismic reactions of a person. Shakespeare anticipated the clinical use of patterning from which to draw inferences in his classic line, "Methinks the lady doth protest too much." The essence of this point is that inconsistencies in behavior are revealing of the true nature of the underlying state.

I would still maintain, in the face of the gradually changing vogue away from a need-oriented conception of apperceptive fantasy, that needs are reflected in fantasy (when they are not expressed motorically). The point is that they are not reflected directly. They interact with ego-control processes, and, of course, qualities of the external stimulus as well. Thus, what emerges is a complex product which is a resultant of the interplay of many forces. In my estimation, the only way in which these forces will be disentangled is through the study of the multiple aspects of response and their patterning. This argument applies not only to apperceptive fantasy, but to other behavior samples, for example, introspections or self report, physical behavior, and physiological reactivity. Singly these different aspects of behavior often provide a markedly different picture than when they are taken in combination. We must get over our hunger for a single assessment tool (based upon a single behavior segment) to infer the complex forces which characterize the structure and dynamics of human personality.

REFERENCES

1. Atkinson, J. W. (Ed.): *Motives in Fantasy, Action, and Society.* New York, Van Nostrand, 1958.
2. Atkinson, J. W., and McClelland, D. C.: The projective expression of needs: II. The effect of different intensities of the hunger drive on thematic apperception. *J. Exp. Psychol., 38*:643-658. 1948.
3. Bleuler, E.: Autistic thinking. In D. Rapaport (Ed.), *Organization and Pathology of Thought,* New York, Columbia Univ. Press, 1951, Pp. 399-437.
4. Broverman, D. M.: Jordan, E. J., and Phillips, L.: Achievement motivation in fantasy and behavior. *J. Abnorm. & Social Psychol., 60:*374-378, 1960.
5. Brozek, J., Guetzkow, H., and Baldwin, Marcella V.: A quantitative study of perception and association in experimental semistarvation. *J. Pers., 19:*245-264. 1951.
6. Clark, R. A.: Projective measurement of experimentally induced levels of sexual motivation. *J. Exp. Psychol., 44*:391-399. 1952.
7. Dollard, J., and Miller, N. E.: *Personality and Psychotherapy.* New York, McGraw-Hill, 1950.
8. Estes, W. K.: Stimulus-response theory of drive. In M. R. Jones (Ed.), *Nebraska Symposium on Motivation.* Lincoln, Neb., Univ. Nebraska Press, 1958, 35-69.
9. Feffer, M.: The cognitive implications of role-taking behavior. *J. Pers.,* (in press).

10. Gardner, R. W.: Cognitive control principles and perceptual behavior. Presented at Symposium on Perception, Joint meeting of Kansas and Southern Psychol. Assn., April 16, 1959.
11. Holt, R. R.: The nature of TAT stories as cognitive products: a psychoanalytic approach. In J. Kagan and G. S. Lesser (Eds.), *Contemporary Issues in Thematic Apperceptive Methods.* Springfield, Thomas, 1960.
12. Jones, H. E.: The galvanic skin reflex. *Child Development, 1*:106-110, 1930.
13. Klein, G.: Need and regulation. In M. R. Jones (Ed.), *Current Theory and Research in Motivation: a Symposium.* Lincoln, Neb., Univ. Nebraska Press, 1954.
14. Lazarus, R. S.: Ambiguity and nonambiguity in projective testing. *J. Abnorm. & Social Psychol., 48*:443-445. 1953.
15. Lazarus, R. S., Baker, R. W., Broverman, D. M., and Mayer, J.: Personality and psychological stress. *J. Pers., 25*:559-577. 1957.
16. Lazarus, R. S., Yousem, H., and Arenberg, D.: Hunger and perception. *J. Pers., 21*:312-328, 1953.
17. Levine, R., Chein, I., and Murphy, G.: The relation of the intensity of a need to the amount of perceptual distortion. *J. Psychol., 13*:282-293. 1942.
18. Malmo, R. B.: Measurement of drive: an unsolved problem in psychology. In M. R. Jones (Ed.), *Nebraska Symposium on Motivation.* Lincoln, Neb., Univ. Nebraska Press, 1958, 229-265.
19. McClelland, D. C., and Atkinson, J. W.: The projective expression of needs: I. The effect of different intensities of the hunger drive on perception. *J. Psychol., 25*:205-222. 1948.
20. McClelland, D. C., Atkinson, J. W., Clark, R. S., and Lowell, E. L.: *The Achievement Motive.* New York, Appleton, 1953.
21. Murray, E. J.: Conflict and repression during sleep deprivation. *J. Abnorm. & Social Psychol., 59*:95-101. 1959.
22. Piaget, J.: *The Psychology of Intelligence.* London, Kegan Paul, 1950.
23. Rapaport, D.: Toward a theory of thinking. In D. Rapaport (Ed.), *Organization and Pathology of Thought.* New York, Columbia Univ. Press, 1951, 689-729.
24. Sanford, R. N.: The effect of abstinence from food upon imaginal processes: a preliminary experiment. *J. Psychol. 2*:129-136. 1936.
25. Sanford, R. N.: The effect of abstinence from food upon imaginal processes: a further experiment. *J. Psychol., 3*:145-159. 1937.

!6. Singer, J., Meltzoff, J., and Goldman, G.: Rorschach movement responses following motor inhibition and hyperactivity. *J. Consult. Psychol., 16*:359-364. 1952.
!7. Vogel, W., Baker, R. W., and Lazarus, R. S.: The role of motivation in psychoogical stress. *J. Abnorm. & Social Psychol., 56:*105-112. 1958.
!8. Vogel, W., Raymond, Susan, and Lazarus, R. S.: Instrinsic motivation and psychological stress. *J. Abnorm. & Social Psychol., 58:*225-233. 1959.
!9. Werner, H.: *Comparative Psychology of Mental Development.* Chicago, Follet, rev. ed., 1948.

DISCUSSION OF DR. LAZARUS' PAPER

John W. Atkinson, Ph.D.
Primary Discussant

D*r. Atkinson:* Dr. Lazarus has overlooked the fact that the *simple* "direct expression" concept, as he has phrased it, faded out of the research on thematic apperceptive expression of needs by McClelland *et al.,* about the time of the Clark study on sexual motivation (8, 9). That study was part of a research program based on a theoretical conception of inhibition of direct expression of need in thematic apperception (2).

I'd also like to lay to rest any other simple alternative hypothesis. Dr. Lazarus is arguing that the simple "direct expression" idea should be buried, and he offers another simpler one! I believe that acceptance of the alternative he has proposed would also be a mistake.

We know this much: there is good evidence that when certain needs are aroused experimentally, there is a production of need-related imagery within TAT stories (1). This at least suggests that aroused needs are *sometimes* manifested directly in thematic apperceptive imagery. I would agree that there is also evidence, mainly from the clinic but also in some of the experiments in the research program to which he referred, that very intense or conflicted needs are often inhibited (1, 2, 8, 9, 11, 24). That is, the absence of manifest content may sometimes be symptomatic of intense or conflicted need. There is also suggestive evidence that the expression of imagery may represent a misleading denial of the opposite.

The guiding questions in our research on achievement motivation and other motives have been: (a) Under what conditions are motivating states expressed in manifest content? (b) Under what conditions do the motives expressed in manifest imaginative content relate to overt behavior? A lot of work has been done to find answers to these questions; some people at this table have participated in it. For the sake of review, in connection with the first question there is factual evidence indicating that under arousal conditions, hunger (3), ambition (21), fear (29), and anger (13) are all expressed in manifest thematic content.

Now let us turn to the evidence that has been introduced to support an argument that the "direct expression" hypothesis doesn't stand up. First, consider the Murray study in which individuals kept awake for 90 hours were found to express less imagery having to do with sleep in thematic apperception than a control group, when tested near the time when people normally go to sleep. Again let me argue that we shouldn't be too confident about assuming that we already have a good enough theory of motivation to know when a particular need (assuming we mean by this a goal-directed tendency) has been aroused. Let me use an illustration to make my point.

In recent discussions of animal experiments on hunger it has been suggested, by Hebb (16, p. 192) originally, and by others like McClelland *et al.* (21), and Estes (12), that what we think of as hunger, e.g. motivation to eat food, is not a function of simple degree of biological deficit produced by food privation. Rather, hunger as we know it, may simply reflect the extent to which the internal cues associated with a certain number of hours of food deprivation (the so-called "drive stimuli") have been associated in the past with eating, that is, habituation. Hebb has called attention to the possibility that a person reared in our society who later undergoes natural starvation may actually lose his appetite when he has gone without food for a long time. The internal cues accompanying abnormal food privation then become so dissimilar from the cues in the presence of which he has normally eaten that there is no longer arousal of the anticipation of eating. This idea has recently been confirmed in an animal experiment which controlled the maintenance schedule of animals from infancy. An experiment by Birch, Burnstein, and Clark (7), has produced the positive results suggested by this kind of conception of arousal of "hunger." Animals who were fed after 22 hours food privation from the time of infancy showed the increase in activation of behavior, normally thought to be a function of biological need, up to 22 hours. However, there was then a drop in level of activation, too soon to be attributed to debilitation, when hours of food privation were extended beyond 22 hours for the first time. Now, general level of activity is the sort of behavioral manifestation of "motivation" that for fifty years psychologists have thought of as a simple function of degree of biological need defined in terms of hours privation. The explanation offered by Birch *et al.* is that internal cues which have become associated with eating are responsible for the arousal of hunger, or the motivation to eat in a rat (i.e., the arousal of an anticipatory goal response). When you go past the point of deprivation at which the animal habitually eats, the internal cues change and it is no longer hungry.

Now let's consider the sleep experiment. What subject in that experiment had ever had a history which would account for associations between the internal cues produced by 90 hours of sleep deprivation and sleeping? My argument is — none. I make this point simply to illustrate the fallacy of assuming we already know all about the operations that are supposed to control strength of motivation. We don't; and if I read the literature in the *Nebraska Symposium* correctly, the kind of theory of motivation that is gradually coming into focus in the animal work is one that is quietly getting rid of the old concept of biological need as the source of biological drive and substituting, instead, an associative theory, as in Estes' (12), or Spence's (25) treatment of incentive motivation, in which internal or external cues are associated with certain kinds of goal satisfactions. Motivation is aroused when you reproduce those cues. Going without sleep for ninety hours would probably produce a state similar to those occasions when every one of us has been so fatigued we haven't been able to sleep without some coffee to restore the state of normal sleepiness. At this stage, I don't think results corresponding to an inverted U function need be considered crucial. I think they appear crucial only if we presume in advance that we already know all about motivation and the conditions under which it should be aroused.

Now let us turn to the other evidence that has been presented. Dr. Lazarus refers to results in some of his earlier experiments on stress, and he refers at length to a new set of results in his paper today. I feel there are some questions to be asked about TAT methodology or at least in the report of it. I have been trying to make sense out of the n Achievement results in one or two of the earlier stress studies, and I run into things like the use of only two pictures, the repeated use of the very same test after a very short time interval, and the absence of any report of a scoring reliability coefficient or validity coefficient. These are some of the little methodological details that those of us who have been concerned about improving the rigor of thematic content analysis have made a lot of. I am very concerned when I think of the dire consequences of low coding reliability. When two coders correlate .90 in scoring, they account for 81 per cent of the variance in scores. If two coders only agree to the extent indicated by a correlation of .70, they account for only 49 per cent of the variance in scores. There has been a loss of 32 per cent in common variance; and 32 per cent of the variance is big enough to contain a correlation coefficient between .50 and .60. I perhaps lay more stress than many would on this. But when I try to make sense out of experiments that don't come out the way other ones have, and I don't find a report of the coding reliability coefficient or clear indication that stories were actually coded for n Achievement as the manual by McClelland *et al.* specifies, I have to wonder if we are necessarily dealing with the same variable.

Turning to the "crucial" evidence in the n Achievement study cited at length, there was a detail of method that would make it very difficult for me to attempt to explain the results. The little detail — the thematic apperception method wasn't even employed in the study. Some other *ad hoc* instrument that presumably has no history of validity is introduced. The claim is made that this has the same functional properties of achievement imagery scored in a particular way in thematic apperception. Maybe it does and maybe it doesn't. I would not want to lean very hard on an argument for a thesis that rests on the assumption, in the absence of demonstration, that some *ad hoc* test device has the same properties as thematic apperception.

Aside from this, even the negative relationship between what is called n Achievement and behavior is not necessarily crucial because studies of achievement motivation have already shown that what is called the achievement motive (the name imagery of a certain kind in TAT analysis) is not always positively related to behavioral achievement. According to the theory developed in research on n Achievement and performance (1, chap. 42; 4) whether or not achievement imagery in the TAT will be related to performance depends upon the conditions under which the achievement imagery is obtained and the conditions that obtain at the time of performance. Elizabeth French (14, 15), who has done a series of experiments on this problem with a slightly modified apperceptive device, shows the same trends observed in our studies at Michigan. She has shown that "achievement-related" behavior can be produced by the affiliative need under certain circumstances and by extrinsic motivation under other circumstances. We have even performed an experiment to demonstrate that you can deliberately wash out the relationship between TAT need achievement and performance by systematically introducing other kinds of incentives for performance.

These are important methodological points — sometimes they seem to be small details. Yet I feel the hope of moving ahead with thematic apperceptive analysis rests upon the extent to which investigators take these little details seriously.

I am impressed with the a priori plausibility of the general argument Dr. Lazarus has presented. I hardly want to find myself in the position of defending the notion that the only vehicle we should use in attempting to study motivation should be TAT content. Obviously the way to increase our understanding of human motivation is to relate a particular kind of motivational content from thematic apperception to the other kinds of variables that Dr. Lazarus has mentioned — to GSR, to verbal reports about how a person feels under certain circumstances, and to overt performances. I don't want to be pushed into saying thematic apperception *by itself* is the royal road to motivation. However, just to restore the balance, I would like to review a little of what we do know about the correlates of achievement imagery in the TAT. It has been argued that thematic apperceptive measures of n Achievement in college students will relate to "unreal" laboratory behavior but not to "real-life" behavior. The extent to which one can make that distinction suggests that something is wrong with the experiments that have been done. The relevant experiments on human motivation in the so-called lab setting always ought to be realistic, life-like experiences.

Here are a few facts from which to argue that at least within "normal" school and college populations the evidence is stronger for the "direct expression" hypothesis (even willingly granting exceptions) than for any other hypothesis when we deal with a motive which, in a society like ours, can be expressed in behavior without consequent punishment. I mean specifically, the achievement motive. We know from Winterbottom (30) that children eight to ten years old who have a lot of achievement imagery in their protocols are rated by their teachers as being more strongly motivated than others, as more independent, and as taking greater pleasure in success (suggesting the idea that the achievement motive is a capacity for getting greater satisfaction out of success). All that appears to be "real-life" behavior among children.

In studies of college students, we have made some progress in isolating the conditions under which differences in TAT n Achievement are most clearly manifested in the level of performance: When the performance task is presented as an important test of ability and when an effort is made to keep other kinds of motivation for performance, like need for affiliation, at a minimum.

We have developed and tested a theory which accounts for the relationship between TAT n Achievement scores obtained under neutral test conditions and behavior (1). Strong achievement motivation in an individual has *three* implications for his behavior: he will prefer an intermediate degree of difficulty (or risk); he will perform at a higher level; and he will be more persistent at achievement tasks than a person who is weak in achievement motivation. All three hypotheses have been confirmed in life-like experimental studies (5, 6). In one experiment (6), we found that Ss high in n Achievement showed the greatest preference for intermediate risk in a competitive game played during a lab period as the theory suggested. In addition, we found that the high n Achievement group was more persistent; that is, they worked longer on their final exam, as the theory suggested they should. We also found that their exam performance was more efficient; that is, they did better on the exam than individuals who were low in need for achievement.

The theory which related n Achievement to behavior has also been confirmed in a study of vocational aspirations in a recent dissertation by Mahone (19). Subjects who had high n Achievement scores had intermediate aspirations on a scale of occupations; subjects who were low in n Achievement had vocational aspirations either way above or below the level for which they were realistically suited by their general ability. Is this "unreal" laboratory behavior or "real-life" behavior?

In the national survey research that Dr. Veroff is going to talk about tomorrow, one result having to do with real-life achievement behavior is the level of education attained by the respondents. College educated individuals have significantly higher n Achievement than less educated persons (26).

In other words, there is a large body of evidence that suggests that under certain conditions you *can* assess individual differences in the strength of a need or a motive from manifest thematic content.

I will not argue with the notion that sometimes this manifest content may really be substitutive, i.e., a reaction to frustration. Nor will I argue with the notion that sometimes positive achievement content may really represent a denial of anxiety about failure in people who aren't positively motivated. We have seen suggestions of that already. The problem is to state clearly *the conditions under which* this occurs. I think Lazarus' hypothesis suggests some of the conditions under which this phenomenon occurs. We also have evidence from the work of Mussen (22) and Kagan (17) that shows it is possible to tap manifest thematic content for both sides of conflict, aggressive imagery and also anxiety about its expression, to improve the prediction of overt performance.

What we seem to have, in other words, are several different reasonable hypotheses about the meaning of manifest content, including those proposed today. What we need is clarification of the *conditions under which* one or another of these hypotheses should be the basis for our inference about what the content of the TAT means.

Dr. Lazarus: I am not sure we should be talking only about need achievement because I have been talking about the general problem of needs and fantasy. I am always bothered by what I think is the over-generality of the concept of need achievement.

I find it a little difficult to accept the notion that a person who is regarded as a high need achiever, from your own theoretical position, would manifest this need with respect to all types of functioning. For example, I can conceive of a person being strongly achievement oriented with respect to playing the piano but have very little concern with respect to some non-musical activity. One can proliferate the varieties of kinds of activities that might be involved.

Dr. Tomkins: Overt behavior is in many important ways somewhat elliptical. If we observed what someone did from the beginning of his life until he died, there would be certain important gaps in our ability to interpret what the components were which produced the resultants that we observed. No matter how much we refined our observation of behavior, there would still be certain questions. So we go to something like the TAT because by means of language the individual is in a position to say not only what heroes do but what they think and what they feel and how they wrestle with the human situation.

Now, it appears that the projected solution is incomplete and unsatisfactory for the very same reason that we rejected overt behavior in the first place. It now turns out that the feelings, thoughts, and conflicts in a story become elliptical under certain conditions. This is indeed paradoxical but understandable on the same basis that a person doesn't do everything he feels like doing. The same factors that are at work in making his behavior the elliptical thing it is, can also, under certain conditions, make his fantasy statements of behavior elliptical.

REFERENCES

1. Atkinson, J. W.: (Ed.), *Motives in Fantasy, Action, and Society.* Princeton, New Jersey, Van Nostrand, 1958.
2. Atkinson, J. W.: Explorations using imaginative thought to assess the strength of human motives. In M. R. Jones (Ed.), *Nebraska Symposium on Motivation,* 1954. Lincoln, Univ. of Nebr. Press, 1954, 56-112.

*3. Atkinson, J. W., and McClelland, D. C.: The projective expression of needs. II. The effect of different intensities of the hunger drive on thematic apperception. *J. Exp. Psychol., 38*:643-658. 1948.

*4. Atkinson, J. W., and Reitman, W. R.: Performance as a function of motive strength and expectancy of goal attainment. *J. Abnorm. & Social Psychol., 53*:361-366. 1956.

5. Atkinson, J. W., Bastian, J. R., Earl, R. W., and Litwin, G. H.: The achievement motive, goal-setting, and probability preferences. *J. Abnorm. & Social Psychol., 60.* 1960.
6. Atkinson, J. W., and Litwin, G. H.: Achievement motive and test anxiety as motives to approach success and to avoid failure. *J. Abnorm. & Social Psychol., 60.* 1960.
7. Birch, D., Burnstein, E., and Clark, R. A.: Response strength as a function of hours of food deprivation under a controlled maintenance schedule. *J. Comp. & Physiol. Psychol., 51*:350-354. 1958.
8. Clark, R. A.: The projective measurement of experimentally induced levels of sexual motivation. *J. Exp. Psychol., 44*:391-399. 1952.
9. Clark, R. A.: The effects of sexual motivation on phantasy. In D. C. McClelland (Ed.), *Studies in Motivation.* New York, Appleton, 1955, 132-138.

*10. Clark, R. A., Ricciuti, H. N., and Teevan, R. C.: An investigation of the hope of success and fear of failure aspects of need for achievement. *J. Gen. Psychol., 53*:182-186. 1956.

*11. Clark, R. A., and Sensibar, Minda R.: The relationships between symbolic and manifest projections of sexuality with some incidental correlates. *J. Abnorm. & Social Psychol., 50:*327-334. 1956.

12. Estes, W. K.: Stimulus-response theory of drive. In M. R. Jones (Ed.), *Nebraska Symposium on Motivation,* 1958. Lincoln, Univ. of Nebr. Press, 1958, 35-68.

13. Feshbach, S.: The drive reducing function of fantasy behavior. *J. Abnorm. & Social Psychol., 50:*3-11. 1955.
14. French, Elizabeth G.: Some characteristics of achievement motivation. *J. Exp. Psychol., 50:*232-236. 1955.
15. French, Elizabeth G.: Motivation as a variable in work-partner selection. *J. Abnorm. & Social Psychol., 53:*96-99, 1956.
16. Hebb, D. O.: *The Organization of Behavior.* New York, Wiley, 1949.
17. Kagan, J.: The measurement of overt aggression from fantasy. *J. Abnorm. & Social Psychol., 52:*390-393. 1956.
18. Lazarus, R. S., Baker, R. W., Broverman, D. M., and Mayer, J.: Personality and psychological stress. *J. Pers., 25:*559-577. 1957.
19. Mahone, C. H.: Fear of failure and unrealistic vocational aspiration. Doctoral dissertation, Univ. of Michigan, 1958.
20. McClelland, D. C.: Risk-taking in children with high and low need for achievement. In J. W. Atkinson, (Ed.), *Motives in Fantasy, Action, and Society.* Princeton, New Jersey, Van Nostrand, 1958, 306-321.
21. McClelland, D. C., Atkinson, J. W., Clark, R. A., and Lowell, E. L.: *The Achievement Motive.* New York, Appleton, 1953.
22. Mussen, P. H., and Naylor, H. K.: The relationships between overt and fantasy aggression. *J. Abnorm. & Social Psychol., 49:*235-240. 1954.
23. Rosen, B.: The achievement syndrome. *Amer. Soc. Rev., 21:*203-211. 1955.
24. Scott, W. A.: The avoidance of threatening material in imaginative behavior. *J. Abnorm. & Social Psychol., 52:*338-346. 1956.
25. Spence, K. W.: *Behavior Theory and Conditioning.* New Haven, Yale Univ. Press, 1956.
26. Veroff, J., Atkinson, J. W., Gurin, G., and Feld, Sheila C.: The use of thematic apperception to assess motivation in a nationwide interview study. Unpublished paper. Survey Research Center, Ann Arbor, Michigan, 1959.
27. Vogel, W., Baker, R. W., and Lazarus, R. S.: The role of motivation in psychological stress. *J. Abnorm. & Social Psychol., 56:*105-112. 1958.
28. Vogel, W., Raymond, Susan, and Lazarus, R. S.: Intrinsic motivation and psychological stress. *J. Abnorm. & Social Psychol., 58:* 225-233. 1959.
29. Walker, E. L., Atkinson, J. W., Veroff, J., Birney, R., Dember, W., and Moulton, R.: The expression of fear-related motivation in

thematic apperception as a function of proximity to an atomic explosion. In J. W. Atkinson, (Ed.), *Motives in Fantasy, Action, and Society*. Princeton, New Jersey, Van Nostrand, 1958, 143-159.

*30. Winterbottom, Marian R.: The relation of need for achievement to learning experiences in independence and mastery. In J. W. Atkinson, (Ed.), *Motives in Fantasy, Action, and Society*. Princeton, New Jersey, Van Nostrand, 1958, 453-478.

---

*The items marked by asterisk (*) are reprinted in reference number 1.

THEMATIC APPERCEPTION IN A NATIONWIDE SAMPLE SURVEY[1]

Joseph Veroff, Ph.D.
Survey Research Center
University of Michigan

IN THE spring of 1957, 1619 men and women, constituting a representative sample of the adult population of the United States,[2] told stories in response to pictures. These stories were taken down verbatim by interviewers of the Survey Research Center and coded for motivational contents (n Achievement, n Affiliation and n Power) as described in Atkinson (1). This information was then punched into IBM's finest assortment of cards and fed to the machines, and the results from these maneuvers are now being explored by a team of us – John Atkinson, Gerald Gurin, Sheila Feld and myself. Some of these explorations I would like to discuss with you today.

One of the most interesting of the substantive findings that we have encountered thus far has to do with the relationship of the achievement motive scores of working men to the kind of work they do. Table 1 shows dramatically that the men in the higher status occupations have higher achievement motivation than the men in the lower status occupations.

---

[1]The investigations reported in this paper are based on data obtained within a national sample survey supported by the Joint Commission on Mental Illness and Health. Analysis of these data is supported by two grants from NIMH, USPHS–projects M2181 and M2280.

[2]The individuals interviewed in this survey are a representative cross-section of adults, 21 years of age or older, living in private households in the United States. The sample was selected by a probability method with procedures known as area sampling. For details of this sample, see Gurin, Veroff, and Feld (7).

TABLE 1

PERCENTAGE ABOVE THE MEDIAN N ACHIEVEMENT SCORE BY OCCUPATION[a]

	Percentage Above Median n Ach	*(N)*
Professional men and technicians	60	(68)
Managers and proprietors	59	(71)
Clerical workers	55	(31)
Salesmen	60	(35)
Skilled workers	50	(121)
Semi-skilled workers	52	(88)
Unskilled workers	44	(41)
Farmers	44	(39)

[a]Based on scores derived from procedures outlined in Atkinson (1); these scores have been corrected for correlation with length of protocol, to be discussed in a forthcoming section.

Not a surprising result, you say! Of course you would expect the relationship to be that way! Well, so did we. And so we were at first disconcerted to find some challenge to this original relationship when we related these variables with age of the respondent controlled. In Table 2 the relationship of achievement motive scores and occupation is presented separately for three age periods — 21-34, 35-49, and 50 and over.

TABLE 2

PERCENTAGE ABOVE THE MEDIAN N ACHIEVEMENT SCORE BY OCCUPATION WITHIN AGE GROUPINGS (EMPLOYED MEN ONLY)[a]

Age	*Occupation*	*Percentage Above Median n Ach*	*(N)*
21-34	Professional men and technicians	67	(27)
	Managers and proprietors	60	(20)
	Clerical workers	60	(15)
	Salesmen	53	(15)
	Skilled workers	51	(37)
	Semi-skilled workers	49	(41)
	Unskilled workers	18	(11)
	Farmers	40	(10)
35-49	Professional men and technicians	56	(25)
	Managers and proprietors	55	(23)
	Clerical workers	60	(10)
	Salesmen	75	(12)
	Skilled workers	61	(41)
	Semi-skilled workers	64	(25)
	Unskilled workers	54	(13)
	Farmers	45	(11)

50 and over	Professional men and technicians	53	(15)
	Managers and proprietors	64	(26)
	Clerical workers	40	(5)
	Salesmen	43	(7)
	Skilled workers	38	(42)
	Semi-skilled workers	45	(22)
	Unskilled workers	57	(14)
	Farmers	44	(18)

[a]Does not include nine men whose age was not ascertained.

In the youngest age group, the simple positive relationship between occupational status and achievement motivation holds up. But not so in the middle age or the older age period. What we find for middle-aged men is that they all are at a fairly high level of achievement motivation relative to young men and very old men; all groups except professional and managerial men show an increase from the young age period to the middle age period. Achievement motivation shows a slumping off in the older age period.

Now these findings seem to present enormous possibilities for speculation about achievement motivation and how it is related to age and a man's job. And there is perhaps nothing more richly rewarding than to think that in these results we may come closer to understanding the problems of achievement strivings in American society. Such presumption is good for one's soul on occasion. And so, in spite of the fact that these data presented are based on few cases in some of the groups, and that statistical significance is not considered, grant me some indulgence and allow me to speculate freely about these data. Substantive results coming from the national survey will be viewed in this paper as illustrative points of general issues. With your forbearance then, I begin spinning this web of speculation about the meaning of achievement motivation for men in our society.

In the bloom of young manhood, the world is open to a man's desires. What worlds he conquers depends on what worlds he wants to conquer. The development of his achievement desires in youth predisposes him to seek the work he wants to do as a young adult. At least, romantic doctrine would lead us to believe that if he has been taught to desire excellence he will seek jobs that allow for this satisfaction as an adult; if he has not been taught to desire excellence, his occupational goals will be limited. It is the motives of these young men, the inner pushes for achievement, that underlie the finding that achievement motivation is positively related to their occupational attainment. One thus has evidence that the achievement motivation measure is tapping an important, enduring *predisposition* in men.

Now let us continue our speculations by shifting attention to the middle-aged men. They are relatively high on need for achievement, and their achievement motive scores are *not* related to occupational status. This middle-aged spurt makes sense. At middle age, a man obtains some distance from the omnipresent interpersonal demands put on him by the problems of raising a family and hence at this point in his life cycle can devote more attention to his achievement concerns. The achievement motivation measure is picking up this change in a life situation. This spurt is not in evidence for the top-positioned occupational groups — the professional and managerial groups. Could it be that these groups have a more precocious, overpowering concern with achievement during their earlier years? The amount of effort it takes to become a member of these occupations is initially very strong. For professional and managerial men the demands for the big push toward achievement may by necessity come into their life situations earlier. The decrease in achievement motivation in middle age may reflect a relaxation of achievement goals in the work situation for those high status men.

Now, what about the older men? Except for the managerial-proprietor group, older men show a decline in achievement motivation. As men reach old age, retire from a commitment to life and retrench into solving the problems of death, undoubtedly their energy for achievement concerns is reduced. Again the *situation,* this end phase of man's life cycle, seems to be an important determinant of his motivational pattern.

Now, hold on there, I have to warn myself; what have I done? This speculation is all very interesting, and may even be accurate. But look at the gross inconsistency in the way the motive measures have been interpreted. For the young men, one talks about the achievement motive as a personality characteristic, an enduring predisposition (as the *antecedent* of high occupational status). And with the older men one talks about the life situation they are confronted with and how this affects their achievement motivation (now viewed as a *consequence* of situational factors). Where is consistency? Do the motive measures tap, at one and the same time, enduring predispositions and situational influences? If so, how does one evaluate how much of each of these factors contributes to determination of motive scores?

The theoretical assumption about the measuring instrument in previous usage has been that the motive scores are *joint* functions of the situation — proximal or distal — in which the person finds himself and his *enduring* motive predisposition (1, ch. 42). Indeed the whole background of research establishing the validity of not only the achievement motive measure but also the measures of affiliation and power motivation is a grand testimony to this viewpoint. As you will recall, there are two steps in the development of these motive measures: (1) the measures reflect situational changes: demonstration of differences in motivational contents between two groups of subjects — one experimentally aroused with respect to a motive under investigation, and the other not aroused; (2) the measures reflect dispositional differences in strength of motivation: demonstration that the differences found in the first step can be used as scoring criteria for valid measures of *individual differences* — people showing much imagery diagnostic of the above group differences (high motive scorers) are meaningfully different in their behavior from people showing little of this imagery (low motive scorers). Studies involving the prediction from motive score of choice, intensity or persistence of behavior over time presume that the fantasy measure taps an enduring characteristic of the individual.

A number of studies are especially illustrative of how the motive measure seems to be tapping a predispositional variable. First of all, from the achievement measure, there is better prediction of grades to be attained in school than postdiction of grades already attained (10). Power motive score can predict influence attempts in a two-person decision-making setting (15) a month after the motive measure has been obtained. In the national data, the affiliation motive scores of the young men predict their job satisfaction — those high in affiliation motivation tend to be more satisfied with their jobs than those low. Although this latter case can be interpreted as an indication that affiliation motivation can be increased situationally if one is satisfied with the job, it seems to make more sense to interpret this result the other way: that people with high need for affiliation are more predisposed to look for and find affiliative satisfaction and in the process experience greater job satisfaction. All of these studies are demonstrations to the effect that the motive measures are at least *partially* tapping a relatively enduring predisposition. One of our team of researchers, Feld, is presently completing an important study of the achievement motivation of high school boys which bears very directly on this problem (6). The achievement motivation of these boys was assessed in 1952 when they were about ten years old and in 1958 when they were about sixteen. What this study demonstrates is that over six years there still remains a significant relationship between the motive scores of these boys at two widely separated times. Certainly between the ages of 10 and 16 a boy encounters many situations which may affect his motivation to achieve. Nevertheless, there is a positive relationship between the two sets of scores — suggesting that it is, to some extent, a stable personality characteristic being tapped by the measure.

On the other hand, at each stage of this nationwide survey of apperceptive measures of motivation — in the construction of the measuring instrument, in coding, in derivation of scores, and now in the analysis and interpretation of results — we run headlong into the realization that in addition to the motive predisposition measured by this technique we have to account for the other components undoubtedly reflected in these measures: life situation of the subjects telling stories; the imaginativeness of the respondents; the kinds of pictures used; the test administrators; the way the stories are obtained. These are all factors that can be considered to have had some effects on motive scores in previous research, but in no other study with this technique have all of these components been of paramount concern. But now that we have attempted to adapt an instrument developed primarily in the highly restricted college population to national survey use, we have to consider very seriously these other factors influencing motive scores.

When we had to select a group of pictures to use for all potential respondents in America (not just college students); when we had to use many different interviewers to do the data collection task (and not just one test administrator); when we came to the task of coding responses from people of widely different educational backgrounds (and not just one level); when, as in my introductory example, we have to compare directly the motive scores of such widely different groups as unskilled workers and professional men; we have been and still are extremely sensitive to factors other than motive predispositions affecting motive scores.

Today I would like to present some of the factors in these thematic apperceptive measures of motivation which in one way or another can stand in the way of our interpreting the motive measures as reflecting motivational predispositions. One might say there are certain factors — both dispositional and situational — which we *don't* want reflected in the motive measures. Our efforts to discourage such pesty influences I will discuss in the remaining portions of the paper, along with various theoretical positions about apperceptive measurement that are necessary guides to how we go about our exterminating campaign. Three unwanted effects on thematic apperception to be discussed are (1) verbal fluency; (2) differential meaning of pictures to different subjects; (3) interviewer effects on thematic apperception.

Disposition variable unwanted; verbal fluency. Any time a study demonstrates that the motive being measured with the apperceptive technique is indeed predispositional, one can still always ask: Are you sure you have measured the predisposition you say you are measuring? We faced this problem in our national survey with respect to a possible contaminating predisposition variable, *verbal* fluency.

This is not the first time this problem has arisen in our research. A few years ago two of us scored the stories Roe had obtained from eminent scientists (oral TAT protocols) for achievement motivation. Presumably we were dealing with the inner sanctum of achievement motive scorers — the highest of the highs; the eminent physical, natural, and social scientists of our day. To our surprise there were many apparently low scorers who for the most part turned out to be physical scientists (chemists and applied physicists), and a handful of very high scorers who were with few exceptions dominated by that notable group — young social scientists. Even in their stories these men were unmistakable. They talked a lot and in the process gave a lot of achievement imagery. The low scorers gave unimaginative stories, with little dramatic content and in the process ended up with low achievement motive scores. We can ask ourselves about this study: was the achievement motive measure appropriate for all of the group: The physical scientists, it could be argued, do not *think* verbally, and in fact may have some difficulty in verbal expression. In a certain sense, one might say that the verbal fantasy measure was potentially insensitive as a measure of the motivational processes of these men. The verbal bias frequently attributed to IQ assessment may be also applied to these verbal apperceptive measures. It is indeed this limitation which makes these fantasy measurement techniques difficult with children, for which one relies on less verbal modes of expression (for example, drawing or doll-play).

If one thinks that a verbal fantasy measure might be inappropriate with eminent physical scientists and with children, how then can we think that the measure is appropriate for a national population — for old ladies who are unable to say more than "I don't know, dearie" to the question "What is going on in the picture?" or for an illiterate laborer who cannot (or is not willing, if you will) to "give" any information about his free associations to a picture. Well, in truth, this is a nasty problem in the use of thematic apperceptive techniques with the general population. These instruments have been developed generally in such a confined setting — with college students who represent a select sample with regard to verbal fluency, and clinical patients whose disturbances are often excellent catalysts for imaginative flow. But even in these settings we find some people who are unable to "give" for one reason or another.

A further complication must be noted when one raises the

whole issue of verbal fluency as a contaminating variable for apperceptive measurement. One may interpret a lack of imaginative productivity in these measures as defensiveness, as an unwillingness to think about or report the associations that one has about pictures presented. Two studies, one by Scott (13) and a recent one by Ruscoe (12), have shown that with an intense involvement of motivational concern there is a great decline in the length of story protocols. Under these conditions lack of imagination can be interpreted as defense against an overwhelming need. Indeed this is a common clinical interpretation of lack of responsiveness to the TAT. However important such an interpretation might be, in our work thus far we have asked ourselves only the following question — should lack of imaginative productivity be interpreted as a low score in motivation or as an indication of lack of verbal command? Are we measuring motivation or verbal fluency, or possibly are these one and the same thing?

What we have assumed in this national study is that the motive measures might well be contaminated with this other dispositional variable — verbal fluency. People might get high n Achievement, n Affiliation and n Power scores not because they necessarily had strong dispositions to strive for these goals, but because they told long involved stories and in the process described imagery that was scorable for motivational content. This problem is clearest when one considers someone who does not tell any story at all — who rejects the task. By necessity he ends up with a low n Affiliation score. But one cannot say that this is equivalent to a low score from a person who went on talking about people in stories and never brought up affiliative concerns. Throw the first subject out, someone might say. Okay, but where do you stop? How does one establish the boundaries between protocols to be considered as adequate for measurement and those that are not?

This is a problem we encountered in our national study, and this is how we handled it.

We had every indication that our motive measures were contaminated with an extraneous variable — verbal fluency. We first eliminated from consideration for motive analysis all those subjects who gave us insufficient protocols—protocols too short in imaginative content to justify considering them for measurement. In this group were not only people who flatly refused to take the whole six-picture test (about 2%) but those who rejected telling stories to one or more pictures or refused to answer certain sub-sections within any story or combination of stories. In order to simulate the conditions of test administration in the psychological laboratory, the interviewer asked a series of questions for each story to be told, similar to those used in the written form:

Who are these people? What are they doing?
What has led up to this? What went on before?
What do they want? How do they feel?
What will happen? How will it end?

Judged to be inadequate for our consideration in analysis were respondents' protocols that had more than three stories with answers to one of these questions omitted or that had any story with answers to two or more of the above questions omitted.

You might wonder who these people are whom we threw out with such criteria. Is there any indication that they are respondents with little general verbal fluency or are we throwing out people who are rejecting the task because of defense avoidance? Those eliminated turn out to be predominantly from lower educational levels, as you can note in Table 3.

TABLE 3

THE RELATIONSHIP OF EDUCATION TO PERCENTAGE LOSS OF *S*s FOR FURTHER ANALYSIS OF MOTIVE SCORES DUE TO INADEQUATE PROTOCOLS[a, b]

	Men		*Women*	
Educational Level	*N in Sample*	*Percentage Loss*	*N in Sample*	*Percentage Loss*
No schooling or some grade school (1-6 years)	(107)	32	(125)	28
Grade school (7-8 years)	(138)	25	(160)	18
High school (9-11)	(139)	12	(209)	16
Completed high school	(169)	12	(266)	7
Attended college	(157)	7	(136)	7

[a]Does not include *S*s whose educational level was not ascertained.
[b]Reprinted from Veroff, Atkinson, Feld and Gurin (16).

What we can conclude, therefore, is that for many people from lower educational levels this sort of technique seems inappropriate.

In examining the remaining protocols we found a significant correlation between the length of the protocols and each of the motive scores. These results are reported in Table 4.

TABLE 4

PRODUCT MOMENT CORRELATIONS BETWEEN RAW MOTIVE SCORES AND LENGTH OF PROTOCOL[a]

	Men *(N=597)*	*Women* *(N=774)*
n Achievement	.28	.25
n Affiliation	.20	.24
n Power	.21	.21

Note: All p values $< .0001$

[a]Reprinted from Veroff *et al.* (16)

What do you do about this? An argument can be made that high scorers on each of these motives measures should be motivated to tell longer stories — to do well at the task (achievement motive), or to do a good turn for the interviewer (affiliation motive), or to develop control over the situation (power motive). Previous results (18) have pointed to another interpretation: that the major determinant of these correlations is an extraneous variable, verbal fluency. Therefore, we corrected all motive scores by adding or subtracting constants from scores at given lengths of protocol so that the average correlation between verbal fluency and motive scores was effectively removed. Whether this correction is a difference that really makes a difference in substantive results is another question. But at any rate we now feel confident that the dispositional variable we are measuring is not verbal fluency. The correlations between length of protocol and motive scores after correction ranged between —.04 and +.05.

Situation effect unwanted: Differential meaning of pictures used to elicit stories in different groups. Apperceptive measurement was founded on the principle that ambiguous stimuli can serve as the basis for fantasy productions diagnostic of a person's dynamics. The way a person brings structure to ambiguity, the imaginative associations he has about unclear situations, will be gauges of his personality. Presumably the fact that the subjects or patients reacted to ambiguous stimuli was the key to the apperceptive device. But this ambiguity turned out to be one of the faults in thematic apperception measurement as well — especially within a very heterogeneous population. When a picture is ambiguous there is great possibility that people or groups of people will differ in what they say is in general going on in a picture. Presumably if everyone agreed that a given picture represented men working at an achievement task, then individual differences in kinds of story told about this situation will reflect individual differences in motivational predisposition to achieve. If people did not agree, to begin with, that the picture basically was about men working at an achievement task, then individual differences in motive scores can not only be attributable to dispositional differences but also to possible differential experience and interpretation of the kind of situation portrayed in the picture as an achievement setting. This is all in the way of saying that if the pictures mean something different for different groups or different individuals, then one might think that the motive scores derived from the stories written about these pictures might not be sensitive measures of strength of motivational predisposition, but might be better reflections of social group experiences with given situations.

The cue value of a picture, the motivational structure of the picture, the objective stimulus properties of pictures, are rarely assessed in this kind of measure. A few studies can and have undertaken such work, but what is important for our consideration here is that one has evidence to support the viewpoint most clearly expressed by Atkinson (1) that the person's motive scores are joint functions of his own predispositions and his expectations based on his past contacts with situations portrayed in the stimulus pictures presented to him. To select pictures that would be similar in meaning for all social groups in American society and at the same time equally sensitive to three different social motives was a major task. We pre-tested a number of different pictures in Detroit residence samples, pretested some with college students, and finally arrived with one set of six pictures for men and another set for women. The sex difference with regard to pictures in a thematic apperceptive measure is so important (5, 17) that we decided from the very beginning to have two separate sets. We felt that two different sets would insure greater validity of scores for each sex, although using different sets of pictures for men and women meant we can no longer directly compare the motive scores of men and women. Over and above this first decision, we chose pictures that would present a variety of situations actually encountered by men and women. The logic of this has been outlined elsewhere. Briefly, selecting pictures of a variety of situations — work and interpersonal — should cut down on the possibility of bias resulting from the use of pictures which allow only certain social groups to express motivational imagery in their stories.

Parenthetically, it may be of some considerable interest to this group that the pictures which seem to stimulate the most readily scorable stories from the respondents were ones that seem to be of intermediate structure. Pictures that were vague (for example, one used in previous studies on Affiliation — a man looking out of a doorway) obtained very little imagery of any kind from the representative sample. Pictures that were highly structured, encompassing a lot of details in the pictures, produced fairly stereotyped responses from this sample. What is needed for variability of usable protocols in heterogeneous populations therefore seems to be pictures that are somewhere in between the quality of vague unstructured stimuli and definitely structured ones.

If there are so many problems about the differential stimulus values of pictures to different kinds of people, why then did we use pictures? Force of habit undoubtedly played a strong part. I say this somewhat facetiously, although there is some reasoning behind it. Since so many of the previous researchers in the area have used pictures, we felt that a study that could possibly bridge assessment techniques developed in the clinic and the laboratory with survey methods should simulate methods of the previous researchers as far as it could. There have been instances of the successful use of verbal stimuli for these motive measures (for example, Winterbottom, 19). Nevertheless, our hunch was that especially with non-verbal subjects, verbal stimuli can be very poor in engaging apperceptive processes for a spontaneous story. Stories told to verbal stimuli would perhaps accentuate the verbal fluency bias even more than stories based on picture cues. We would have the verbal bias on the *input* as well as the output side of our measure. The attraction of pictures for this kind of fantasy measure is that it seems to draw most people into an imaginative story fairly easily. And so we have stood by our use of pictures for this survey.

We have as yet no way of estimating with any certainty how effective we were in selecting unbiased pictures for this broad survey population. If by using total motive scores we obtain meaningful results for blue-collar workers and white-collar workers, rich and poor, city people and farmers, then we have some indirect evidence that the measures allow at least some expression of the motivations of most social groups. In our preliminary analysis thus far, the motive measures of most groups show theoretically meaningful relationships to other variables. As a result we have confidence that there is at least partial validity of the scores of all groups. One group that seems to be showing little in the way of relationships of motive scores to other variables is the oldest group of subjects. It could very well be that we have selected pictures which depict people who are sufficiently different in age from people 55 and over so that the measure minimally involves apperceptive processes reflecting motive dispositions.

It has been a general assumption of our work that the closer the situation being portrayed in the pictures to the life situation of the individual the more readily he can identify with characters in the story and hence the more likely the motive measures will be good estimates of motivational behavior in the person's ongoing daily activity. To ask an older person to tell a story about a younger person involves retrospective fantasy. What meaning this has for valid estimates of ongoing motivation has been questioned by Atkinson in a study with college students (2). In that study college students wrote stories in response to the picture of the boy with violin (TAT I). The n Achievement scores derived from this picture did not predict total scores derived from other pictures depicting adult situations. Atkinson concludes that the retrospection involved in telling stories about a boy represents a different psychological process from that which is measured in future-oriented stories about adults.

A direct way of testing the effectiveness of the selection of pictures for one group contrasted to another is to select a picture or set of pictures that might have particular relevance for just one of these groups (Group A), and to see whether motive scores derived from these pictures have more power in predicting a relationship to another variable for Group A than they have for the other group. We have an opportunity to demonstrate such a possibility with our data from the national study. We have performed two analyses of different meanings of pictures to different groups that bear on this general problem. One analysis has to do with the meaning of the achievement motive measure for white- and blue-collar workers; the other has to do with the meaning of achievement motive measure for women from educational groups.

One of the problems we had in selecting pictures which stimulate achievement motivation concerns was whether or not to use any pictures that may easily be construed as a work situation. What we were worried about was the fact that any particular work situation may have relevance for only a select group of people. If we present a picture of a man in a shirt and tie at a desk, how much relevance does this situation have for the achievement affiliation or power motivation arousal of a semiskilled worker? And a picture of machines might very well precipitate more meaningful motive thoughts for the blue-collar workers. We did want to present work situations, since we thought they were crucial ones for arousing achievement concerns. We thought the best solution would be to include both types of work situations — white-collar and blue-collar, and our pictures do include two specifically white-collar situations and a blue-collar situation. Our reasoning behind this solution runs like this. The total motive score for any individual is the sum of the scores for *all* pictures used. The assumption is that in the long run the most meaningful single score for motivation would be an average score across many different situations, even if there were situations included that were not immediately relevant for the person. The strength of a person's motivation can be thought of as being not only dependent on how much *directed* concern he has in a given affective dimension, but also how many *different cues* can give use to such direction. For example, if one wanted to know how a person was going to try to influence his parents, his spouse, his children, his supervisors and friends in the neighborhood, then a measure based on a variety of cues would probably do the over-all best job. On the other hand, if one is to make the best specific prediction about a person in a *given* situation (e.g., how hard he would try to influence his child), we might predict that motive scores derived from pictures close to that situation (parent-child scenes) should be most effective.

The fact that we do have both a blue-collar situation and white-collar situations represented in the pictures gives us an opportunity to assess the validity of this latter statement in another context. We can see whether the achievement motive score derived from pictures of white-collar workers and those derived from pictures of blue-collar workers have the same power in generating relationships between achievement motivation and the psychological variables relevant to the jobs of blue-collar workers and white-collar workers.

We have available two such job measures on this national sample as part of another study (7). The first measure deals with job satisfaction — answers to the question:

Taking into consideration all the things about your job, how satisfied or dissatisfied are you with it?

For the purpose of this analysis we distinguished only two groups: those people who mentioned any dissatisfaction in their answer to this question, in contrast to those who only said they were satisfied. The second variable is perception of achievement gratification from the job. This variable was measured with the following question, which followed directly after the above question in the interview:

What things do you particularly like about the job?

For the analysis of this question, the major coding decision was whether or not an achievement satisfaction is mentioned. Considered as achievement satisfaction were such statements: "I like the responsibility"; "I can use my ability"; "I'm good at it"; "Your work is appreciated"; "It's interesting."

Using these two measures we have found that for the young men in most of the occupational groups the total achievement motive score relates to these two variables about reactions to the jobs: at least for young men (21-39), people high in achievement motivation are more likely to be dissatisfied with their jobs, and at the same time recognize achievement gratifications from their work.

The strength of these relationships varies considerably from occupation to occupation. The trends are considerably stronger in the white-collar workers. Among the young white-collar workers these two trends are in evidence for both professional and managerial groups; and among blue-collar workers both of these trends are present only for the skilled workers. And so we selected these groups to represent the white-collar workers and the blue-collar workers. We already know then that for both these groups the total achievement scores (encompassing scores derived from both blue- and white-collar situations) predict dissatisfaction on the job and the perception of achievement gratifications, at least to some extent (more so for the white-collar than blue-collar workers). The crucial question for our purpose is whether or not scores derived from the separate pictures (blue- vs. white-collar situations) are better or worse predictors of these relationships for each of these groups.

In Tables 5 and 6 are some data that we hoped would answer these questions.

TABLE 5

STRENGTH OF RELATIONSHIP BETWEEN JOB SATISFACTION AND THREE ACHIEVEMENT MOTIVE SCORES (FOR BLUE-COLLAR WORKERS AND WHITE-COLLAR WORKERS)[a]

	Achievement Motive Scores Based on Stories Written About:		
Subjects	*Pictures of White-Collar Workers*	*Picture of Blue-Collar Workers*	*All Pictures*
Blue-collar workers (N=50)	.01[b]	—.14	—.13
White-collar workers (N=59)	—.01	—.29	—.26

[a]White-collar workers are young (21-39) professional and managerial men; Blue-collar workers are young (21-39) skilled workers.

[b]Phi coefficients.

TABLE 6

STRENGTH OF RELATIONSHIP BETWEEN PERCEIVING ACHIEVEMENT SATISFACTION ON THE JOB AND THREE ACHIEVEMENT MOTIVE SCORES (FOR BLUE-COLLAR WORKERS AND WHITE-COLLAR WORKERS)[a]

	Achievement Motive Scores Based on Stories Written About:		
Subjects	*Pictures of White-Collar Workers*	*Picture of Blue-Collar Workers*	*All Pictures*
Blue-collar workers (N=50)	.10[b]	.01	.06
White-collar workers (N=59)	.20	.18	.20

[a]White-collar workers are young (21-39) professional and managerial men; Blue-collar workers are young (21-39) skilled workers.
[b]Phi coefficients.

Fortunately or unfortunately, the tables raise more questions than they answer, but the answered and unanswered questions are extremely pertinent to the general topic of picture cues in apperceptive assessment. I offer these tables merely as an illustration of a methodological problem and ways of solving it. In these tables we have estimates of the degree of relationship between job satisfaction measures and three different achievement motive scores. The first score is based on stories told in response to the pictures of the white-collar situations; the second score is based on the picture of a blue-collar situation; and the third score is based on all pictures used. The statistical significance of these relationships and the differences between these relationships[3] are not of concern for the present discussion. What is of concern is which set of scores generates the strongest relationships with these two variables for blue-collar workers in contrast to white-collar workers.

We do find in these tables that there *is* a difference in strength of relationship between achievement motive and these job satisfaction measures, depending on which set of motive scores is used. However, the pattern of results is not altogether as expected.

Two interesting results warrant our attention. One is that the achievement motive scores from blue-collar pictures are better than scores from white-collar pictures in predicting job

[3]Phi-Coefficients are attenuated—especially for the pictures of white-collar workers—because the percentage of subjects giving any achievement imagery to these pictures is low.

dissatisfaction for *both* white-collar workers and blue-collar workers. And achievement motive scores based on stories of white-collar pictures predict better than scores based on stories of blue-collar pictures the perception of achievement gratifications on the job for both groups of men. This pattern of results supports our assumption that the safest over-all measurement of achievement motivation — the scores that would in the long run produce the most meaningful network of relationships with other variables — would be the scores based on a variety of situations. What this pattern of results does not support, at least in this particular case, is that one can predict better using motive measures based on the stories of situations most like the one the subject is actually in. We did not get what we expected; if there was a real bias in the pictures, then scores from blue-collar stories would generally predict better for blue-collar workers than white-collar workers, and scores derived from stories of white-collar pictures would predict better for white-collar workers than blue-collar workers.

The other interesting result is a contradiction to the above expectation. White-collar workers seem to be responding *more* meaningfully to the blue-collar situation than the blue-collar workers — that is, the achievement motive scores based on the blue-collar situation seem to be generating more fruitful relationships to other variables for white-collar workers than for blue-collar workers. These results seem inconsistent with this tentative assumption that the potentially most valid motive scores are derived from stories about situations that are closest to the life situations of the subjects being tested. We recognize the possibility that starting from different assumptions others might have anticipated these results. One can point to the possibility that in situations too much like the one a person is actually in, defensive distortion, suppressions of associations can occur. It could be that one might obtain a better assessment of achievement motivation of blue-collar workers about white-collar characters and vice versa.

This kind of assumption seems quite reasonable when one is dealing with motives that are highly tinged with anxiety components — sexual and aggressive motivations in particular. Indeed, experimental results from one study investigating the projective expression of experimentally aroused fear would support this idea. In that study, soldiers under different degrees of fear arousal, defined as different distances from the site of an exploding atomic bomb, told stories in response to pictures. The more fearful soldiers were able to express this increased fear more easily in response to a picture of women and children than they were in response to pictures of soldiers. It seems sensible to speculate that these results represent a projection of fear upon women and children — a fear which they regard as unmanly. That the same kind of situation was operating for the white-collar workers is a possibility — perhaps a very intriguing one — but we have insufficient information about this problem to make such an interpretation.

Another analysis of the differential meanings of pictures was done with women's protocols. Obtaining valid achievement motivation scores for women has always been a problem for this apperceptive technique. At first we thought it was because the group of us starting the research on women were men and hence lacked insight into the mysteries of femaleness and need for achievement. But female researchers fared no better with the task.

A major problem has been whether to use pictures of women in a career achievement scene or pictures of women doing things at home. Nothing definitive had been established to guide us in regard to this question when we selected pictures for the national survey. So, as before, when this problem arose with blue-collar and white-collar pictures we decided to include both kinds of situations — we have one obvious career work picture and two homemaking scenes (upholstering a chair and cooking). It is thus possible to get these three different achievement motive scores for women: a total n Achievement score based on all pictures; a score based only on stories about the career picture; and a score based on homemaking pictures. The question we then can ask is whether scores derived from either the career or homemaking pictures mean something different (relate to another variable differently) for one group as opposed to another.

We have an opportunity to answer this question in the following context. Housewives in this national study were asked the following question:

> *Different people feel differently about taking care of a home — I don't mean taking care of children, but things like cooking and sewing and keeping house. Some women look on these things as just a job that has to be done — other women really enjoy them. How do you feel about this?*

For our present analyses we coded out all people who mentioned disliking some aspect of homemaking — included in this group are people who say, "I don't like cooking," "I hate it all," or "It's just a job to be done."

We thought that achievement motivation of women might have something to do with the way they respond to this question. Furthermore, we thought that this relationship might be different for women at different educational levels. And so we related the total achievement motive scores of women to their expressed dissatisfaction with housework, separately for grade school, high school, and college educated women. And what we find is a similar relationship (although small) for all groups — the high achievement motive scorers in each group tend to express less dissatisfaction about housework than low achievement scorers. These results can be seen in Table 7.

TABLE 7

Strength of Relationship Between Dissatisfaction with Housework and Three Achievement Motive Scores (For Full-time Housewives)

Subject	*Achievement Motive Score Based on Stories Written About:* *Picture of A Career Work Setting*	*Pictures of Household Action*	*Pictures All*
Grade School-educated housewives (N=155)	–.12	–.10	–.10
High School-educated housewives (N=258)	–.09	–.11	–.12
College-educated housewives (N=72)	.11	–.17	–.06

At first this seems like a shattering result: According to social commentators of our day, the sore point about women's role in America is their confinement to their home, their frustration with unfulfilled achievement strivings in the masculine world. From this viewpoint, one might expect the high Achievement motive scorers to say, "The housewife's lot is not a happy one." But when we realize that the scores from the stories of the home-making scenes were contributing twice as much to the total scores of most women as the score from the career picture, we then had some rationale to account for these results. If a woman sees achievement possibilities in household activities, then we can understand how this might contribute to seeing satisfaction with these activities in her life experience. When one looks at the relationship between achievement motive scores based only on stories about household work (see Table 7 again), then the same slight trend is obtained for all educational groups. The women high on achievement motivation tend to be less dissatisfied with their role. The relationship is slightly stronger for college-educated women when we use these scores (specific to stories of housework) than when we used total motive scores.

Now what happens to this relationship when one uses as a basis for measuring achievement motive scores derived from the story of the work-career setting? In Table 7 the relationship between these scores and housework satisfaction is reported for each educational group. In these comparisons we do have evidence of the differential meaning of this picture for college-educated women as opposed to the others. What we find in this table is that for grade school- and high school-educated respondents the relationship between achievement motivation (as measured in the career picture) and housework satisfaction is consistent with the results based on scores derived from the other pictures — the higher the achievement motive, the greater the satisfaction with housework. *Not so* with the college-educated women. For these women, the higher their scores on an achievement motive measure based on a career picture, the more the dissatisfaction with housework. Our social commentator can breathe more easily. Now we do have some evidence that achievement concerns can interfere with housework satisfaction, but only for a particular group — the most highly educated. This phenomenon occurs only when we are tapping achievement concerns in the context of a career picture. You might wonder about possible differential responsiveness to these sets of pictures — high in one and low in the other. Of those college-educated women who respond with achievement imagery in the career context and not in the housework context, 61% express some dissatisfaction. Only 30% of the remaining college-educated women expressed dissatisfaction. This difference is statistically significant.

In this second analysis of differential meaning of pictures to different groups, therefore, we can conclude that the picture of career women seems to be measuring the general achievement concerns of the majority of high school- and grade school-educated women, while it seems to tap the more specific conflict in concerns about career achievement in the college-educated women.

Differential meaning of pictures for white- and blue-collar workers, or for grade school- or college-educated women, would better be tested in conditions where we would have more adequate control of the pictures used. Two important variables that should be considered in any such systematic analysis are: The cue value of the picture in eliciting a particular motivational content and the order of presentation of the pictures. For the foregoing comparisons to be completely valid one would have to have equal cue value for achievement motivation in both white- and blue-collar pictures, and in career and household pictures (which we did not have) and these pictures would have to be presented in random order to different subjects.

Another way we can ask the question we have been asking about different meanings of pictures to different groups is: are the scores based on different pictures reliable estimates of motivation? If we split the measuring instrument in half would the two halves be highly related to one another in *all* groups? However, in a systematic study of split-half reliability one again has to construct subsets of pictures of equal cue value. We deliberately selected a variety of cues — both because we wanted different kinds of situations represented and because we wanted to measure three motives at once. Therefore we cannot handle the problem of reliability in this study.[4]

As I said when I introduced these data, the results may raise many questions. The specific results, however, are not crucial to the general problem I wanted to emphasize. These two analyses were introduced to serve as an illustration of what can be done in the way of investigating the meaning of the stimulus in apperceptive assessment to one social group in contrast to another. What we have to recognize as we make broad sweeping contrasts between social groups is that part of the variability in motive scores is undoubtedly determined by differential expectations about the situations portrayed in the pictures we used to elicit the stories.

Unwanted situational effects: interviewers affecting motive scores. In contemplating a national survey of these measures, we were very concerned about another uncontrolled situational variable — the fact that we would have to, and did, employ 159 different interviewers (27 men and 132 women) to collect these data for us. The use of 159 interviewers could mean 159 different stimuli affective motive scores — over which we had little control.

We made every effort to standardize the test administration. The four questions that have been asked in the written form of these motive measures were again asked by all the interviewers in slightly modified form, as we have noted. And contrary to all their training, the interviewers were warned not to probe except under specified conditions. Even with these efforts at

[4]Scoring reliability is another question entirely. The research with these motive measures has in large part depended on the fact that the measuring tools—human coders—could be easily taught the coding rituals with a very high degree of reliability. In the national study we were able to maintain strict standards although the stories were based on some completely new pictures and each coder scored about 3200 stories (a tedious task, I would say). The nine coders we used each scored 2 stories of each subject for only one motive. The average score reliability was .77 with the highest average reliability for achievement motive scoring (the grandfather scoring scheme) and the lowest average reliability for power motive scoring (the infant scoring scheme). Although we have a slight decrease in scoring reliability from the usual coefficients, its value is sufficiently high to guarantee usable data for research purposes.

standardization, previous research with the motive measure would tell us that the interviewers might still have effects on scores. Birney (4) has recently demonstrated how two different test administrators (one instructor; the other a student) can produce differential n Achievement scores in college students. Presumably the status of interviewers should remain fairly constant from respondent to respondent. But there are sex, age, and general style differences in the interviewers which might have a profound situational effect that we would want to know about.

To estimate this effect we had to go through elaborate elimination procedures. One difficulty with a study of interviewer differences in a national study is that the interviewers are not randomly assigned to the respondents in the population. Each interviewer sees respondents in a particular location and may be assigned to a particular income group, or foreign-speaking group or the like. To eliminate this contamination of respondent variability with interviewer variability we selected interviewers for study who would be potentially similar to the kind of respondents they would have to deal with. Such interviewers were women, white, working in non-metropolitan sampling points, who interviewed at least four respondents. Interviewers to be considered had to be paired with another qualified interviewer from the same sampling point so that interviewer differences within sampling points could be assessed. With these limitations we were able to amass eight pairs of interviewers for male respondents and fifteen pairs of interviewers for female respondents. The motive scores of the respondents interviewed by these pairs were broken down into component variances and an analysis of variance was performed. The following components were analyzed out of the total variance of motive scores: variances attributable to respondents, sampling points and interviewers. These analyses, separate for males and females (Tables 8 and 9), show that there is an interviewer effect on n Achievement scores for women and on n Power scores for both men and women.

The latter shows the strongest effect when you interpret the interclass correlation derived from this analysis as proportion of the variance in motive score possibly contributed by interviewer differences (14, p. 243). Interviewer variance increases the

TABLE 8

ANALYSES OF VARIANCE OF MALES' MOTIVATION SCORES (*S*S WITHIN INTERVIEWERS WITHIN PSUS)[a]

Source of Variation	df	Mean Square	F	Component Variance for Interviewers	Interclass Correlation[b]
n Achievement					
PSU	7	96.77			
Interviewer within PSU	8	97.78	1.38	6.81	.09
*S*s within interviewer	48	70.42			
Total	63				
n Affiliation					
PSU	7	186.00			
Interviewer within PSU	8	135.13	1.33	8.47	.08
*S*s within interviewer	48	101.27			
Total	63				
n Power					
PSU	7	220.00			
Interviewer within PSU	8	170.13	2.65*	26.51	.29
*S*s within interviewer	48	64.06			
Total	63				

$^{*}p < .05$.

[a]Limited to cases of white female interviewers of non-metropolitan PSUs who interviewed at least four *S*s giving adequate measures.

[b]Ratio of interviewer component variance to *S* variance plus interviewer component variance.

Reprinted from Veroff *et al.* (16).

men's n Power score variance by 29%, the females' n Power score by 18%, and the females' n Achievement score by 18%. Actually, we were encouraged by these results. In the first place these findings must be considered maximal estimates of interviewer effects because this estimate of interviewer effects undoubtedly includes some respondent selection which we cannot control. Some of the interviewers may still be assigned special kinds of respondents. And secondly, although we have to recognize that there is potential situation effect on motive scores contributed by our interviewers, and that this will act to cut down on potential reliability of the measuring instrument, the fact that it is not any more than it is is reassuring.

One reason we may have minimal interviewer influences on

TABLE 9

ANALYSES OF VARIANCE OF FEMALES' MOTIVATION SCORES (*S*s WITHIN INTERVIEWERS WITHIN PSUs)[a]

Source of Variation	*df*	*Mean Square*	*F*	*Component Variance for Interviewers*	*Intraclass Correlation*[b]
n Achievement					
PSU	14	118.00			
Interviewer within PSU	15	174.40	1.90*	20.70	.18
*S*s within interviewer	90	91.24			
Total	119				
n Affiliation					
PSU	14	90.14			
Interviewer within PSU	15	72.13	.88	−2.33	−.03
*S*s within interviewer	90	81.44			
Total	119				
n Power					
PSU	14	86.14			
Interviewer within PSU	15	107.27	1.88*	12.61	.18
*S*s within interviewer	90	56.84			
Total	119				

*$p < .05$.

[a]Limited to cases of white, female interviewers of non-metropolitan PSUs who interviewed at least four *S*s giving adequate measures.

[b]Ratio of interviewer component variance to *S* variance plus interviewer component variance.

Reprinted from Veroff *et al.* (16).

motive score is that we have already taken out the variance attributable to length of protocol from the scores. Verbal fluency is undoubtedly highly affected by interviewer differences.

In conclusion: We started out this present exploration into various dispositional and situational influences on thematic apperception — wanted and unwanted — as a way of warning ourselves to step lightly on the treadmill of speculation. With the data we have at our disposal, an accumulation of information about three important social motivations of a cross-section of Americans, we have literally one of the very few studies that can perhaps serve to describe by direct assessment some major personality features of various social groups in America. Furthermore, this study may represent a prototype of what might be involved in an empirical study of American national character.

If we take the motive measures for granted, speculation can run rampant. Undoubtedly we would like to speculate, and most likely will speculate, about religious differences in motivation, class differences, generation differences, and so on. But such speculations, however interesting, if not backed up by considerable questioning of the apperceptive measure itself and what it measures, can be no better than considered but unsure guesses about the American scene.

In reviewing various features of the apperceptive measures of motivation, it has become clear that we will be measuring both dispositional tendencies and situational influences within a cross-section of the American population — some wanted, some unwanted. Of these latter unwanted factors, some can be eliminated (verbal fluency, test administration); others still remain (picture differences and interviewer differences). As a result we can never be sure about which factor of a combination of factors was operating in determining motive scores. We will have to offer our best guesses. Hopefully, if we are aware that these are guesses and not hard facts derived from a fancy measuring instrument, then we can be further along in promoting the research that will change these sophisticated guesses into tested assertions.

REFERENCES

1. Atkinson, J. W.: (Ed.) *Motives in Fantasy, Action, and Society: A Method of Assessment and Study.* Princeton, N. J., Van Nostrand, 1958.
2. Atkinson, J. W.: Studies in projective measurement of achievement motivation. Unpublished doctoral dissertation, Univ. of Michigan, 1950.
3. Birney, R. C.: Thematic content and the cue characteristics of pictures. In J. W. Atkinson (Ed.) *Motives in Fantasy, Action, and Society*. Princeton, N. J., Van Nostrand, 1958, Pp. 630-643.
4. Birney, R. C.: Experimenter effect on the achievement motive. Unpublished manuscript. Amherst College, 1956.
5. Davenport, J. W.: The projective expression of the achievement motive in relation to career orientation and social satisfaction in home economics freshmen. Unpublished master's thesis, Univ. of Mass., Amherst, 1953.
6. Feld, Sheila: Studies in the origins of the achievement motive. Unpublished doctoral dissertation, 1959.

7. Gurin, G., Veroff, J., and Feld, Sheila: *Americans View Their Mental Health: A Nationwide Interview Study.* New York, Basic Books, 1959.
8. Haber, R. N. and Alpert, R.: The role of situation and picture cues in projective measurement of the achievement motive. In J. W. Atkinson (Ed.) *Motives in Fantasy, Action, and Society.* Princeton, N. J., Van Nostrand, 1958, Pp. 644-663.
9. Jacobs, B.: A method for investigating the cue characteristics of pictures. In J. W. Atkinson (Ed.) *Motives in Fantasy, Action, and Society.* Princeton, N. J., Van Nostrand, 1958, Pp. 617-629.
10. McClelland, D. C., Atkinson, J. W., Clark, L. A., and Lowell, E. L.: *The Achievement Motive.* New York, Appleton, 1953.
11. Murray, H. A.: *Thematic Apperception Test Manual.* Cambridge, Harvard Univ. Press, 1953.
12. Ruscoe, G.: An investigation of approach and avoidance within the concept of power motivation. Unpublished honors thesis, Univ. of Michigan, 1959.
13. Scott, W. A.: The avoidance of threatening material in imaginative behavior. *J. Abnorm. & Social Psychol., 52:*338-346. 1956.
14. Snedecor, G. W.: *Statistical Methods.* Ames, Iowa, Iowa State College Press, 1946.
15. Veroff, J.: Power motivation related to influence attempts in a two-person group. Unpublished manuscript, Princeton Univ., 1956.
16. Veroff, J., Atkinson, J. W., Feld, Sheila, and Gurin, G.: The use of thematic apperception to assess motivation in a nationwide interview study. Unpublished paper, 1959.
17. Veroff, J., Wilcox, Sue, and Atkinson, J. W.: The achievement motive in high school and college-age women. *J. Abnorm. & Social Psychol., 48:*108-119. 1953.
18. Walker, E. L. and Atkinson, J. W.: The expression of fear-related motivation in thematic apperception as a function of proximity to an atomic explosion. In J. W. Atkinson (Ed.) *Motives in Fantasy, Action, and Society.* Princeton, N. J., Van Nostrand, 1958, Pp. 143-159.
19. Winterbottom, M.: The relation of need for achievement to learning experiences in independence and mastery. In J. W. Atkinson (Ed.) *Motives in Fantasy, Action, and Society.* Princeton, N. J., Van Nostrand, 1958, Pp. 453-478.

DISCUSSION OF DR. VEROFF'S PAPER

William E. Henry, Ph.D.
Primary Discussant

Dr. *Henry:* I should like to say just one or two minor things in discussing Dr. Veroff's paper. The mode of approach has raised so many issues and has offered so many possible solutions that I want to merely emphasize a couple of things.

The first point has not yet been stated explicitly in our discussions. It is clear that either some of us are operating on the basis of one logic and others on another logic, or some of us are using one logic at one time and another at another time. Let me call it the difference between the notions of "motives" and "motivation," and suggest that one logic implies that a motive is a thing that can be isolated and that specific relationships of that thing to various other things can be explored, as in many ways Dr. Veroff has explored them here. This leads to the question of whether or not when one says "motive" one should not say instead, as Dr. Holt has said here, "scores." That is, are "motives" the exact equivalent of "scores" (e.g., need Achievement scores)?

I bring this up in part to note that by calling need Achievement scores only *responses,* or even by saying, "After all, we aren't making assumptions about motives; we refer, after all, merely to a behavior sample," does not in effect get us out of the dilemma of what relationship the score bears to the motive called need Achievement. This applies to other needs as well. What relationship do these scores have to continuing, recurring principles (needs) which we assume guide the choices of action made by people? We can also ask, what relationship does a single motive have to what some of us are inclined to think of more as "motivation"? By inserting the term motivation, I merely call attention to the fact that we ordinarily assume that one does not know much about motivation unless one sees certain motives operating in context with other events involving the same person or with other information about related motives.

I am sure that part of our logic stems from the fact that we are doing both of these, i.e., we refer to motives in terms of specific responses and behavior samples and we also attempt to examine motives in context with other events about the person. When one says that it is only a behavior sample, only a response, one claims a certain methodological cleanness which is entirely justifiable. I am not complaining about that. It is quite different and important, however, to ask, "How can you get good TAT stories when you are not sure that the interviewers were highly skilled clinicians?" Now, the interviewers used in this study were not highly skilled clinicians. But if you are not interested in good TAT stories which would permit elaborate clinical analyses and which sample a wide range of motivationally stimulating areas, then you are interested in something quite different.

The question is one of how you move from treating need Achievement as just a response (whether you call it motive or just response) to the relationship of that score to persons, to personality, or to some recurring dynamic principles (such as needs). Dr. Veroff indicates his concern about this issue in describing a distinction between the dispositional and the situational; he is obviously concerned about this problem. Dr. Veroff has made the choice to deal with need Achievement as a single thing. The moment it is dealt with as a single thing, which presumably has limits and dimensions that can be described, then you are coping with the problem of what was the context you tore it out of.

Now, some of us would feel that Dr. Veroff has indeed torn it out of a context, and hence our questions ask how does the score articulate with what we consider to be the person, whether a single person or a group psychology. Others of us would think that Dr. Veroff has not artificially segregated the score because motivation does not come in a morass of intertwined dynamics but is really composed of isolated, describable units.

While I would quite agree that we would be way off if we

assume that we know all about motivation and are merely trying to get good tests of it, at the same time I think the difficulty that some of us experience is not with following the procedures and logic, or agreeing that this procedure or logic is better than another, but with the questions of, "So what? What does it mean now?" This stems from these differential viewpoints as to whether or not you have indeed torn it out of some context and hence perhaps do not know what it is you have torn out. If you do not know what it is that you have torn out of context, the fact that need Achievement scores relate to other variables in a discernible way may indeed be greatly influenced by casual factors, like the interviewer, like social class, and maybe in what may turn out to be random (and as yet unknown) ways.

Part of the evidence that what you have torn from context is not random is the fact that there are certain explainable, predictable, and subsequently reasonable relationships that are being discovered. The thing that interests me in particular about Dr. Veroff's paper is that I take some of the explorations to be of the order of providing this context, this meat, this body, and perhaps, therefore, some articulation to the rest of what we think we know about persons via, in one case, your efforts to demonstrate its dispositional quality. While I would take these efforts to be insufficient as yet, they do seem to be moving in the right direction. Accepting the exploration of the picture meaning, even though you attach it to the meaning of the outside stimulus, nonetheless does have some of the qualities of an interactional system which potentially can provide more body and meaning.

Two other things that I am particularly interested in are relevant to this issue. One is affiliation and the other is power. I do not ask the question of how affiliation and power behave independently, but rather how does the constellation of achievement, affiliation, and power behave? This latter question is relevant, for example, to the extent to which you use the scores to describe personality changes with age.

Now, some of those personality changes with age that you described seem to make a great deal of sense, in the light of other material. At the same time, in terms of any personality material that I have personal acquaintance with, achievement, while it is a crucial issue at any age, always seems far more meaningful to at least certain age groups (that is, the forties and fifties) with at least a seeming connection to other issues. The choice of affiliation, achievement, and power is not random. They are not merely the first three on some long list. These three motives are, in one sense or another, crucial. Presumably, the implication is that there are interrelationships among them. I think that the interrelationships among them found within specific groups of persons would be of enormous interest.

The other exploration I would like to see pursued, and this may be due to my lack of familiarity with some of the literature, is to examine the variations of any one need, such as achievement, within some specific group of persons. Dr. Veroff has assigned certain meanings to high and low achievement scores by relating these scores to such categories as age, occupational level, etc. This does give meaning to the score. But what I would like to see is further explorations in the essentials of this – a group of persons who are all, let us say, professionals, some of whom are high on need Achievement, and others low on this variable. Then, it would be interesting to relate need Achievement scores in this specific group of persons to other varieties of data about those persons, beginning with affiliation and power, perhaps, or with other behaviors, other tests, other personality measures. It seems to me that this might be one way to put a specific need back in its context, and would considerably extend the meaning of the score beyond what is indeed already being done by relating it to broad social categories.

Dr. Veroff: I should like to make just one or two points in response to Dr. Henry's questions. First, we would like very much to use the motive scores in a kind of "chemistry periodic" fashion. Perhaps compounds of these motives may mean something different than any of these taken separately, and in fact research on this in our setting has been fruitful. One nice thing is that these scores are not related one to another for the total group. Different combinations of scores are very likely to appear. What I did a couple of weeks ago was to take various occupations, and within each occupation, find out whether there were any particular patterns or scores peculiar to any of them. So you see that this is something we would like very much to do.

Second, we contemplate relating motive scores to other variables in the near future. Let me tell you one model we are using for this. It is a simple model. We wanted to do a role-motive analysis of this order. We analyze a given social role in terms of its demands on motivation and then think of a given person fitting in or not fitting into the demands of the particular role. Let us take the occupational role. Here we have what might be called a "plug in a socket" analysis. If the plug (person's motives) fits the socket (role) then there should be gratification. If it does not fit then there should be some disturbance in the role behavior.

We did this with power motivation in regard to occupation. What we did within each occupational group was to take those persons who had much supervision on the job and those who did not. Then we took the high-power and low-power people and found out whether the high-power people within those jobs of different supervision demands were more satisfied than the low-power people. We do find support for our model; anyhow, this is the kind of analysis we will be doing.

Finally, I would like to affirm your position that the richer the description you have of a person, the more likely you are to be able to predict or understand his behavior. I think that we have focused upon something out of simplicity. It gets very complicated to do it all at one time.

Dr. Henry: I should like to make a personal comment. There is a sense in which some of us here have been identified with the projective techniques in which, one might say, you gentlemen are not. Dr. Atkinson said yesterday that he had not conceived of the notion that he was investigating fantasy or anything even related to it in his need Achievement studies. For him, a "projective" technique is involved only because the instrument appears to have certain advantages in gathering scorable data. For him, it was irrelevant that *other* people call it a projective technique. A number of us have put a lot of effort into exploring the intimacies of the projective instruments, such as the TAT, into the idiosyncrasies of the performance, into the subtleties which a full and well-taken TAT permit in the analysis of a single case. This leads us to suggest that there is no single element in a given TAT record that has any meaning in and of itself. This obviously leads us to say that everything is interrelated with everything else, a viewpoint which I still hold. I do not think that anyone strongly disagrees.

However, there is another purpose, another intent within another framework of concepts, which makes the scoring of needs an equally appropriate, usable, feasible, reasonable thing to do. This is in part why we point out that the rapport between interviewers and subjects was not absolutely the peak of what many of us would say it ought to be when we are teaching clinical students. But for the scoring of needs, it does not bother me one whit. The fact that when you take a few little bits of material from these records and call them "need Achievement," the fact that you are distorting the true psyche of that individual, also does not concern me. Your objectives are quite different, the contexts are quite different. Within this context, the answer to whether this is appropriate or inappropriate is to be found within the logics of your various procedures and nowhere else — its appropriateness will not be found within the logics of the *clinical* use of the instrument. Clinical use has a different context using, I would say, different concepts. I would even think that when we talk about achievement in the clinical context we do not mean achievement-motive-score, although it obviously bears a relationship.

There are some issues related to the use of the TAT in the clinical context that have some relevance to your procedures in scoring need Achievement. You have obviously concerned yourself with some of those, such as in the exploration of picture meaning and so on. But I do not see any contradiction whatsoever between these two operations, provided it is perfectly clear that what we call achievement motive in your studies is different from the exploration of achievement which, for example, Dr. Sigel was talking about this morning in inquiring if we could not get more full and elaborate material on achievement through a more elaborate series of interviews. I think that we could get more elaborate material in this way, but I do not take this to be a better route to what you are talking about. I think that you are talking about another matter, and in that context, our logic of fuller, richer, more individualistic, more elaborate material is beyond the point.

THE INFLUENCE OF DRIVE AROUSAL AND CONFLICT UPON FANTASY BEHAVIOR

Seymour Feshbach, Ph.D.
University of Pennsylvania

THE USE of verbalized fantasy in the assessment of motives which may be a source of conflict presents a number of difficult and challenging problems to the clinician and to the research psychologist. There are those problems which pertain to the specification and measurement of any motive regardless of its conflict-eliciting properties. Secondly, there are those issues which arise in connection with the identification of conflict situations, with the cognitive and motivational consequences of conflict and, in particular, with the manifold and devious forms in which conflicts may find expression in fantasy. This second set of problems will provide the central focus of the present paper. Nevertheless, some general statements regarding the conceptual framework in which motives and drives are placed will be necessary in order to clarify the subsequent discussion of conflict and fantasy.

A THEORETICAL GUIDE

A Mediating Stimulus Model. An organism is said to be motivated when its behavior appears to be "persistent" and "directed." For our immediate purpose, we can ignore the thorny issue of the role of drive, drive-stimuli, and habits in providing direction to the organism's activities. In order to designate the direction of behavior, we assign a label to the motive based upon a class of stimulus situations which have such properties as terminating the organism's activity, increasing the probability of occurrence of a response associated with or leading to the situation, or being preferred by the organism in comparison with some other class of situations. In assessing motivation, whether it be n Achievement, n Affiliation, or n Aggression, one attempts to ascribe not only a label to the motive but also some kind of rank or number. Nominal scales have very little utility under conditions where almost all members of the population demonstrate to some degree the characteristics being measured. In order to make predictions, we want to be able to assert that individual A has a greater amount of n Achievement than individual B. What precisely is meant by such an assertion? One can suggest at least three different implications: (1) Many more situations elicit achievement motive in A than in B; (2) The intensity of the achievement motive aroused in A by some particular situation is greater than the corresponding intensity aroused in B; (3) The range of behaviors influenced by the achievement motive is greater in A than in B. These three dimensions are not independent but they are by no means theoretically equivalent. Need Achievement in A may be equally aroused by a prospective examination, the sight of a competitor, and a visit from his father. B may be predominantly responsive to paternal stimuli but, when aroused, the intensity of his motivation as measured by the effort he expends in overcoming obstacles may be considerably greater than that of A. Moreover, A's achievement motivation may be largely reflected in studying whereas B may strive to achieve high standards of athletic as well as academic accomplishment.

This analysis is obviously guided by a model of motivation in which response-produced mediating stimuli carry the burden of accounting for variations in the intensity and direction of behavior.[1] The model, which is essentially an adaptation of

[1]The mediating drive stimulus is considered to be independent of the incentive value of the goal. However, incentive value is, in part, a function of the intensity of the drive stimulus. If the drive is weak, then incentive value must be small; however, if the drive is strong, then incentive value can vary over a considerable range. The incentive value of a situation is assumed to exert a direct energizing function on the reaction potential of some particular behavior or act. In the case of acquired drives, it frequently occurs that the goal situation is identical to the situation that arouses the drive. In this instance, a distinction is made between the cue properties of the situation and the energizing properties as represented in its incentive value. Offering a reward to a subject may "remind" him of his material wants. The incentive value of the reward is then a function of the size of the reward and the intensity of the subject's material desires.

Leonard Doob's formal treatment of social attitude (8) distinguishes between variations in the number and kinds of arousing stimuli to which the mediating response is attached, in the strength of these S-R relationships, in the intensity of the response-produced drive stimuli, in the number and kind of instrumental responses and goal situations which serve to satisfy this motive, and in the incentive value of the goal situation. The term model is meant to suggest a mode of analysis rather than a precise theoretical formulation. Its major utility lies in suggesting the kind of questions that might be raised rather than in predicting answers to these questions. A major disadvantage in comparison to comparable models such as those proposed by Atkinson (2) and by Rotter (23) lies in the complexity and number of mediating links which are assumed to intervene between a stimulus and the organism's response. Nevertheless, it will be argued that the data of human motivation, performance, and fantasy require a complex model of this order which distinguishes between the conditions of motive arousal and the conditions of motive satisfaction. In contrast, Atkinson, in his novel treatment of this problem, makes the expectancy of motive satisfaction the condition for motive arousal. One consequence of this approach, which is also characteristic of other research using fantasy as a measure of motivation, is a failure to distinguish between characteristic individual differences in drive disposition — e.g., differences in the intensity of achievement aspirations in response to varying situations and characteristic differences in the mode of coping with the drive — e.g., passivity vs. active striving.

Some Further Theoretical Distinctions. The necessity for making finer discriminations than has generally been the case is perhaps most apparent in the treatment of those achievement-oriented subjects characterized by "fear of failure." These individuals are generally viewed as being in conflict because of the tendency to anticipate failure in an achievement situation. Thus McClelland (17, p. 326) notes that "individuals with fairly high motivation will fail to express it even in fantasy because of basic anxieties about achieving." This observation was based on a number of studies which indicated that individuals with moderate or low n Achievement scores tended to be defensively oriented in a variety of different test situations. An attempt by Clark, Teevan, and Ricciuti (6) to produce differences in achievement imagery by experimentally manipulating "fear of failure" and "hope of success" was unsuccessful. In addition, subjects characterized as either "fear of failure" or "hope for success" on the basis of rather complex level of aspiration measures, showed similar TAT response patterns. However, a group scoring in the middle of the fear of failure-hope for success continuum obtained higher total n Achievement scores and manifested less positive goal imagery and more negative goal imagery than either of the two extreme groups. This somewhat complicated finding is partly accounted for by assuming that the fear of failure group is so anxious over goal attainment, they tend to repress deprivation imagery and enhance positive goal imagery.

Atkinson (1) offers an interesting alternative explanation of these data to the effect that "hope for success" and "fear of failure" behavior in a level of aspiration situation is fundamentally similar, representing alternative means of avoiding failure. In any event, the difficulty still remains of distinguishing between low n Achievement scores based on avoidance of failure and low n Achievement scores which simply reflect a weak achievement motive. I suggest that part of the difficulty lies in the ambiguity of the phrase "fear of failure." It has been most frequently used to connote "anticipation" of failure as, for example, when it is contrasted with "hope for success." However, in the traditional treatment of level of aspiration, a distinction is made between expectancy of failure and anxiety or fear over failure. In an ingenious formulation of risk-taking behavior, Atkinson (1) extends this distinction and contrasts the influence of fear of failure with that of n Achievement. The assumption is implicity if not explicitly made that the high n Achievement scores on the TAT have uniform significance. I suggest that this assumption is untenable; that the sources, both situational and developmental, of high or low scores on other measures of "motivation" are by no means clear-cut. For example, it is quite possible that high n Achievement scores may be as much a consequence of anxiety associated with failure as pleasure associated with success. I would like to describe some data which I believe are consistent with this view and are inconsistent with the assumption that achievement imagery is inversely related to anxiety over failure.

In a dissertation by Glass (12), hope for success and expectancy of failure were experimentally manipulated, much in the same manner as in the Clark, Teevan, Ricciuti study, and the effects of this variation upon Thematic Apperception type stories were observed. The subjects consisted of male college undergraduates who, under varying conditions of expectancy of success or failure, were administered a modified digit-symbol substitution task and an anagram problem. The "hope of success" instructions were designed to give the impression that there was something to be gained but nothing to be lost in performing the test. Thus, the subjects were told that scores above the 25th-35th percentile were associated with academic success while lower scores were unrelated to academic performance. Expectancy of failure was induced by a comparable procedure, the difference being that low scores (below the 60th-70th percentile) predicted academic failure while high scores were presumably unrelated to academic performance. Fantasy material was elicited from the subjects following their performance on the two intellectual tasks. Consistent with the Clark, Teevan and Ricciuti study, Glass found no difference between the hope of success and expectancy of failure groups in the frequency or content of Achievement imagery. He had also administered the Mandler-Sarason Test Anxiety Scale, and found no difference in achievement scores between those subjects scoring above the median and those scoring below the median on the Test Anxiety Scale. However, there was a significant interaction between Test Anxiety and the variation in experimental instructions. The high anxious subjects responded with more achievement imagery under anticipation of failure than under the hope for success conditions, while the reverse effect held for the low anxious subjects. The mean n Achievement scores of the high anxious-fear of failure and low anxious-hope for success groups are almost identical while the corresponding scores for the high anxious-hope for success group and low anxious-fear of failure group were also quite similar.

Why should high anxious subjects respond with increased achievement imagery scores when the chances of failure are enhanced and the possibilities of success minimized, and the low anxious subjects respond with increased imagery when the possibility of failure is minimized and the chances of success are enhanced?

I suggest that high anxious subjects are especially concerned about failure and that their achievement motivation is engaged when failure is made a salient aspect of a test situation. Low anxious subjects are relatively unmoved by the anticipation of failure, but become aroused by the anticipation of success. A high n Achievement score tells us that the subject is running hard toward an achievement goal (either in fantasy or in more realistic life activities). Whether he is running toward a "carrot," so to speak, or away from a "stick" cannot be ascertained from the n Achievement score alone. Since, in this instance, the difference in the source of the motivation may make a difference in the behaviors mediated by the motive, one may have to posit at least two types of achievement motivation. In this connection, Downing (9), in an unpublished dissertation, has found that among a group of subjects who consistently obtained high n Achievement scores, those subjects obtaining high scores on the Taylor Scale displayed significantly different behavior in a level of aspiration situation than those with low manifest anxiety scores. To state the argument more generally, most fantasy measures of motivation are probably not undimensional.

Though the TAT *may* more clearly reflect human motivation than any other instrument that we have available, it is not the x-ray that will lay bare the naked pattern of the organism's inner drives undisguised and uncomplicated by the transformations of fear and guilt. However, the Thematic Apperception Test, by virtue of the same complexity, may permit the development of procedures for discriminating between low drive and inhibited high drive, between compensatory and representational fantasy, and between the sources of drive arousal and the conditions of drive gratification. There have been a number of interesting strides in this general direction and it would seem useful at this point to examine in detail the effects of conflicting motives upon fantasy behavior.

CONFLICT AND FANTASY

Response Competition. The concept of conflict falls within a category of terms such as motive, fear, set, drive, etc., that resemble each other in the diversity of meanings they manage to convey in the psychological literature. Without attempting a formal and rigorous treatment of conflict phenomena, a few distinctions can be made among these various meanings which are pertinent to the problem of ascertaining the influence of conflict upon fantasy behavior. It is helpful to distinguish between the conflict resulting solely from response competition and the conflict resulting from a special form of response competition — approach vs. avoidance — in which a particular situation elicits anticipation of both reward and punishment. Both types of conflict influence the assessment of motive through fantasy but in rather different ways. The approach-avoidance conflict from the viewpoint of this discussion is the more critical since, as it will be subsequently argued, it is this type of conflict that results in defensive and compromise behavior. Response competition is of interest when the measure of motivation depends upon relative differences in response strength and where little information is available regarding the absolute strengths of the habits or the degree of intensity of the drive stimuli being compared. Thus, given a TAT card which elicits an Achievement theme from subject A and a Hostility theme from subject B, one cannot conclude that subject A has a greater n Achievement than subject B. It may well be that n Achievement is equal for both subjects but that B has stronger hostile strivings. Given a series of TAT cards in which the frequency of achievement themes is greater for subject A and the frequency of hostility themes is greater for subject B, the same problem still obtains.

To extend this argument to its extreme, it is theoretically possible, although empirically unlikely, that a high theme count could reflect either a strong or weak response tendency depending upon whether the competing response tendencies elicited in the situation were strong or weak. The difficulties in interpretation resulting from response competition are not insuperable and can be largely circumvented by appropriate selection of stimulus materials. Perhaps the simplest procedure is to utilize stimuli which have a fairly high probability of eliciting the same theme, let us say n Achievement, but vary with regard to the probability of eliciting other themes. Because the cognitive restraints of the stimuli minimize the degree of systematic response competition, the variations obtained in achievement imagery can be more readily interpreted as a function of the strength of an achievement-oriented disposition. Experimental investigations of a number of motives have pointed to the importance of using stimulus cards which have a high probability of eliciting imagery relating to the motive being assessed. As an incidental note, if one's task is to predict some overt behavior such as fighting in the play yard and the TAT stimuli are very similar to the play yard stimuli, then the issue of the absolute strength of the disposition is irrelevant with regard to the prediction of the criterion. If Johnny's affiliative responses to the TAT and to the playground situation are greater than Richard's so that Johnny displays less combativeness in response to the TAT and in response to the actual playground situation, then it does not matter if his combative tendencies are actually equal to those of Richard.

APPROACH-AVOIDANCE CONFLICTS

Displacement. The above example suggests the presence of another factor which has been ignored in the above discussion — namely, inhibition[2] of the response disposition being assessed. A low imagery score can be a function of weak motivation, strong response competition, and finally of inhibition of the responses elicited by the motive. We now turn to a consideration of this second and, for our purposes, more significant type of conflict. The effects of motivational conflict upon verbalized fantasy is a challenging and in many ways puzzling problem. The theoretical model most widely applied to this problem is some form of Miller's conflict theory. In these applications, fantasy behavior is viewed as a response to a generalized stimulus. When direct expression of the goal response is inhibited but appears in the

[2]Inhibition is not being used in the technical Hullian sense but rather is broadly meant to suggest any tendency leading to avoidance of expression of an approach motive.

subject's fantasies, one refers to this process as displacement.

The phenomenon of displacement can be predicted by assuming that the avoidance or inhibitory gradient falls off more rapidly than does the approach gradient. According to this model, the displaced response can be either weaker or equal to, but never stronger than, a generalized response which would occur if no inhibition was operating (19). This consequence of the model has never been directly tested, although there is indirect evidence which indicates that if anxiety is elicited by some drive stimulus, the expression of that drive in fantasy will be diminished (4, 16, 22). And yet the rationale which guided the development of the Thematic Apperception Test and other projective techniques was based on the assumption that such techniques are particularly sensitive to covert, repressed material. The pictures presumably provide a screen upon which the subject casts his private fantasies and expresses his forbidden impulses. There is also the implication that if drives are accepted and find expression in everyday life, they are less likely to dominate a subject's fantasies than if the same drives were a source of conflict. Fantasy behavior is here conceived to be a kind of substitute goal response which is employed when more direct expression is inhibited or not feasible. Similarly, the Freudian "hydraulic" model of libidinal processes implies that as pressure (repression) is applied at one point in the system, there is increased tension in the system and consequently a greater tendency for the libidinal drives to "break through" at some other point in the system where the repressive forces are weaker. Further, to the extent that projection in the classic psychoanalytic sense is involved in TAT fantasy, one would expect repression to result in an increase in expression of the anxiety-arousing impulses. There is an apparent discrepancy between the traditional conceptions of TAT-elicited fantasy and certain implications of displacement theory as currently applied. If two theoretical positions lead to different implications, then the resolution of the differences is primarily an empirical matter. However, in the case of TAT fantasy, the behavior being assessed is extremely complex and is probably influenced by more factors than are dealt with in the simplified displacement and hydraulic models that have just been described. A closer look at the theories and the behavior is necessary.

It is not necessary to discuss here the theoretical and heuristic importance that Miller's conflict model has had for personality theory and research. Our essential concern is with the implication of this model for fantasy behavior. In the application to fantasy, it has been generally assumed that the avoidance gradient drops off more rapidly than does the approach gradient with increasing distance from the goal or with increasing dissimilarity from a drive-arousing stimulus. These assumptions may be empirically correct but as Miller (19) himself has noted, they should not be invariably applied. Miller suggests that the difference that has been observed in the slope of the two gradients is a consequence of the source of the motivation. Fear is conceived to be an acquirable drive which is aroused by environmental cues. The farther the subject gets from the instigating situation, the weaker are the drive-arousing cues. However, with a primary drive such as hunger, the intensity of the drive stimulus is largely dependent upon internal processes and consequently these primary drives are less subject to external stimulus controls. Approach behavior stimulated by hunger will therefore decline less rapidly than avoidance behavior stimulated by fear with increasing distance from the goal. If the approach motive is, in Miller's terms, a secondary drive it will also be subject to arousal by environmental cues and approach behavior should then diminish with distance from the goal at the same rate as avoidance behavior. Thus, Katz (15) has shown, using human subjects, that when the approach and avoidance motives are stimulus-linked, there is no difference in the slopes of the approach and avoidance gradients. In studies of fantasy behavior, where displacement theory has been applied, the approach motives — e.g., sex and aggression — are manifestly stimulus-linked and the theoretical basis for assuming a difference in gradient slopes is unclear.

Of course, differences in learning conditions rather than in degree of similarity could account for these apparent gradients. If the subject has been punished for overt aggressive expression but has never been punished for privately rehearsing aggressive thoughts, then one would expect a form of displacement which, however, is a function of differential reinforcement. This type of analysis is especially applicable where fear has been attached to an overt response rather than to the mediating drive stimuli. Where fear is directly attached to the drive stimulus, then as the behavior model outlined at the beginning of this paper suggests, all behavior mediated by this drive stimulus should be less likely to occur or should be diminished in intensity. To complicate the matter further, there may be variations in the degree of fear or guilt attached to different intensities of a drive as a result of differential learning experiences.

The effect of inhibition of a motive upon its expression in fantasy is a complex problem which warrants considerably more attention than it has been given and requires distinctions that are not generally made. Thus, while frustration and guilt are both sources of inhibition, their effects on fantasy are probably quite dissimilar, because frustration is much more likely to be linked to an overt response than is guilt, which is more likely to be linked to the mediating drive stimulus.[3] An adolescent whose progress toward an achievement goal is hampered by disappointments and failures may compensate by increased achievement imagery in his fantasy life.[4] The fantasies, however, of an adolescent who feels guilty about his aspirations are more likely to reveal a lesser amount of achievement imagery than if no guilt were experienced.

This discussion has been concerned with motivational aspects of inhibition and has yet to consider the cognitive implications. The issue here pertains to the effect of lack of awareness of one's motives upon their projection in fantasy. Thus, it is often assumed, and I believe it to be a reasonable assumption, that the greater the degree of unawareness of a motive (especially one

---

[3]Of course, if all the means by which one attempts to attain a goal are continually blocked and hampered, then frustration-produced responses may become attached to the drive stimulus. Also there are undoubtedly many instances in which guilt is attached only to a particular instrumental means of gratifying a drive.

[4]Where the fantasy-eliciting stimuli are highly similar to the frustration-producing situation, then, as in Crandall's (7) study, the subject's fantasies may be strongly colored by negative reactions to the frustration.

with strong affective components) the more likely it will be that the motive will appear in the subject's fantasies, in his judgment of other people, and in other behaviors in which projection is possible. I cannot offer a rigorous rationale for this expectation except to suggest that lack of awareness eliminates an essential cue which the subject has learned to utilize in discriminating between his own feelings and those of other people. The amount of primary generalization may thereby be increased and the extent to which the expression of the affect is subject to cognitive controls is reduced. An experiment recently reported by Robert Singer and myself (10) which deals with the effects of inhibition of fear on the perception of fear in others yielded results which are consistent with these conjectures. A group in whom fear had been aroused and who were encouraged to deny their feelings judged the stimulus person as significantly more anxious than a comparable group who had been encouraged to express their feelings. Although the interpretation of this experiment is rendered somewhat ambiguous by the possibility that the operations for inducing inhibition may also have increased the subject's anxiety, the empirical findings indicate that inhibition of an affect facilitates the degree of projection of the affect.

There is still another source of empirical findings and theorizing which indicate that inhibition should enhance projection. I refer to the experimental studies based on Heinz Werner's sensoritonic theory (25). The Rorschach studies, for example, indicate that inhibition of motor expression tends to increase M responses (18, 24). Whether one is dealing here with a vicarious expression of tension or rather with an increase of tension due to frustration is unclear, but again the data suggest that inhibition will increase this particular form of displacement. The effects of inhibition on displacement depend, then, on a number of processes which may combine to exaggerate the degree of displacement or may counteract and minimize displacement phenomena since the same factors which produce unawareness may also produce avoidance of stimuli associated with the inhibited motive. It may be possible experimentally to differentiate some of these processes by varying the anxiety- or guilt-provoking properties of the TAT stimuli as well as varying the degree of inhibition of the motive under investigation.

In considering the effects of "inhibition" upon displacement, we have had very little to say about the behavioral consequences, if any, of conflict as such. Thus, in predicting from Miller's conflict model, one essentially has to determine the strengths of the approach and the avoidance tendencies at some point in the stimulus continuum and then summate them algebraically. The term "conflict" is used by Miller in a purely descriptive sense and has no special theoretical status. Miller's analysis has been extended by Brown and Farber (3) in a theoretical paper which argues that a situation of conflict or frustration has drive and cue properties and thus, for Brown and Farber, the notion of "conflict" enjoys the status of a hypothetical construct. The problem remains, however, of specifying the behavioral implications of this construct. This task is in large measure an empirical one, and our purpose will be best served if we restrict the consideration of conflict effects to verbal behavior. There are two types of verbal effects that are of special interest: 1. Changes in the response indices of the motive being measured (approach behavior). 2. Changes in other types of verbal content which, for want of a better name, will be temporarily referred to as "defensive" (i.e., compromise, disguised) responses.

With regard to the first type of response index, we are again confronted with the problem of displacement but now must consider the consequences of conflict-produced stimuli upon displacement. Whiting and Child (26), in their study of the relationship between certain child-rearing practices and beliefs about illness, review this problem and are able to account for certain aspects of their data only by assuming an increase in drive level resulting from conflict. With this assumption, Whiting and Child (26) are able to demonstrate that at certain points on the stimulus continuum, a high anxiety group should manifest significantly stronger approach tendencies than a low anxiety group; that is, their modified displacement model predicts that "the habit potential of extremely displaced responses will be greater with high anxiety." This prediction cannot be made from the Miller model. However, the Whiting and Child model does not predict that all displaced responses will be stronger with high anxiety and consequently one is unable to ascertain in advance of collecting the data whether a high inhibition group will manifest more or less of some displaced response than a low inhibition group. For reasons already noted, it is also difficult to make predictions from the Miller model in any concrete situation. In fact, in most studies of verbalized fantasy where Miller's displacement model has been applied, the application has been on an ad hoc basis. Insofar as the TAT and similar fantasy material are concerned, a partial solution to this general difficulty may be provided by determining whether there is a discriminable category of verbal responses which are markedly affected by conflict and which may provide some indication of the presence of a drive even when the usual response indicators of that drive are absent due to inhibition.

Conflict-produced Responses. A dissertation directly relevant to this issue and, unfortunately, never published, was carried out a number of years ago by S. Gellerman (11), who was interested in the effects of experimentally induced aggression and inhibition on word association response sequences. College student volunteers were randomly assigned to one of the 4 treatment groups generated by the two levels of aggression and inhibition employed in this study. Thus one group was insulted and also subjected to an inhibiting procedure, a second group was insulted only, a third group was inhibited only, while the fourth or control group was not subjected to any motivational manipulations. Aggression was aroused by exposing the students to a few nasty unwarranted comments regarding their lack of any real interest in science and education while inhibition was induced by informing the subjects that the test to be administered measured emotional maturity and that the test score would be recorded in the Dean's office. All groups took a modified version of the word association test, giving a sequence of 10 responses to each of 5 aggressive stimulus words and 6 neutral or buffer stimulus words. Previous research had indicated that only associations to the aggressive stimuli discriminated the effects of motivational arousal. The word association responses could be reliably classified into 3 categories: aggressive, defensive and neutral. These defensive responses were presumed to represent a compromise or interaction resulting from the conflict of aggression and inhibition. More specifically, among the statements included in this category were terms of rescue (save, succour), protection (bombshelter, shield), disapproval of aggression (crazy, inhuman, horrible), punishment (jail, gallows), and prevention (stop, avoid). It is apparent that the "defense" category is rather inclusive and contains responses that are direct indices of inhibition as well as responses that represent more of a compromise or substitution. Operationally, however, it is difficult to make this distinction and since both types of defensive reactions should increase as a function of increased aggression and increased inhibition, they were grouped together.

In developing a simple model to predict the outcome of the experimental manipulations, the number of defensive responses was assumed to be a positive function of the size of both the approach tendency and the inhibitory tendency. Inhibition was directly linked to aggression in that it was assumed that a given inhibitory tendency would "convert" a constant proportion of aggressive responses into defensive responses; thus, the greater the degree of aggression, the higher the absolute number of defensive responses. Apart from the Gellerman experiment, there are insufficient data to evaluate the merits of this particular assumption. The main consequences of this assumption — namely, that defensive behavior in the sense of compromise behavior can be high only if the approach motive is strong and that the degree of inhibition is often directly linked to the strength of the approach motive — seem to be reasonable hypotheses. The principal results of the word association study were consistent with expectations based upon these hypotheses. The aggressive group who were not subjected to the inhibitory instructions had the greatest number of aggressive associations; the mean number of aggressive associations of the aggressive-inhibited group was similar to the means for the control groups. Moreover, the aggressive-inhibited group, as predicted, manifested the greatest number of defensive responses. While in the preliminary study, the aggressive group had more defensive as well as aggressive responses than the control subjects, this difference in defensive behavior was not replicated in the final study.

The principal value of this experiment is that, like Clark's (4, 5) study of the influence of sexual arousal on the TAT, it demonstrates that one can discriminate between the verbal behavior or fantasies induced by low drive and induced by inhibited high drive. The distinction between "approach" indices of a motive and conflict-induced indices of a motive can be readily applied to Clark's data. Clark was especially concerned with reconciling the following findings: 1. Under non-alcoholic conditions, a group exposed to sex-arousing stimuli produced significantly less manifest sexual imagery and significantly more sex-symbolic responses than the control subjects. 2. Within both the experimental and the control groups, a curvilinear relationship was obtained between manifest sex responses and symbolic sex responses such that the groups displaying the highest and least amount of manifest sex imagery obtained the highest sex symbol scores. This relationship was especially marked in the sex condition.

Let us equate manifest sexual imagery with approach responses (a category which describes a response gradient varying from statements of intercourse, to kissing, to dating behavior) and symbolic sex responses with conflict-induced behavior. If, as Clark assumes, both sex drive and anxiety or guilt over sex is greater in the experimental group than in the control group, the experimental group should have more defensive responses than the control group. The difference in manifest sex imagery would depend upon the comparative strengths of the approach and avoidance tendencies and could not be predicted without some prior knowledge of relevant parameters. The curvilinear relationship obtained in the intragroup analysis could result from variations in the degree of sexual arousal and variations in the degree of anxiety over sexual feeling. One would have to assume that the high manifest sex imagery-high symbolic response group had a stronger approach tendency and a weaker avoidance tendency than did the low manifest sex imagery-high symbolic response group. While this (ad hoc) explanation is perhaps no more parsimonious than that offered by Clark who, in addition to drive-induced anxiety, also assumes variations in fantasy response-produced guilt, it does have the advantage of being more amenable to experimental test since one can manipulate the degree of sex arousal and degree of inhibition.

However, it is probably premature to be concerned about subtle distinctions in underlying mechanisms when we have only the rudiments of empirical relationships about which to theorize. More immediate needs are the systematic manipulation and assessment of approach and inhibitory tendencies, a distinction between and an analysis of stimulus and response displacement, and with regard to defensive behavior, a distinction between inhibitory (avoidance) responses and compromise responses. We need to further develop and systematically apply conflict indices when verbalized fantasy is used to assess motivation. Unless such a procedure is followed, one cannot be confident that one is measuring an inhibited motive rather than a weak motive or vice versa. For example, in the Mussen and Scodel (21) study, the lower mean sexual response score obtained by the group exposed to slides of nude females presented by a stern, professorial figure in comparison to the sex response score obtained by a group exposed to the same slides presented by a young, informal graduate student may have been a function of lower sex arousal rather than inhibition of sexual responses.

Hokanson and Gordon (13) recently reported a study in which the aggressive fantasy content of high scorers on a Manifest Hostility Scale decreased under conditions of drive arousal as compared with a neutral condition while the aggressive fantasy content of low scorers increased under drive arousal. The authors present data which indicate that the degree of drive arousal was equivalent for the High and Low Scorers. However, the difference may not have been a function of inhibition of hostile expression in the High Scorer group (because the approach gradient intercepts the avoidance gradient at a higher point under conditions of drive arousal) but possibly of differences between the high manifest and low manifest aggression group in the tendency to use fantasy as a means of expressing aggression when aroused. I do not mean to imply that these alternative explanations more adequately account for the data than the explanations offered by the authors; only that these alternatives can be excluded by an analysis of changes in response indicators of conflict.

A preliminary study just completed by M. Hurvich, at the University of Pennsylvania, presents similar problems. In this study concerned with the effects of the arousal of dependency motivation upon TAT type fantasy, the reading of a "case history" was used to arouse n Dependency. Two forms of the case history were compared. One form, the dependency-deprivation condition, described a series of development situations in which a child sought help from his parents but this help was not provided. The second form was quite similar except that the child's requests were consistently gratified. Hurvich found that the dependency-gratification condition produced significantly more dependency themes than either the dependency-frustration or a control condition. Is the lower score of the dependency-frustration group a function of inhibition of dependency responses or of a lesser degree of motive arousal? The assessment of conflict indicators would decide this issue. An important task for future research is the identification of these conflict-produced fantasy responses as they relate to particular drives.

SUMMING UP

This discussion of conflict and fantasy behavior has traveled a long and sometimes indirect route. Yet there are a number of remaining issues which warrant attention but will be neglected here. We have not considered the consequences of conflict indices obtained in fantasy production for the prediction of overt behavior. Of particular relevance to this issue is Pittluck's (22) study of aggression in which she was able to demonstrate a positive relationship between fantasy aggression and overt aggression only after taking into account response indicators of conflict. Mussen and Naylor (20) and Kagan (14), who were concerned with the same problem, reported a significant positive correlation between fantasy and manifest aggression without the use of conflict indicators. Lesser (16), who systematically explored a variety of anxiety indices, found a substantially greater correlation between a combined aggression, aggression-anxiety fantasy index and overt aggressive behavior than between overt aggression and either fantasy aggression or aggression-anxiety when considered separately.

It is by now evident that we should not expect to find a simple, uniform relationship between "covert" fantasy expression of a motive and "overt" behavioral expressions. The proper question is not "what is the relationship?" but rather under what conditions would we expect to find a positive, inverse or negligible correlation. As has been indicated at various points in this discussion, the influence of conflict upon this relationship is a complex one. Whether or not the inhibitory responses are associated with a particular instrumental act or are connected to the mediating drive stimulus is one among a number of considerations that must be taken into account before predicting the direction of the relationship. Essentially, one has to determine whether similar conflict-producing cues are present in the situation in which fantasy is assessed and in the situation in which the non-fantasy behavior is elicited. A procedure which might be very helpful in this regard is the systematic use of TAT stimuli in the formation of stimulus gradients in order to study displacement effects. This possibility might be best reviewed in a context of a discussion of the properties of TAT stimulus cards.

It is evident that the problems that touch upon the area of motivational conflict and its assessment through fantasy are too complex and too varied to be considered in one paper. We have chosen to restrict our discussion to, and hopefully have demonstrated the value of, the following points:

1. The conditions of motive arousal should be distinguished from the conditions of motive gratification. Thematic Apperception Test responses are behavioral outcomes of a complex process in which there may be variations in the source of motive (drive) arousal, in the intensity of the motive aroused, and in the manner with which the subject characteristically copes with this motive under the conditions provided for expression of the motive.

2. The effects of response competition as such can be distinguished from the effects of the particular kind of response competition involved in approach-avoidance conflicts. Both forms of conflict influence fantasy behavior but in different ways. It

is assumed that only the latter type of conflict results in defensive or compromise fantasy responses.

3. Current theoretical models of displacement have very limited utility with respect to predicting fantasy behavior. Inhibition of expression of a motive leads to various motivational and cognitive consequences which must be assessed before one can predict displacement effects.

4. Approach-avoidance conflicts result in compromise and defensive behavior which, at least for some motives, are reflected in verbal responses. A promising area of future research is the development of fantasy response indicators of conflict and the use of these "defensive" indicators in the assessment of motivation.

REFERENCES

1. Atkinson, John W.: Motivational determinants of risk-taking behavior. *Psychol. Rev., 64*:359-372. 1957.
2. Atkinson, John W.: Thematic apperceptive measurement of motives with the context of a theory of motivation. In J. W. Atkinson (Ed.) *Motives in Fantasy, Action, and Society.* New York, Van Nostrand, 1958, Pp. 596-616.
3. Brown, J. S., and Farber, I. E.: Emotions conceptualized as intervening variables. *Psychol. Bull., 48*:465-493. 1951.
4. Clark, R. A.: The projective measurement of experimentally induced levels of sexual motivation. *J. Exp. Psychol., 44*:391-399. 1952.
5. Clark, R. A., and Sensibar, M. R.: The relationship between symbolic and manifest projections of sexuality with some incidental correlates. *J. Abnorm. & Social Psychol., 50:*327-334. 1955.
6. Clark, R. A., Teevan, R., and Ricciuti, H. H.: Hope of success and fear of failure as aspects of need for achievement. *J. Abnorm. & Social Psychol., 53*:182-186. 1956.
7. Crandall, V. J.: Induced frustration and punishment—reward expectancy in thematic apperception stories. *J. Consult. Psychol., 15*:400-404. 1951.
8. Doob, L. W.: The behavior of attitudes. *Psychol. Rev., 54*:135-156. 1947.
9. Downing, Robert W.: The relationship between the mode of expression of achievement motivation in imaginative thought productions and anxiety level, level of aspiration and performance. Unpublished doctoral dissertation, Univ. of Pennsylvania, 1957.

10. Feshbach, S., and Singer, R. D.: The effects of fear arousal and suppression of fear upon social perception. *J. Abnorm. & Social Psychol., 55*:283-288. 1957.
11. Gellerman, S.: The effects of experimentally induced aggression and inhibition on word-association response sequences. Unpublished doctoral dissertation, Univ. of Pennsylvania, 1956.
12. Glass, H. L.: The effects on fantasy of achievement motivation based on "fear of failure" and "hope of success." Unpublished doctoral dissertation, Univ. of Pennsylvania, 1957.
13. Hokanson, J. E., and Gordon, J. E.: The expression and inhibition of hostility in imaginative and overt behavior. *J. Abnorm. & Social Psychol., 57*:327-333. 1958.
14. Kagan, J.: The measurement of overt aggression from fantasy. *J. Abnorm. & Social Psychol., 52*:390-393. 1956.
15. Katz, L.: The effects of constant versus variable approach motivation on human conflict behavior—A test of Miller's hypothesis. Unpublished doctoral dissertation, Univ. of Pennsylvania, 1956.
16. Lesser, G. S.: Conflict analysis of fantasy aggression. *J. Pers. 26*:29-41. 1958.
17. McClelland, D. C., Atkinson, J. W., Clark, R. A., and Lowell, E. L.: *The Achievement Motive.* New York, Appleton, 1953.
18. Meltzoff, J., Singer, J. L. and Korchin, S. J.: Motor inhibition and Rorschach movement responses: a test of the sensory-tonic theory. *J. Pers. 21*:400-410. 1953.
19. Miller, N.: Theory and experiment relating psychoanalytic displacement to stimulus-response generalization. *J. Abnorm. & Social Psychol., 43*:155-178. 1948.
20. Mussen, P. H., and Naylor, M. K.: The relationships between overt and fantasy aggression. *J. Abnorm. & Social Psychol., 49*:235-240. 1954.
21. Mussen, P. H. and Scodel, A.: The effects of sexual stimulation under varying conditions on TAT sexual responsiveness. *J. Consult. Psychol., 19*:90. 1955.
22. Pittluck, Patricia.: The relationship between aggressive fantasy and overt behavior. Unpublished doctoral dissertation. Yale Univ., 1950.
23. Rotter, J. B.: *Social learning and clinical psychology.* New York, Prentice Hall, 1954.
24. Singer, J. L., Meltzoff, J., and Goldman, G. D.: Rorschach movement responses following motor inhibition and hyperactivity. *J. Consult. Psychol., 16*:359-364. 1952.

25. Werner, H. and Wapner, S.: *Sensory-tonic field theory of perception. Psychol. Rev., 59:*324-333, 1952.
26. Whiting, J. W. M. and Child, I. L.: Child training and personality; a cross-cultural study. New Haven, Yale Univ. Press, 1953.

DISCUSSION OF DR. FESHBACH'S PAPER

Kenneth Purcell, Ph.D.
Primary Discussant

D*r. Purcell:* Dr. Feshbach has made a good case for the multidimensionality of current fantasy measures of motivation. Using Glass's (7) data, he has illustrated the point by showing that high anxious subjects obtain higher need achievement scores under anticipation of failure whereas low anxious subjects obtain higher need achievement scores under hope of success. This seems quite in accord with tradition in psychology. Just as there has been found more than one dimension of rigidity, and of anxiety, and more recently, of masculinity-feminity, so there is more than one dimension of need achievement. However, the interesting finding here is that different antecedent conditions – different experimental manipulations – evidently generate indistinguishable fantasy content when applied to individuals differing on a second variable – in this case, level of anxiety. As in the Clark (4) study, it is assumed that certain experimental procedures can be used to define genotypically different groups which then turn out to be phenotypically similar on need achievement scores. Whether more refined analyses can tease out differences in achievement imagery produced by operationally different procedures remains a question for study. My own hunch is that it can be done. It may require a more detailed scoring procedure embodying, for example, a category such as instrumental actions to avoid achievement situations, or realistic versus unrealistic achievement. Such categories are not part of the usual scoring system. Or it may demand a more varied set of stimuli designed to engage the motive to avoid failure as opposed to the motive to achieve. Pictorial cues may not be sufficiently distinctive to allow a differentiation between motives as closely related as these. Perhaps story completion tasks would be a useful technique to apply. Plot situations permitting varied solutions may be described to subjects in a way so as to contrast essentially failure-avoidance situations with those of achievement.

Feshbach argues strongly that the conditions of motive arousal must be distinguished from those of motive gratification. He feels that Atkinson (2), in making arousal contingent upon expectancy of gratification, has been led to neglect such matters as the variation in amplitude of the achievement response to varying situations. As I understand Atkinson's viewpoint, the role of expectancy is of special importance in assessing the relationship between measures of motive strength and performance of a particular act. A positive relationship exists only when the expectancy of satisfying a given motive through a given performance sequence has been aroused. Since expectancy, defined as the subjective probability that a given performance will result in incentive attainment, is of variable magnitude, the model appears to have no difficulty in predicting intensity differences in achievement aspiration responses for different situations. Nor does the model appear to have any special problem in dealing with the finding that chemistry students respond with more need achievement imagery to laboratory picture stimuli than do physical education students. The nature and magnitude of the incentive, as well as expectancy and motive measures, enter into the motivation formula.

As a matter of fact, Feshbach himself seems to have inadvertently slipped into using the expectancy hypothesis to account for motive arousal. At first glance, Glass's findings (higher need achievement for high anxiety Ss with failure set and for low anxiety Ss with success set) seem to challenge the conception that motive arousal is a function of the subjective likelihood of goal attainment. To quote Feshbach, "Why should high anxious subjects respond with increased achievement imagery scores when the chances of failure are enhanced and the possibilities of success minimized, and the low anxious subjects respond with increased imagery when the possibility of failure is minimized and the chances of success are enhanced?"

Dr. Feshbach suggests that "high anxious subjects are especially concerned about failure and that their achievement motivation is engaged when failure is made a salient aspect of a test situation. Low anxious subjects are relatively unmoved by the anticipation of failure, but become aroused by the anticipation of success." By translating into slightly different terminology one can say that high anxious subjects are especially motivated to avoid failure and that their expectancy of satisfying this motive is obviously greater in a situation where failure is a distinct possibility than when the possibility for failure does not exist. The same line of reasoning applies to the low anxious-hope of success group. Motive arousal may be said to be dependent upon the opportunities perceived by the subject for motive satisfaction — in this case the opportunity for success. None of this denies Feshbach's important point that quite different sources of motivation appear capable of producing similar motivational content in fantasy.

The distinctions made by Feshbach between the various forms of response competition, and between inhibition attached to an overt response as contrasted to inhibition attached to a mediating drive stimulus, are extremely well taken. The latter distinction particularly is held to be of considerable importance in theories of psychopathology and psychotherapy. I refer to the guilt-producing lack of discrimination between the thought and the action frequently reported in schizophrenia and to the significance which therapists assign to developing such discriminations. Efforts to operationalize this distinction and to identify its thematic consequences are sorely needed. Perhaps Lazarus' suggestion for forced kinds of erotic or aggressive stories represents a useful technique in this task.

Turning now to a discussion of the effects of approach-avoidance conflicts on defensive verbal content we find, in the Gellerman (6) results reported by Feshbach, a nice demonstration of the way in which defensive indicators can be applied to discriminate between a low approach motive and an inhibited high approach motive. However, I would question one of the assumptions stated by Feshbach as underlying this experiment; namely, that the degree of inhibition is often linked to the strength of the approach motive. Two studies, each dealing with aggression as the approach motive may be briefly mentioned here. One is reported in a monograph by Jensen (8). He studied the TAT productions of three groups, one aggressive in socially acceptable ways, the second aggressive in socially unacceptable ways, and the third a passive group. Although there was a highly significant positive relationship between overt aggressive behavior and socially disapproved TAT aggression, the latter was associated with a conspicuous absence of punishment themes or defense against aggression. The results are quite similar to those which I obtained in studying a delinquent population (9). In fact, in the main Gellerman study, the aggressive subjects had no more defensive responses than the control subjects, although this difference had appeared in a preliminary study. It would also appear, on theoretical grounds, that the acquisition of inhibition motives of varying intensities may proceed relatively independently of the acquistion of approach motives of varying intensities.

Feshbach has drawn repeated attention to the importance of deriving response indicators of conflict if we hope to distinguish between approach response competition, weak drive and inhibited high drive. Besides illustrating some simple but effective techniques for independently manipulating approach and avoidance response gradients, he has suggested the beginnings of a distinction between compromise and avoidance types of fantasy content. In this connection, I would like to suggest the potential usefulness of more formal, relatively content-free, indices of conflict. For example, Wyatt (12) makes the point that fantasy production in response to pictures is principally an organizing, synthetic function of the ego. Based on this conception he describes the rudiments of a system for scoring thematic content for different types of inconsistency presumed to reflect disruptions in ego functioning. Perhaps such a scheme can be made to discriminate successfully between weak motive and inhibited strong motive since the latter would presumably place greater stress upon the synthetic function of the ego. If we accept the view that fantasy expressions of a motive are determined not only by the motive but also by the intervention of ego processes (and I believe this to be the case) then systems to assess adequacy of ego functioning in thematic productions may be especially valuable. Instances in which content material is relatively barren because of excessive blocking or other ego defense mechanisms are cases in point.

Before closing my comments I would like to make a slight digression to a related issue. The title of Feshbach's paper is "The Influence of Drive Arousal and Conflict Upon Fantasy Behavior." It occurs to me that an equally interesting paper might have been written with the title "The Influence of Fantasy Behavior Upon Drive Arousal and Conflict." In fact, Feshbach himself could have written it since he has accomplished some highly interesting work in this area. Probably the most commonly accepted view is that imaginative expression may be one form of motive gratification or drive reduction. Certainly clinical psychologists lean heavily upon this assumption in their daily practical use of a theory of personality functioning in psychological evaluations. The phrase "uses fantasy as an outlet for discharging aggressive or sexual tensions" must strike a familiar chord with most of you. The experimental evidence, although limited, tends to be consonant with this view. There is Feshbach's (5) own study on the drive-reducing function of fantasy as well as the serial position effects recently reported by Reitman and Atkinson (10). The latter referred to the fact that achievement motive scores derived from pictures in the first four positions of an eight-picture sequence successfully predicted performance differences whereas those derived from the last four positions did not. There was also a significant positive relationship between the size of the motive scores for the first four positions and the amount of decrease in these scores based on the last four positions. It was suggested that achievement motivation might have been reduced through fantasy expression.

However, I would like to call your attention to the possibility that the process of producing thematic material may not only *arouse* avoidance motives, but under certain conditions may also *increase,* rather than reduce, approach motives. Clark (3), in his now well-known study on the influences of sex stimulation on TAT content, has utilized the concept of fantasy response-produced avoidance motives in order to explain certain of his findings. Furthermore, in a situation generating *high-approach, low-avoidance* gradients, it may be that fantasy produces cues which result in heightened motivational states. Fortunately, in Dr. Holt's presentation at this conference there appeared a brief quotation which allows me to appeal to the authority of Freud. To quote Holt quoting Freud: "Some patients consciously realize them (fantasies) in action and thus imagine and actually bring about assaults or sexual aggressions." Thus, once again the principle is illustrated that if one is diligent enough in the finding and careless enough in the application, one can support anything from something said by Freud.

Conceiving of a class of fantasy behaviors as fractional anticipatory goal responses does, however, suggest a theoretical rationale for this statement. As you know, drive properties have been assigned to the anticipation of punishment. Now Spence (11) has done the same thing for the anticipation of reward objects and, even more recently, Amsel (1) has argued that anticipation of frustration has drive properties. With this in mind it might be worthwhile to review an aspect of the data in the Gellerman experiment. You will recall that the procedure in the word association test consisted of Ss giving a sequence of ten responses to each of the stimulus words, some aggressively toned and some neutral. Among the groups studied were an aggressive inhibited group and an aggressive uninhibited group. The latter group had the greatest number of aggressive responses while the former group did not differ from control groups on this dimension. It would be of interest to re-examine the associations to determine whether the frequency of aggressive associations changed in any systematic fashion during the response sequence. Specifically, I would look for a build-up of such associations as characteristic of the aggressive uninhibited group.

It should be noted that this line of reasoning is not dependent upon what conception one holds of the etiology of fantasy expression of a motive; e.g., that it occurs only when motor discharge is blocked or that there is a parallelism between motor and fantasy expression of a motive. In either case, the question remains: what are the conditions under which fantasy, once produced, may reduce or further arouse a motivational state?

A practical facet of this same problem lies behind one of the fateful questions frequently raised by educators and parents in our era of delinquency consciousness. Namely, do violence-infused comic strips and TV productions in some way instigate further delinquent behavior? Most psychologists reply in the negative to such a query, noting that delinquent behavior existed long before comics and TV and that we are merely showing the effects of a greater awareness of such phenomena. The point of view I am suggesting now would propose a qualified "yes" to such a question, reasoning that delinquents are characterized by high-approach, low-avoidance gradients with respect to aggression and are just the kind of people for whom fantasy would serve as a medium for aggressive self-stimulation. Non-delinquents, on the other hand, persons with either weak or inhibited strong approach motives are, for different reasons, not likely to experience an arousal of approach motive that would lead to overt delinquent behavior. In the case of weak motives the magnitude of arousal will not be great and in the case of strong inhibited motives there should be simultaneous strengthening of the inhibitory controls.

The only data bearing on this issue of which I know consists of an unpublished reanalysis of TAT stories which I collected from delinquents and non-delinquents in an earlier study. The series of 10 TAT stories were examined for changes in number of aggressive themes and frequency of manifest aggressive imagery. Delinquent Ss showed a significant increment on both these indices in the last 5 cards whereas no change was evident in the non-delinquent group. In other words, the significant differences which existed in the first half of the series became larger in the second half. However, since this study was not designed to test the hypothesis, uncontrolled variables do not permit a clear-cut interpretation of the finding. For example, the possibility exists that the picture stimuli in the latter half of the series were differentially superior cues for arousing aggressive motives in the delinquent as opposed to non-delinquent subjects.

A paradigm for beginning to evaluate this question would consist first of experimental manipulation or natural selection of various groups differing on approach-avoidance gradient combinations. After or simultaneous with this would come motive arousal followed by induced fantasy to motive-relevant cues. Interest would focus on the role of induced fantasy in altering the intensity of motive states and, in particular, on the direction of intensity change as a function of the relative height of approach-avoidance gradients. Dependent measures of motive state might consist of perceptual techniques such as threshold measures or even certain motor learning or performance tasks which would reflect degree of motivational arousal.

Dr. Feshbach: The problem of the effects of aggressive fantasy on subsequent behavior could take several hours of discussion. Before we get to that issue, I would like to first consider those comments made by Dr. Purcell which are directly relevant to the paper. One minor source of contention arose from a statement I made regarding the relationship between inhibition and aggression, or inhibition and approach responses. The assertion that the degree of inhibition is often directly linked to the strength of the approach motive seems to me to be a reasonable hypothesis. I did not state that strong manifestations of inhibition necessarily imply a strong approach motive. In general, though, evidence of inhibition suggests the presence of an approach motive; that is, one does not show anxiety over sex as a rule unless sex responses are aroused.

A second issue raised by Dr. Purcell has to do with the Glass (7) experiment and the distinction between the conditions under which drive is aroused and the conditions under which drive is gratified. While certainly relevant, the Glass experiment was not cited in connection with that particular issue. In reviewing that experiment, I was trying to demonstrate that fear of failure does not necessarily lead to a conflict regarding achievement and that, in fact, a situation in which failure is made very salient can engage achievement motivation.

Dr. Purcell: Does Glass rely on the expectancy hypothesis?

Dr. Feshbach: I think John Atkinson's (2) theoretical model linking expectancy to motivation can account for all kinds of data; otherwise, he never would have developed it. Moreover, the model is particularly suited to level of aspiration and achievement situations. I believe, however, that this approach presents nany problems when one deals with other kinds of motives. 'or example, it seems to me, as I read the theory, that one impli- :ation would be that a person would not get angry at someone vho is provoking him unless he felt his anger could be gratified. t seems more reasonable to me to first determine the conditions vhich lead to arousal of anger in the person and then separately :onsider the expectancy for gratification of that anger through 'arious kinds of outlets.

Dr. Lazarus: Can't you make the same argument in the case)f dependency? For example, the person may have strong de-)endency needs even though his expectation of getting them ;ratified is very low. I like the point about the separation of he possibility of need from the cognitive expectancy of grati- ication. It makes more sense to me, at least.

Dr. Feshbach: With regard to the gratification or reduction)f hostility, our approach to this knotty problem has been pri- narily through the use of so-called substitute, vicarious out- ets. Recently, we have been concerned with procedures for ·educing aggression which do not lead to aggressive discharge)ut which are probably far more effective, namely, eliminat- ng the conditions which stimulate hostility in the first place. For example, if you act extremely nasty to a person he may ;et angry because essentially you have lowered his self-esteem. However, through various procedures, if he learns that you were upset at the time and you really did not "mean it person- illy," he is no longer threatened and should therefore no longer)e angry. It has not been discharged, but it has been reduced.

Dr. Murstein: The question regarding these procedures is, how- ever, "What is the long range effect?" For example, in cases :hat Dr. Atkinson refers to as showing a "sawtooth effect," you ;et a temporary reduction momentarily, which is not lasting at ill, and then it returns. This, of course, is not Dr. Feshbach's problem, but this might be an important issue in the future to see whether we really have achieved a reduction or a temporary satiation of expression.

Dr. Feshbach: There are many distinctions that have to be made, and I would agree that this is one of them; that is, the difference between extinction of the response itself or satiation of it versus changes in the drive leading to the response.

I might comment parenthetically about fantasy behavior and its effects upon subsequent aggression. It is no longer useful to ask the question whether fantasy reduces a motive or not. The question should rather be, "Under what conditions does fantasy stimulate and under what conditions does it reduce subsequent aggressive behavior?" For example, we have been able to take the same fight film and demonstrate that witnessing the film can lead to either an increment or decrement in subsequent aggressive behavior depending upon the initial state of hostility of the person witnessing the film. If a person is very angry when he witnesses the film, he can then utilize it functionally (at least that is what we think happens) and the number of aggressive word associations decreases, in comparison to witnessing a neutral film. If the subject is not angry at the time, the number of aggressive word associations after witnessing the hostile film tends to increase. The finding regarding the rise is not as striking as the finding regarding the decrement. We have data obtained from children, but based on too few subjects, which suggest that if an aggressive attitude toward a doll figure is induced by telling a story in which the doll is depicted as being nasty and malicious, the consequences of "vicarious" aggressive play with a substitute for that doll object will be markedly different than if a neutral attitude had been induced toward the doll. For those children who had been initially aggressive toward the doll, participation in aggressive activities reduced the subsequent aggression to the doll; however, if they had been initially neutral toward the doll, participation in aggressive activities resulted in an increase in the subsequent number of aggressive responses toward the doll.

Dr. Lazarus: It occurs to me that many psychologists have postulated that fantasy will reduce anger, but I don't think anybody has postulated that fantasying will reduce sexual excitement. I said that half facetiously, but it occurs to me what you propose about the value of fantasy seems to really depend upon the nature of the drive that you are talking about.

Dr. Holt: Are you talking about telling stories, or are you talking about having an internal daydream?

Dr. Lazarus: Internal daydream.

Dr. Holt: Because, in a way, telling a sex story is a kind of sexual behavior. You get a discharge from that more than you can by having a daydream.

Dr. Lazarus: Does the discharge you are supposed to get from telling a sexy story have any relation at all to the discharge that is involved in sexual experience. In other words, I don't know whether these are the same things. I wonder if telling a sexy story hasn't really a very remote connection with having erotic daydreams, images, or what not.

Dr. Atkinson: Is the issue here whether or not there is a persistence of the stimulus that is producing the motive? For example, in the case of hunger I would think that imagining food wouldn't satisfy hunger because you don't really remove the instigating stimulus. This result suggests that in the case of aggression, the stimulus for the aggression is not there after the fantasy aggression is produced.

REFERENCES

1. Amsel, A.: The role of frustrative nonreward in noncontinuous reward situations. *Psychol. Bull., 55*:102-119. 1958.
2. Atkinson, John W.: Thematic Apperceptive measurement of motives within the context of a theory of motivation. In J. W. Atkinson (Ed.) *Motives in Fantasy, Action, and Society.* New York, Van Nostrand, 1958, Pp. 596-616.
3. Clark, R. A.: The projective measurement of experimentally induced levels of sexual motivation. *J. Exp. Psychol., 44*:391-399. 1952.
4. Clark, R. A., Teevan, R. and Ricciuti, H. H.: Hope of success and fear of failure as aspects of need for achievement. *J. Abnorm. & Social Psychol., 53*:182-186. 1956.
5. Feshbach, S.: The drive-reducing function of fantasy behavior. *J. Abnorm. & Social Psychol., 50*:3-11. 1955.
6. Gellerman, S.: The effects of experimentally induced aggression and inhibition on word-association response sequences. Unpublished doctoral dissertation. Univ. of Pennsylvania, 1956.
7. Glass, H. L.: The effects on fantasy of achievement motivation based

on "fear of failure" and "hope of success." Unpublished doctoral dissertation. Univ. of Pennsylvania, 1957.

8. Jensen, A. R.: Aggression in fantasy and overt behavior. *Psychol. Monogr., 71*:13. 1957.
9. Purcell, K.: The TAT and antisocial behavior. *J. Consult. Psychol., 20*:449-456. 1956.
10. Reitman, W. R. and Atkinson, J. W.: Some methodological problems in the use of thematic apperceptive measures of human motives. In J. W. Atkinson (Ed.) *Motives in Fantasy, Action, and Society.* New York, Van Nostrand, 1958, Pp. 664-683.
11. Spence, K. W.: *Behavior Theory and Conditioning.* New Haven, Yale Univ. Press, 1956.
12. Wyatt, F. A.: A principle for the interpretation of fantasy. *J. Proj. Tech., 22*:2229-245. 1958.

PSYCHO-LOGIC: A PERSONALITY APPROACH TO PATTERNS OF THINKING

Edwin S. Shneidman, Ph.D.

Central Research Unit
Veterans Administration Center, Los Angeles
and
University of Southern California

"Thought is common to all." (Heraclitus)

Everyone Thinks With Some Kind of Logic. The assertion is made that everybody thinks logically. This is contrary to the usual notion, for throughout the history of thought the word "logic" has had a rather limited, fixed, honorific meaning. "Logic" has pretty much meant *the* logic, and *the* logic has for centuries meant Aristotelian logic or, in the twentieth century, specific extensions, modifications, or denials of Aristotelian logic. Further, the converse of being "logical" (i.e., reasoning according to rules of logic without error) was being "illogical." Many examples of this notion can be given from various psychological sources. Even that amazing logician, Sherlock Holmes, once told Dr. Watson, in *The Adventure of the Copper Beeches,* that "Misdeeds are common. Logic is rare. Therefore it is upon the logic rather than upon the deed that one should dwell" (14). If, by stating that logic is "rare," Holmes meant that few people use logic, then we must disagree. Perspicacity, rigorous thinking, sagacious inferences, or brilliant insights may be rare, but logic — the use of deduction, induction, reasoning, systematic thinking, mentation, cerebration — is ubiquitous.[1] (If, on the other hand, Holmes means by "rare" that a man's logic is unique, idiosyncratic, and reflects the style of that man, then he is anticipating our own position.) One identifies a man not by whether

[1]Voltaire is quoted as having said that common sense is not so common. We would take the opposite position that logic is not so rare.

or not he thinks logically, but how he thinks logically. The point of view is propounded that everyone thinks logically (when he "thinks"), but that an individual's logic will have idiosyncratic features. The goal of this presentation may now be anticipated: It is to present a scheme which will permit one to construct conceptual relationships between idiosyncrasies of an individual's logic and idiosyncrasies of other aspects of the individual's personality.

What is Meant by "Logic" and "Logical." It might be conceded at the outset that the term "logic" and "logical" ought not to be used at all, inasmuch as what is being discussed can be better described by the phrases "patterns of thought" or "ways of thought." The reader is encouraged to substitute these phrases in his own mind whenever he sees the word "logic" in this essay used in other than its traditional sense.

Ordinarily, people look at ways of thought, by and large, either as *proper* ways of thought, that is, those connected with mental health — "Right minded people are right thinking people" — or as improper ways of thought, that is, those connected with pathology. Further, this connection is made more-or-less globally for the individual in question.[2] We shall suggest that this formulation — of connecting correct thought with logicality and connecting incorrect thought with illogicality — is not a very useful dichotomy to believe. Rather we shall suggest that the "marriage" between expressions of patterns of thought and other aspects of that individual's personality is one that is binding whether "in sickness or in health." Thus the essence of our suggestion will be that of connecting ways of thought with other characteristics of the individual and attempting to indicate that personality is reflected in thought. Our attention, therefore, will be directed to thought. Apropos this goal, we believe that both the Aristotelian logic and "the new logic" have left so much of the individual out of the examination of thought processes that it is impossible

---

[2]There is a little of what Thorndike called the "halo effect" operating here, in that if a "healthy" individual is found to be using what might be called unhealthy patterns of thought, one tends to excuse him by saying something like: "He thinks pretty straight in most things, except he tends to get mixed up when he discusses this particular subject."

to understand either thought itself or the personality using those approaches.

In a later section of this paper we deal with the "sin of psychologism." At this point it is sufficient to declare that we propose to examine thinking as a psychological process. Further, we would hope that empirically determined patterns of thought can be connected with empirically determined aspects of the personality.

We would make a further suggestion regarding the definition of "logic." It may be useful to think of logic without confusing the difference between what is valid and what is psychologically satisfying. The traditional conception of "psychologism" has to do with mixing a logical process with a psychological process. We would take the position that there are no purely "logical" processes, and that the traditional (*a*psychological) position in relation to logic really confuses the two issues of the validity of a psychological process with the effectiveness of that same psychological process; it substitutes an autistic for a realistic way of thinking. We would believe that it makes more sense to take the position that a way of thinking that tries to answer conditions *outside* the organism is simultaneously satisfying to a variety of *inner* needs.[3]

The goal of this presentation may be clarified by comparing it with that which Piaget sets for himself in his *Logic and Psychology* (30). He states, in his introduction:

> The aim of this book is not to discover how psychological theories may be formalized by means of logic, but to study the application of logical techniques to the psychological facts themselves, and especially to the thought structures found at different levels of intellectual development.

Our chosen task is not "to study the application of logical techniques to the psychological facts," but rather to suggest the application of empirical and correlational techniques to both the

---

[3]If, as William James said, "...our beliefs are really rules for action and... to develop a thought's meaning, we need only determine what conduct it is fitted to produce" (21), then I would paraphrase: our logics are really aspects of our modes of thought and to develop a logic's "sense" or meaning, we need only determine what manner of personality saw fit to produce it.

ways of thought ("logical" facts) and to the other psychological characteristics of the individual.

It appears that there have been two senses in which the term "logic" has been employed: (a) "Logic" has been used as characteristic of realistically effective ways of thinking; and (b) "Logic" has been used as a *reconstruction* of a *symbolic* system which, *if* it *were* applied, would be effective. This latter system is a model, which need not correspond — and often does not seem to correspond — to the ways in which individuals do in reality think, not that individuals are "illogical" but rather that individuals simply develop their patterns of thought in ways different from those indicated in the logicians' symbolic systems.

Is it then the logic of Russell or of Carnap rather than the logic of Aristotle that is being discussed? No. The logic that I am interested in does not now exist, or at least does not go under the name of logic. Perhaps of the current names, "philosophy of science" or "scientific method" comes closest.[4] Dewey implied this same point of view when he entitled his text *Logic, the Theory of Inquiry* (13). Apropos of Dewey, we are interested in the processes that people use when they attempt to solve problems — truth-processing transformations — rather than, as is the focus of Aristotelian or contemporary logic, the transformation of symbols. We would hope that the scheme presented in this essay would make it possible to translate thinking into forms of thought in such a way that the work that one as a theorist has to do in making this transformation illuminates the psychological processes that the individual thinker traversed.

Thinking has to do not only with proper use of symbols (which is critical and important) but also with perception, attitudes, set, etc., which are also critical and important.[5] Our position leads us to state that if internal and external factors affect an

---

[4]In *some* ways it is similar to Veatch's *Intentional Logic* (41) — a logic within the context of philosophic realism.

[5]My conclusion while at the dinner table that my wife is subtly enforcing my reducing diet may be based on my erroneous visual perception that the cream pitcher, which is actually filled, is empty; 20/20 foresight may not be unrelated to good vision; conversely, poor perceptions may make for 20/200 thinking. Perceptions and attitudes are part of thinking.

individual's choice of improper thinking, then they also affect an individual's choice in *proper* thinking. Ordinarily, logicians believe that "personality" enters the picture if an individual has made an error in thinking, but not if he has reasoned correctly. What kind of logic is that?

Two general points can be made: (a) One does not know much about an individual if all one knows is how he conforms or does not conform to specific formal patterns of thought; and (b) the *ways* in which individuals think are not accurately described in those areas in which logicians have their proper sphere of discourse. There is, therefore, a need for a description and elaboration of characteristic *individual* ways of mentation, as Whorf has done for some major linguistic groupings (47). Thus what is needed is an expansion of the cognitive map of thinking (as has been done in psychology for perception). "Logic" without psychology is arid; it has an essential mechanistic and artificial flavor to it and, by virtue of these attributes, loses much of its potential meaningfulness and becomes, instead, a kind of high-level esoteric auto-cerebral exercise.

Psychological Investigations of Logic. Within psychology itself, the investigations and theories concerning the place of logic in the study of man have been of essentially five types:

(A) The use of the *principles* of logic in the analyses of psychological processes. In this connection, the application, by Tomkins (40) of Mill's canons of induction to the analysis of the Murray Thematic Apperception Test (27) is perhaps the best example. In Tomkins' work, the psychological analysis of an individual's test protocol becomes, for the interpreter, a living exercise in inductive logic. Another example of this type is the stimulating work of Abelson and Rosenberg (1) in which they attempt to construct a psychological-mathematical model — based on a definition of cognitive elements (actors, means, ends) and the relations between them (positive, negative, null, ambivalent) — for use in the experimental analysis of attitudinal cognition. In their article they "propose a set of rules by which an individual imputes or discovers new symbolic sentences by combining two old sentences with an element in common."

(B) *The use of principles of logic to clarify expositions of psychological theory.* Examples of this genre might include Fine's use of logical principles to support his advocacy of the clinical approach to psychological problems (16); Shneidman's method of successive co-variation, which he calls "a method of educing the present correlates of perception" (35); Wertheimer's (posthumously published) description of two logical structures involved in discrimination between different stimuli by animal or human subjects (46) and Witkin's book on *Personality Through Perception* (48).

(C) *Investigations of the effects of various experimental variables on the logical thinking of normal subjects.* Along these lines are studies on the effect of drugs on syllogistic reasoning by Andrews (3), work by Beier (6) on the effect of induced anxiety on intellectual functioning, the work of Woodworth and Sells (49) on the effects of negative premises on syllogistic reasoning (which they call "the atmosphere effect"), etc.

(D) *Investigations of the developmental aspects of logical reasoning.* The important work of Piaget (29) and Werner (44) on the development of different types of reasoning in individuals of various ages immediately comes to mind.

(E) *The investigation of the logic and reasoning of aberrant individuals, limited largely to schizophrenics and brain-damaged patients.* The literature here is a vast one and includes references to such names as Goldstein (18), Kasanin (23), Vigotsky (42), Storch (37), Van Domarus (43), Arieti (4),[6] Cameron (10), Sullivan (38), etc. The point we wish to make about these studies is that there has been an apparent *dichotomization*

---

[6]Gottesman and Chapman (19), in an article entitled "Syllogistic Reasoning Errors in Schizophrenia," report: "Normal and schizophrenic subjects were given a 40-item multiple-choice syllogism test in order to compare them on the erroneous conclusions which they reach from premises which, by traditional logic, yield no conclusions whatsoever. These included eight items which measured the tendency to conclude the identity of subjects on the basis of identical predicates, an error which Von Domarus and Arieti have described as distinctively schizophrenic. The results clearly failed to substantiate the predictions inferred from Von Domarus and Arieti. On the test as a whole the schizophrenics made more errors than normals. The present investigators' main hypothesis was confirmed in that the schizophrenics showed qualitatively similar error patterns to the normal subjects."

between the assumed two types of logic: normal, healthy (Aristotelian or neo-Aristotelian) logic versus the aberrant, autistic, pathological processes of insane or organically damaged individuals. Only in Kantor, Herman, and Rapaport — all reported in Rapaport's volume (31)[7] — are there any faint suggestions of the possibility of a continuum of logics. More recently, Matte-Blanco (25) has written about the logic of the system Unconscious, in which he elucidates two principles of the "thinking of the unconscious" — first, that the Unconscious treats each person, object, or concept "as if it were a member or element of a class which contains other members" and, secondly, that "the system Unconscious treats the converse of any relation as identical with the relation, i.e., it treats relations as if they were symmetrical." The scheme is intriguing, but it is nonetheless presented as dichotomous with normal, rational, conscious thinking. The "reasoning of the unconscious" may, or may not, always involve these errors of thinking according to Aristotelian rules.

The Availability of a Wide Variety of Various Logical Processes is Suggested and the "Logics of Suicide" Are Described. The suggestion is made that it may be possible to fill in the interstices between "normal" logics and (schizophrenic or organic) pathologic. The assumption would be that an individual's idiosyncratic logic relates to the over-all psychological state of the individual. In our own work, we came to some of these formulations from an analysis of the implied logic contained in (a) genuine and simulated suicide notes and (b) suicidal and non-suicidal Thematic Apperception Test protocols.

Perhaps, at this point, our method of investigation needs to be described. We have attempted to set up what might be termed an "experiment" in suicide. We mean by this that we attempt to use that technique which distinguishes many scientific endeavors, namely, Mill's methods of difference and residues, in which we compare data from individuals who have committed suicide with comparable data from other individuals who have attempted suicide or who are non-suicidal, so as to point up

---

[7] Rapaport also includes fascinating references relevant to logic by Ach, Buhler, Bleuler, Cantor, Schilder, and Silverer, as well as his own erudite comments on this topic.

the unique attributes and characteristics of the suicidal individuals. Specifically, we have obtained data — case histories, psychological test records, suicide notes, records of therapy notes, diaries, etc. — for over four hundred individuals who have committed suicide, and then have advertently obtained similar data (case histories, psychological tests, suicide notes, etc.) from control groups of individuals, that is, individuals who have attempted suicide, threatened suicide, or who are non-suicidal. Our procedure is to strip the data of the identifying information (and parenthetically this can be done even to the case histories by changing the last few pages so as to give them a suicidal ending — we call this the technique of the "fictional denouement"); we are then in a position to do "blind analyses" of all the case histories, all the psychological tests, all the genuine and pseudo-suicidal notes. We do our analyses and then, so to speak, "break the key" and see what characteristics accrued specifically to those individuals who committed suicide, what characteristics accrued specifically to those individuals who attempted suicide or threatened suicide, or were non-suicidal.

It should be stated that we obtained the data on committed suicides from the Los Angeles County Coroner's Office and the California and Veterans Administration hospitals; the data for the attempted and threatened groups at the Los Angeles Suicide Prevention Center; and the data for non-suicidal individuals from fraternal and labor groups.

What things can be said about the logic of suicidal individuals? As the result of our analysis of some of the cognitive processes implicit in the suicide notes we have formulated a tentative schematization of three types of suicidal logic, each with its own psychological counterpart and each with its own implications for treatment. We call these three types: Logical, paleological, and catalogical.

The *logical suicides* are typically individuals who are in physical pain. The process of their deductions (as seen in the reasoning which is implicit in their suicide notes) is quite acceptable according to the usual standards for valid reasoning. They commit neither deductive nor semantic fallacies. They betray no basic confusions concerning either the nature of the self or the nature of reality. Our psychological label for this type is *surcease suicide*. They are individuals who desire surcease from pain, and they reason, correctly, that death will give them this. From this formulation there are some implications for treatment, specifically that treatment would have to give relief from pain (perhaps through use of analgesics, sedatives, or surgery) and would have to provide companionship by means of active milieu therapy such as clubs, activities, home placements, etc. A sample of such reasoning inferred from such a suicide note might be as follows: I hurt and desire freedom from this pain; if I am dead I will not have this pain; therefore I shall kill myself and feel pain no longer." We may not condone the act but we cannot gainsay the "logic" of this reasoning.

The *paleological suicides* constitute the second type. These are individuals who are delusional and/or hallucinatory, that is, they show the traditional hallmarks of psychosis. In their reasoning they make deductive fallacies by violating the rules for making logical identities. (In our opinion, this has been over-simplified by Von Domarus and Arieti when they call it reasoning in terms of the attributes of the predicate.) Also, psychotics lose the distinction between themselves and objects in the external reality and thus confuse the self and reality. Our psychological label for this kind of individual is *psychotic suicide*. Certainly, not all suicides are psychotic, but psychotics can be — because their communications are generally so poorly understood — unpredictably suicidal. Treatment for them has to deal primarily with the psychosis and only subsequently with suicidal tendencies, if they remain. Treatment should include protecting the individual from his own psychotic impulses. An example of psychotic syllogistic reasoning might be: "Death is suffering; I am suffering; therefore I must die." Whatever the formal characteristics of his logic, the psychotic is the least predictable of all suicides. When the psychotic patient expresses suicidal notions, he is a double-barrelled risk. The psychotic is unpredictable because he may not only respond to the injunctions of hallucinated voices to kill himself, but he is also in constant danger inasmuch as the activating mechanism for this explosive mixture may depend on the hair trigger of a dereistic thought, an hallucinated command, or a fleeting affective state. One, fortunate enough to hear these expressions, should communicate them immediately to responsible individuals.

Logical and paleological suicide aside, the third type of suicide we call *catalogic suicide.* Here the reasoning is characterized not by deductive fallacies — errors in the form of the argument — but rather by *semantic* errors, wherein the error is dependent on the meanings of the terms occurring in the premises or conclusions. An example of a semantic fallacy is as follows: "Nothing is better than hard work; a small amount of effort is better than nothing; therefore a small effort is better than hard work." Here the fallacy is not dependent upon the form of the argument but rather on the ambiguous meaning of the terms "nothing" and "better." Another example of a semantic fallacy, this time with suicidal content, is as follows: "If anybody kills himself, then he will get attention; I will kill myself; therefore I will get attention." The fallacy here is concealed in the concepts contained in the word "I." Specifically the confusion is between the self as it is experienced by the individual himself and the self as he feels himself thought of or experienced by others. Actually, this is not so much a fallacy in the words of the reasoning, but rather it is a confusion about the self or fallacious identification; hence we call it a psychosemantic fallacy — and it may well occur whenever an individual thinks about his death, inasmuch as an individual cannot really imagine his own complete cessation. Another semantic fallacy has to do with the nature of existence and the confusion of the real world — our only world — with a possible hereafter. We call the reasoning that involves these semantic fallacies *catalogic* because it is destructive. It is destructive not only in the sense that it destroys the rules for semantic clarity but also in that it destroys the logician.

Catalogic is not only contaminated by semantic fallacies but it has a second characteristic: the penchant toward dichotomous thinking. Dichotomies abound in thinking. There are a number of psychological phenomena which express themselves in terms of opposites: doubt vs. certainty, insecurity vs. security, passivity vs. aggression, expectation vs. satisfaction, hope vs. despair, dependence vs. emancipation, acceptance vs. rejection, chance vs. organization, sacred vs. profane love, right vs. wrong, good vs. bad, and most relevant for our discussion, life vs. death. To think dichotomously is to make happy adjustment difficult to achieve. It puts one in what Bateson, Jackson *et al.* (5) call a "double bind" position. It's all or none: if one is not perfect then he is nothing. One "goes for broke" all the time. And it can be lethal. Consider: ordinarily if one does not like some aspects of his life (like his job or his spouse or his general situation) then one thinks of changing these aspects, but if an individual organizes his world dichotomously and if the topic of *life* is introduced into his consciousness, then he must, logically, think not of some other way of living, but of *death* as the alternative.[8] The dichotomous thinker is an individual who, to paraphrase from Hamlet, is haunted by his own polarities.

The world is filled with dichotomies, paradoxes, contradictions, duplicities, inconsistencies, and double binds. The essence of adjustment is to be able to view these apparently frustrating insoluble situations as what Fromm (17) called existential dichotomies rather than — as the schizophrenics and semantic suicides do — as historical or real dichotomies. Existential dilemmas — like the researcher's choice between precision and relevance — are always with us, but we can get along with them and live with aspects of both horns of the apparent dilemma and resolve them in this way. Adjustment therefore lies in the fundamental abilities to make subtle discriminations and distinctions, to wink at disparities, to sense what is appropriate at the moment, to understand what rules must be broken, and on occasion even to do what one thinks is right rather than to act on one's principles.

Under the category of *catalogic* suicide we have subsumed two psychological types: *semantic* suicide and *sociologic* sui-

---

[8]The similarity to Binswanger's description (7) of his patient is striking: "But Ellen cannot even wait for the end! The slow dying off (rusting, withering, languishing, becoming stale and earthy) is hateful to her. Every day she feels herself fatter, which according to her own statement means getting both older and uglier. Here too we find the all-or-none principle at work: 'If I cannot remain young, beautiful and thin,' we hear in her words, 'then rather—Nothingness.'"

cide. *Semantic* suicides are typically individuals in their 20's, 30's, and 40's who feel helpless and confused emotionally and feel pessimistic about the possibilities of making meaningful interpersonal relationships. Their confusions in semantics and logic are "referred," like referred pain, from other root problems, primarily those of psychological identification. Treatment would focus on the possible non-dichotomous choices and on the clarification of the concept of the self. The goal of treatment would be to have the individual establish meaningful interpersonal relationships so that his search for a stable identification would not be barren.

The other kind of catalogic suicide, also marked by semantic confusions and dichotomous thinking, is the *sociologic* suicide. These are individuals whose conscious cultural and religious beliefs, especially about the hereafter, permit them to view suicide not as death but rather as transition to another life. Inasmuch as the beliefs concerning the concept of death in relation to the self play a primary role in the suicide, the treatment would have to clarify deeply entrenched religious and cultural beliefs and deal with the semantic implications of the concept of death for that individual. Thus one sees that there are aspects of the logical and psychological environment which facilitate the acceptance of erroneous premises and invalid conclusions, and which account for many individuals making tragic deductive leaps into oblivion.

As a result of our tripartite classification of logics (logical, paleological, and catalogical) we reflected that if there were more than *two* types of logic (normal versus grossly aberrant) there might be several types of logic among most (non-suicidal) people, each of these "logics" possibly with some corresponding psychological characteristics. Thus the possibility existed for developing a systematic "psycho-logic" which might explore relationships between "logical states" and "psychological states" within an individual.

This notion of the pervasiveness of dichotomous thinking has been the object of attention by many others. Metfessel (26) has written about "The All-or-None Nature of Emotional Thinking;" Cherry in his recent book *On Human Communication* (11) goes so far as to state that "Dualism or twin thinking seems to be a natural human quality;" and Ruesch and Kees, in their recent book on *Non-Verbal Communication* (32), have stated as follows:

"Western thought, including scientific logic, has been largely based — or was until recently — upon an Aristotelian approach, which in turn is rooted in the Greek grammar and its subject-predicate language *structure*. . . . This is not true, for example, in Chinese logic and language, in which the subject-predicate dichotomy is avoided. It is not without interest that the tremendous advances made in Western technology developed only when scientists adopted a language (mathematics) that was not bound by the subject-predicate dichotomy." This quotation would almost seem to suggest — at least it did so to me — that our behavior may be filtered through our logic as some have proposed it is filtered through our language.

The suicidal ways of reasoning — and all non-suicidal ways of reasoning too — may be funnels through which the individual thinks about himself, his world, and his place in it. They may be similar to the role ascribed by linguists to different language types. Most of us would agree that one of the most provocative current concepts in the field of psycholinguistics is the Sapir-Whorf hypothesis. Briefly, this concept states that the ways in which we think and perceive are ultimately dependent upon the structure of our language. This hypothesis has received considerable interest of late, especially through Carroll's edited book of selected writings of Whorf, called *Language, Thought, and Reality* (47). It is interesting to speculate and to attempt to extend this concept into the area of individual psychology. I mean not only the notion that the differential per capita suicide rate between Hopi and Standard-Average-European groups may be attributed to differences in their language structure, but indeed that *each individual constitutes his own culture* — and perceives and *reasons* in ways which may, in part, be idiosyncratic for him, or at least different from some other humans. Certainly the projective techniques with their concepts of style of the man, private world, idiosyncratic perception, idiographic record, may be the psychological counterpart of the Whorfian linguistic concept.[9]

Dr. Roger Brown in a publication entitled *A Study in Language and Cognition* (8) has stated that Whorf suggested that each language imposes and perpetuates a particular world view and that the speakers of a language are partners to an implicit agreement to see and think of the world in a certain way, not the only possible way. In the same sense, each individual with his separate biological and psychological history imposes his particular view of the world. It is as though he has made an unspoken agreement with himself to see and think of the world in a certain way — not the only possible way. Brown reminds us that Orwell in his novel *1984* describes a totalitarian country of the future in which the dictator invents a language called "Newspeak" in which it is impossible not only to express but

---

[9]Kantor, in his book *Psychology and Logic* (22), says several things which sound almost directly on this point: "Logic is the work of man. Naturally then, the activities comprising this work along with the resulting products inevitably reflect his psychological and cultural frames of reference. We have only to glance at the doctrinal history of logic to have demonstrated that particular logical tenets and systems are conditioned by the ideology of the thinkers involved.

"What a logician believes systems to be, and his notion of how they are built up depend, for instance, upon his knowledge and understanding of the nature of mentality.

"Similarly, we may ask what view the logician holds concerning language and symbols. Are words the bearers or correlates of psychic processes called thoughts?

"To know the influences operating in the formation of any type of logic is not only to understand that logic but also its intimate relations to other disciplines. Does the logician, for instance, derive his views from the mathematical disciplines, the biological sciences or from the fields of rhetoric, law, argument, and debate? Incidentally, too, the form in which the logic is set up, whether verbal or symbolic, is conditioned by psychanthropic influences.

"The logician perhaps more than other intellectual workers, with the possible exception of the mathematician, has unwittingly assumed that he operates in more or less complete isolation from human circumstances. Such an assumption is decidedly erroneous. Nothing is more certain than that differences in logical doctrine are ascribable to the influence of social, political, historical, and specific scientific conditions. To neglect these points is to risk the danger of embracing a theory developed under particular cultural circumstances, only to regard it as the one universal and sufficient doctrine."

even to think a rebellious thought (28). If it is true for cultures that language is not a cloak following the contours of thought but that language constitutes molds into which infant minds are poured, why should this not be equally true for individuals? An interesting clinical example can be cited. Greenson in an article called "The Mother Tongue and the Mother" (20) tells of a patient who could not discuss certain problems in English, and it was not until the psychotherapist had her talk in German that she was able to talk about certain conflict-ridden areas. Indeed the patient herself indicated that she had really different concepts of herself in the two languages.

The notion that one can proceed without some idiosyncratic modes of logical perception or ways of thinking, unrelated to any pervasive style or manners of approach, seems contrary to our data. Nietzsche referred to this notion of perception-without-theorizing as the "dogma of immaculate perception." It appears rather that each man's thoughts, language and logic — and his subsequent actions — are filtered through his perceptual apparatus and are consistent with his other patterns of thinking.

Might it be possible to say anything at this point about the relationship of logic to language? Perhaps this: that *within* any language type there are two kinds of logic: (a) *conventional* or conforming or consensual modes of thinking which are tied to the framework of that language, (as, for example, the scope and limitations of our Aristotelian logic are established by the subject-predicate format of the Greek grammar with which Aristotle operated); and (b) *concisional* or confected or idiosyncratic modes of thinking, which do not, at the moment of their existence, follow those modes of reasoning that are conventional to that language type. By definition, most people are conventional most of the time; thus when an individual is neologistic in his language, heretical in his thought content, or unconventional (for his language) in his thought pattern, the result is attention-getting along some dimension. Heretofore, interest has focused almost exclusively on the conventional modes of thinking; it is time that more systematic exploration was done on the dark side of the moon.

The Core of the Suggestion is Presented — Twice. In the interests of clarity of exposition, we shall present our proposal in a two-stage process: first as an Aristotelian or neo-Aristotelian might present this idea and then, after the reader has followed the trend of our thinking couched in conventional terms, a restatement of our proposal in empirical and pragmatic psychological terms, unhampered by anachronistic trappings and in language acceptable to our own thinking.

A. *In Aristotelian terms.* To follow the presentation of this idea in Aristotelian terms, the reader is asked to imagine four columns or categories of contents — indicated in Table 1 — as follows:

The *first* column is labeled "Logical Fallacy" in which would be listed the Aristotelian and neo-Aristotelian fallacies of logic, such as the fallacy of the major premise, the fallacy of four terms, etc. The *second* (and most iconoclastic) column involves one's taking the position that all logical formulations can be thought to demonstrate some sort of straightforward reasoning (for *that* individual who is doing the reasoning) if one only supplies the suppressed premises or suppressed logical conditions which would *controvert* the apparent error. The label of the second column is "Logical Conditions under which the Fallacy is Controverted," and in it would be listed, for each logical fallacy, that logical condition under which the fallacy is controverted or cancelled out. The *third* column, labeled "Concomitant Psychological State," would indicate the psychological state that would be consistent with, or "explain," the individual's proposing the logical condition (Column II) which would controvert the logical fallacy (Column I). The *fourth* column would be labeled "Psychological Symptoms or Psychiatric Diagnoses" and would indicate the psychiatric conditions that would go with the psychological states indicated in Column III.

An example across the four columns may be given: A patient on a locked ward is heard to say that he is Switzerland (an example quoted by Arieti, Bleuler, and Jung). On the face of it, this appears to be illogical — despite the white hair on his peaked head. After listening to him further, however, one is able to reconstruct the following syllogism by supplying the suppressed premises. He is saying, "I don't like this locked ward, I want to get out of here, I love freedom; Switzerland loves freedom; therefore I am Switzerland." So, in Column II we would indicate the crucial item, i.e., the logical condition under which this fallacy would be cancelled out or controverted. It is this: If the patient adopted the implicit assumption that Switzerland is the *only* member of the class that loves freedom, and if he loved freedom, then it would follow, without logical error, that he would have to be Switzerland. Now for Column III. What are the psychological states that would permit, be consistent with, and even force this kind of logical process? This kind of reasoning (where only one member of a large class is admitted to consciousness) would seem to reflect an intense *narrowing* of the focus of attention (or intense psychological barriers against the widening of it). In Column IV, we would indicate the probable psychological symptoms or personality characteristics that would be consistent with a narrowing of focus. Several come to mind: intense concentration, withdrawal, oblivion to ordinary stimuli, hypesthesia — catatonic schizophrenia. The constriction of attention may be the psychological concomitant of the logical state which shows itself in the difficulty that the emotionally disturbed person has in grasping other than what is immediately before his mind. It may, at the extreme, be similar to what one sees in the paleological behavior of the catatonic schizophrenic where the individual can be so focused on his own thoughts that he can let a cigarette burn through his fingers without his, so to speak, being aware of it.

Table 1 gives other examples of this process. The second example, involving "obsessive (or dichotomous) logic," is from Binswanger's extensive discussion of "The Case of Ellen West," reprinted in Rollo May's *Existence* (7). The third example — illustrating again that the thought and the thinker should somehow not be separated and that logical thinking is a ubiquitous characteristic of thinking organisms — is from the context of "the logic of discovery" or "the logic of productive thinking." Wertheimer,[10] in his exciting book, *Productive Thinking* (45), recites what he calls "The Famous Story of Young Gauss." The

TABLE 1—SOME POSSIBLE CORRELATES BETWEEN TRADITIONAL LOGICAL FALLACIES AND PSYCHOLOGICAL STATES

USING AN EXAMPLE OF:	COLUMN I TRADITIONAL LOGICAL FALLACY	COLUMN II LOGICAL CONDITION UNDER WHICH THE LOGICAL FALLACY (I) IS CONTROVERTED	COLUMN III CONCOMITANT PSYCHOLOGICAL STATE THAT IS CONSISTENT WITH THE INDIVIDUAL'S PROPOSING THE LOGICAL CONDITION (II) THAT WOULD CONTROVERT THE FALLACY (I)	COLUMN IV PSYCHOLOGICAL SYMPTOMS OR DIAGNOSES THAT LABEL THE PSYCHOLOGICAL STATE (III)
BIZARRE LOGIC	From Von Domarus and Arieti. Identification in terms of attributes of the predicate. e.g.: Switzerland loves freedom; I love freedom; therefore I am Switzerland."	If one supplies the implicit premise that Switzerland is the *only* one that loves freedom (and if I loved freedom), then it would follow, without logical error, that I would have to be Switzerland.	The reasoning reflects a psychological state in which the focus of attention is narrowed—in this case to *one* attribute of the class (of freedom lovers), or the boundaries against the widening of the focus of attention are fixed.	Intense concentration or conflict; withdrawal; oblivion to ordinary stimuli; hypesthesia; catatonic schizophrenia.
DICHOTOMOUS LOGIC	From Binswanger's "The Case of Ellen West," as reported in May. The logical fallacy of dichotomization. e.g.: At age 16 her motto is "Aut Caesar aut nihil" (Either the greatest or nothing). Before her death she says: "If I cannot remain young, beautiful and thin, then rather—nothingness."	If one supplies the implicit assumption that the aspects of the universe under discussion are organized in a *binary* manner, then it would follow logically that the alternative to leading a perfect *life* is death. The implicit premise is "No M is S and P" or "Not (P and Q)."	The reasoning reflects a psychological state in which the basic identifications are confused, the basic attitudes toward self-control are ambivalent, and there is a general polarized approach to concepts and people, with unhappy vacillation between the extremes of the dichotomized polarities.	Obsessions; abulia; fixed ideas; anxiety; general impotence; rumination; suicide.

PRODUCTIVE LOGIC	From Wertheimer. Question to the young Gauss: "What is the sum of 1 + 2 + 3 + 4 + 5 + 6 + 7 + 8 + 9 + 10?" Response: correct answer (55) in amazingly fast time.	One can do the task correctly and quickly if one sees (makes the assumptions) that (a) there are *pairs* of numbers (1 + 10, 2 + 9, 3 + 8, etc.) each of which totals 11; (b) there are 5 such pairs; (c) 5 times 11 equals 55. The principle is represented by the formula: $n + 1 \times \frac{n}{2}$.	What are the psychological states with which this performance is consistent? High intelligence, active curiosity, open mind (freedom to explore intellectually), inquiring mind that is original but not destructive, freedom from fear of teacher (of authority generally? of father?)	Genius
THE "LOGIC" OF A SLIP	From Freud. My example: A student telephones me at a late hour to ask for a good deal of information for a paper he is writing; he keeps me on the 'phone a very long time. Finally, in answer to one of his questions, I refer him, rather sharply, to the library. As I hang up I feel sorry at being so abrupt with him and I say: "I am sorry I can help you" — having "meant" to say the opposite.	The pattern of thinking may be reconstructed as follows: "I have this special knowledge and am therefore in a position to help you with your paper; you call me at an inconvenient time and keep me on the telephone inordinately long; I am annoyed that this has occurred; I am sorry that I am in a position to help you."	Here the psychological states are those of irritation, annoyance, guilt.	Rudeness; a "psychological" slip.

story is that Gauss, then a boy of six, was in school when the teacher asked the class, "Which of you will be first to get the sum of one plus two plus three plus four plus five plus six plus seven plus eight plus nine plus ten?" Gauss, of course, was first by a mile, and explained his "short-cut" to the amazed teacher and "non-plussed" pupils by pointing out that there were five *pairs* of numbers each of which have the sum of eleven, and that five times eleven was fifty-five. It is diagrammed in our schematization in Table 1. Here again, as for the other examples, the critical step is that indicated in the second column: what are the conditions (in this case, of arithmetic computation) which would substitute for the traditional (and in this case, pedestrian) steps of adding one and two, adding three to that sum, four to that sum, etc.

One last example — using slips of the tongue — can be given from an area considered, by hallowed tradition, to be "squarely in the center" of Freudian psychology. What can one say, therefore, about the *logic* of slips? Simply that, in practically every case, a slip can be schematized as though it were an *enthymeme*. (Webster's *Dictionary* definition: "Enthymeme — an argument in which one of the propositions, usually a premise, is understood but not stated.") The thinking process can be reconstructed so as

---

[10]It is interesting, too, to quote what Wertheimer has to say in the introductory section of this book in regard to the relationship between traditional logic and the productive processes of thought. He says: "In the course of the centuries there arose again and again a deep-felt dissatisfaction with the manner in which traditional logic handles such processes. In comparison with actual, sensible, and productive processes, the topics as well as the customary examples of traditional logic often look dull, insipid, lifeless. To be sure, the treatment is rigorous enough, yet often it seems barren, boring, empty, unproductive. If one tries to describe processes of genuine thinking in terms of formal traditional logic, the result is often unsatisfactory; one has, then, a series of correct operations, but the sense of the process and what was vital, forceful, creative in it seems somehow to have evaporated in the formulations. On the other hand it is possible to have a chain of logical operations, each perfectly correct in itself, which does not form a sensible train of thought. Indeed there are people with logical training who in certain situations produce series of correct operations which, viewed as a whole, nevertheless form something akin to flight of ideas. Training in traditional logic is not to be disparaged: it leads to stringency and rigor in each step, it contributes to critical-mindedness; but it does not, in itself, seem to give rise to productive thinking. In short, there is the danger of being empty and senseless, though exact; and there is always the difficulty with regard to real productiveness."

to supply the suppressed premise. We would believe that, in the case of slips, the idiosyncratic pattern of thinking may be related not so much to the pervasive aspects of the individual's personality, but rather to specific psychological complexes, conflicts, focal tensions, etc.[11] (as indicated in Column III of Table 1). This type of enthymematic analysis focusses on the suppressed content of the slip and in this way gives clues as to its logical meaning for the speaker. It is a matter of interest (and amusement) that the enthymematic analyses of double-slips yield, as one might predict, twin insights which point to essentially the same conflicts or feelings in the speaker.[12]

It ought to be possible to develop a systematic "psycho-logic" along these lines, showing mutual relationships between characteristics of mentation (logic) and other characteristics of affect and overt behavior. Further, such a scheme should permit one to begin with information at either end (Column I or Column IV of Table 1) and arrive at meaningful data in the other (IV or I) column; i.e., to work from idiosyncratic logic to "personality," or from "personality" to idiosyncratic logic.

---

[11]Our position is not that idiosyncratic ways of thought *have* to be globally characteristic for an individual, but rather the opposite. For example, it would be illuminating to ascertain in what areas (or in what situations or with what topics) a particular individual employs modes of reasoning which are *not* generally characteristic for *him*. It might be just these intraindividual deviations which would account for the "logic of prejudice," the "logic of slips," the "logic of neurosis," etc.

This not-necessarily-global point of view is similar to that recently stated by Arieti, in his discussion of the paleological thinking of schizophrenics (Page 478, *American Handbook of Psychiatry,* Volume I): "It must be emphasized that the schizophrenic does not necessarily adopt paleologic for all or even most of his thinking processes. Especially in the early stages of the illness, paleologic thought is found only when it involves the complexes of the patient. Later, however, it tends to extend to other areas. In this early selectivity for the emotionally determined complexes, paleologic thinking differs from organically determined mechanisms which apply indiscriminately to any content."

[12]Freud mentions that in a "war correspondent's account of meeting a famous General whose infirmities were pretty well known, a reference to the General was printed as 'this battle-scared veteran.' Next day an apology appeared which read 'the words of course should have been "the bottle-scarred veteran."'" My own favorite double-slip is one which appeared in a local newspaper referring to "a detective in the guard farce" and was corrected to read "a defective in the guard force."

B. *In pragmatic and empirical terms.* As a forecast of things to come, what can be said to characterize this second exposition of our idea? The reader may consider it to be multi-iconoclastic, in that:

– It does not elevate Aristotelian (or even neo-Aristotelian) logic.

– It does not seek to incorporate the mathematical approaches to the analysis of thought. (Except between these parentheses, the names of Boole, Frege, Whitehead, etc., do not appear in this essay.)

– It is contemptuous of the specter of "psychologism." We would deny that this "sin" is committed by us – affirming rather that we are simply building a bridge of intervening variables between patterns of thought (the traditional ground of logic) and patterns of affect and behavior (the traditional ground of psychology). But even if the charge of psychologism could be leveled and maintained, we would tend not to attempt to defend ourselves against the charge but rather to dismiss it as trivial.

– It wishes to eschew the traditional, formal, rather rigid nosologies, whether they are Aristotle's nosology of logical fallacies or Kraepelin's nosology of psychiatric illnesses.

And now that we have broken out of Aristotelian country, where do we find ourselves? The place and the feeling are both quite clear: We find ourselves with our feet planted firmly in terra incognita.

The reader will recall that in the "Aristotelian" presentation in the previous section, the four columns were labelled (a) logical fallacy, (b) logical conditions under which the fallacy is controverted, (c) concomitant psychological state, and (d) psychological symptoms and psychiatric diagnoses. How can these rubrics be redrawn? As indicated in Table 2, we propose the following:

Column I would contain a sample of a "Specific Way of Thought." In this category would be delineated verbal and other behaviors from which an individual's (overtly expressed, implied, or latent) idiosyncratic "ways of thought" could be analyzed. This approach would seem to be more useful than that of nosology of syllogistic errors or of fallacies of formal logic.

Column II would concern itself with "General Kinds of Thinking" (and perception and attitudes) would be consistent with (or produce) the sample of thinking (I); i.e., the ways of thought — as well as the individual's beliefs and perceptual distortions — within which the individual's specific way of thought (I) "makes sense." It can be asserted that (even) neurotic or aberrant patterns of thought are realistic, but they are realistic for a reality situation which does not obtain — just as there is a germ of truth in many false beliefs.

Column III would have to do with the "Total Setting of Psychological Characteristics" within which the "pattern of thinking" (II) is likely to emerge. Whorf has analyzed this setting in linguistic and cultural terms; the present proposal would suggest an analysis in personality terms. It occurs to us that a listing of some psychological dimensions which are proximal and relevant to logic (and which might very well affect the cerebrational activities of the logician) might include the following: careful, reliable, consistent vs. unreliable, variable; focussed, constricted, narrowed vs. wide-ranged; cohesive vs. disjointed, loose; gestalt-like, combinatory vs. atomistic, piecemeal; flexible vs. rigid, dogmatic; contrary, negative, iconoclastic vs. conforming, conventional; ambivalent, abulic, over-elaborative vs. decisive, simple, clear-cut; dichotomous, binary, either-or vs. neutralistic, both-and; etc.

Column IV would focus on a "Detailed Personality Analysis of the Individual's Overt Behavior" — broader than a categorization in terms of some psychiatric nosology — that reflects (and encompasses) the total setting (III) within which the individual's patterns of thought (II) occur that gives rise to his specific ways of thought (I).

How can this approach to the rapprochement of thinking and personality be illustrated? The difficulty is not that of finding examples, but rather of presenting illustrations which fit into the confines of page limitations. We shall allude to three kinds of illustrations, sharing with the reader some responsibility to examine for himself from the primary sources the richness of the materials and the many "bridges" (or intervening variables) — Columns II and III — which can be built between a man's

TABLE 2—SOME POSSIBLE CORRELATES BETWEEN WAYS OF THINKING AND OTHER ASPECTS OF PERSONALITY

COLUMN I SAMPLES OF SPECIFIC WAYS OF THOUGHT	COLUMN II GENERAL CONDITIONS OF THINKING WHICH "MAKE SENSE" OF THOUGHT SAMPLE (I)	COLUMN III TOTAL SETTING OF PSYCHOLOGICAL CHARACTERISTICS WITHIN WHICH THE PATTERN OF THINKING (II) IS LIKELY TO EMERGE	COLUMN IV DETAILED PERSONALITY ANALYSIS OF INDIVIDUAL'S OVERT BEHAVIOR THAT REFLECTS THE PSYCHOLOGICAL CHARACTERISTICS (III)
From Fine, DeGroot, and Alekhine. Examples from *Chess:* *A. Alexander Alekhine:* Chess style was primarily one of attack. Loved chess. Great exponent of surprise attack; some marked weakness, especially in his last years, in his defense play.	For Alekhine the purpose of chess-playing was to win, and more, to defeat the opponent. Anything went (because the opponent might be more powerful) and the more one could catch him off guard, the better. For Alekhine, chess is war. (Contrast this with Euwe's comment, below).	Fine calls him a phallic-narcissistic person who used chess as a weapon of aggression, and for whom chess attack represented (unconsciously) sublimation of sadistic urges towards his father.	Reported to have shown sadistic behavior; drank excessively; had megalomaniac tendencies; collaborated with Nazis; married five times, twice to much older women.
B. Max Euwe: Euwe's style is characterized by careful preparation, planning, with emphasis on the opening game. He is deemed to be a careful rather than a flashy player. He can rarely be outplayed at the start. DeGroot reports (on pages 61, 247, and 265) actual quotations from Euwe on how he thinks while he is playing. (33, pp. 298-300).	Chess is just one of his accomplishments. He is also a teacher of mathematics. He has two choices: chess and mathematics. For Euwe chess is an exercise. He says: "I adjust my chess thinking according to the reasoning of theoretical economy. Furthermore, the making of a campaign plan in a game of chess is on the same plane as *factory* planning." (DeGroot).	Essentially a well-adjusted individual for whom chess is not an outlet for deep-seated neurotic conflicts. If chess is a contest for him, the aggression is kept within normal limits, so that victories are not megalomaniac and defeats are not exterminations.	"He is married, has three children, and has lived an exemplary and, by usual standards, reasonably happy life. . . . He is a teacher by profession and has been a teacher to the chess world." (Fine)

From *Thematic Test Analysis:* Description of John Doe's *Quality of Thought:* "There are pathological thought processes and autistic and contaminated thinking. There is rich fantasy material, but it is loosely organized. There is good but somewhat pretentious vocabulary with some impairment of his ability to communicate."	Description of John Doe in terms of the following categories: Pressures, Forces & Press; Motivations, Goals & Drives; Outlooks, Attitudes & Beliefs; Affect, Feelings & Emotions; Self-Concept & Insight into Self; Interpersonal Relations.	Description of John Doe in terms of the following categories: Frustrations, Conflicts & Fears; Psycho-sexual Level; Super-ego, Values & Ego Ideal; Personality Defenses & Mechanisms; Intellect & Abilities; Psychological Postdictions.	Description of John Doe in terms of the following categories: Sexual Thought & Behavior; Self-Control; Reality Contact & Orientation; Symptoms; Etiology; Prognoses & Predictions; Factual Postdictions.
From "The Case of Jay" (34). Jay's specific ways of thinking as he responds to Wechsler-Bellevue questions relating to information and comprehension. (See pp. 297-302).	Jay's "general conditions of thinking," his "ways" of approaching intellectual tasks, his techniques for handling intellectual challenges.	The total personality setting is indicated in the discussion of Jay's psychodynamics — his personal (unconscious) psychological history. (See pp. 449-453; 457-461; 467-470).	The "facts" about Jay's *behavior*—his appearance and demeanor, his family background, his own detailed anamnesis—a verbal picture of the man. (See pp. 329-345).

fragments of thought and his "life style" of general deportment and behavior.

Example No. 1: Our first example comes from the field of chess. The primary source materials are Fine's monograph entitled *Psychoanalytic Observations on Chess and Chess Masters* (15) and DeGroot's book (unfortunately published only in Dutch), *Het Denken van den Schaker* (*The Thinking of the Chessplayer,* 12). Fine's monograph contains psychoanalytic observations on nine chess grandmasters — Staunton, Anderrsen, Steinitz, Morphy, Capablanca, Lasker, Alekhine, Euwe and Botvinnik — and indicates how their different styles of chess thinking (which Fine analyzes) seem to be reflections of their general personalities and of their life styles, and can be explained in terms of the psychodynamics inferred from their case histories. Thus we find, to use two contrasting figures, Alekhine[13] being described as a great exponent of the surprise attack (Column I) in chess whose style was essentially to attack, as contrasted to Euwe, whose emphasis in his chess game was on careful preparation and a great deal of focus on the opening game. Similarly, Alekhine's personality is described by Fine as phallic-narcissistic, a man who used chess as a weapon of aggression, a man for whom the chess attack represented a sublimation of his sadistic urges toward his father (Columns II and III); a man whose overt behavior is known to have included his having been sexually sadistic, alcoholic, intermittently megalomaniac, a Nazi collaborator, married five times, twice to women who were over twenty

---

[13]It is interesting to catch the "flavor" of Alekhine's aggressive, driving, competitive, almost hostile and sadistic approach to his chess games from his comments in his own book, *My Best Games of Chess, 1924-1934* (2). In commenting on some of his championship games, Alekhine says the following: "But as a draw meant as much as a loss to me I did not even take this variation into serious consideration"; "I confess that I did not accept the Pawn-offer quite independently of a would-be distaste for defensive play, but because I actually do not like to be mated—and this unpleasantness would most likely occur after this play"; "This game shows once more that, if White has any fighting ambitions, he must avoid in this variation the Pawn exchange at the fourth move"; "This tame rejoinder would be convincingly refuted (as a winning attempt, of course) in the present game. It has since completely disappeared from the master's practice"; and "But this risky offer mainly is explained by my being a half-point behind Fine and having to win at all costs in order to be first . . ."

years older than he, etc. (Column IV). By way of contrast Euwe, who had great competence in both chess and mathematics, was able to see one (chess) as a contest and the other as not, and able in all to keep his aggressions within normal limits (Columns II and III); his overt behavior includes his leading a well ordered life as a school teacher of mathematics, being married, having three children and leading an exemplary, reasonably happy life (Column IV). Similar relationships between style of chess thinking and style of over-all living can be made for the other seven world champions discussed by Fine.

DeGroot's book, though it predates Fine's work by ten years, can be seen as being completely consistent with Fine's work. DeGroot actually interviewed and tested world champions (including Fine himself) on the occasion of their meeting for chess matches in Amsterdam. His comments would seem essentially to corroborate the general point made by Fine. His descriptions of Euwe's thought processes (pages 61, 247, and 265) are especially illuminating. One catches the flavor of Euwe: the thoroughness, the careful planning, the theoretical economy, the placid personality. There is no chance of confusing either his chess style or his character with other (very different) world champions, such as Alekhine, Lasker, Capablanca, etc.

The point of these examples from chess is, of course, to illustrate how the specific samples of cerebration that take place in chess thinking are by no means entirely cerebral — in the sense of cold, unemotional logic — but that even among chess masters there are idiosyncratic ways of chess thinking which reflect the pervasive aspects of their personalities.

Example No. 2: The second example comes from what might be called the idiographic tradition of contemporary psychology, that is, the attempt at scientific investigation by means of an intensive study of a single case. In this instance the primary source material is a book, *Thematic Test Analysis* (33). The book reports a study in which the protocols for various psychological tests (the Rorschach, the Thematic Apperception Test, the Make-A-Picture-Story Test, the Minnesota Multiphasic Personality Inventory, Wechsler-Bellevue Intelligence Scale, etc.) for one 27 year-old male, Caucasian subject (called John Doe) were distributed to 22 well known psychology test experts for them to do "blind" analyses, i.e., without their knowledge of any of the facts of the case except the race, sex, and age of the Subject. From the 22 very different reports which were written, several hundred discrete items of personality description were abstracted; these later were then subsumed under 20 categories which, when taken *in toto* were deemed to constitute a comprehensive description of any individual's personality. These categories and the specific statements made about John Doe are given in detail on pages 298 to 300 of the book. In terms of our present schematization, we would say that John Doe can be understood by reordering the information in terms of our proposed four columns — see Table 2 — as follows:

Under Column I, we would put the category "Quality of Perception, Language and Thought"

Under Column II, we would subsume the following categories:

- — Pressures, Forces, Press
- — Motivations, Goals, Drives
- — Outlooks, Attitudes, Beliefs
- — Affects, Feelings, Emotions
- — Self-concept, Insight into Self
- — Interpersonal Relations

Under Column III, we would put these categories:

- — Frustrations, Conflicts, Fears
- — Psychosexual Level and Development
- — Super-Ego, Values, Ego Ideal
- — Personality Defenses and Mechanisms
- — Intellect and Abilities
- — Psychological Postdictions

Under Column IV, we would place the following:

- — Sexual Thought and Behavior
- — Self-Control, Ego Strength, Ego Capacity
- — Reality Contact, Orientation
- — Symptoms, Etiology
- — Prognoses, Predictions
- — Factual Postdictions

With this schematization it becomes a relatively easy task to bridge the gap between John Doe's quality of thought and aspects of his overt behavior, using Columns II and III (which indicate his internal motivations, his self-concept, his attitudes, his personality defenses, etc.) as the intervening variables which help us to understand how the quality of his thinking grows out of the character of his personality.

Example No. 3: This example also comes from an individual case study in psychology. In many ways it is similar to Example No. 2, cited above. This is called "The Case of Jay" and was reported in the *Journal of Projective Techniques* (34). Although Jay was administered a number of psychological tests and in spite of the fact that there are fascinating blind interpretations of these tests by Robert Holt, Pauline Vorhaus and the ubiquitous Reuben Fine, it is upon the relatively structured intelligence test protocol and its interpretations that we wish to focus in this example. Jay was administered the Wechsler-Bellevue Intelligence Scale. He was asked questions of direct information ("Who is president of the United States?"); and of similarities ("In what way are a tree and a fly alike?"). It happened that Jay was an extremely bright fellow so that his "score" is high, but his score is of secondary interest compared to the *quality* of his responses. In the discussion which appeared in the *Journal of Projective Techniques,* Kutash interprets the Wechsler-Bellevue Scale and delineates a personality picture from Jay's aproach to this intellectual task. But the task is crowned by Bell's astute and detailed analysis of the nuances of language and details of ways of thought from which an accurate, illumined picture of the total personality emerges. It is this kind of exercise which we believe provides a meaningful use of ways of thought and the role that these ways play in the context of the total personality — much more meaningful than any analysis of errors of syllogistic reasoning according to Aristotelian and neo-Aristotelian rules.

The process we are proposing, as illustrated by "The Case of Jay," is indicated sketchily in Table 2. The limitation of space imposed by the table and our text has left us fretful — but we have somewhat mollified our feelings by referring the reader to "The Case of Jay," with appropriate page references in the table to specific passages in the reprint, so that the reader will be able to catch the flavor of Jay's specific ways of thought (Column I), can read the extensive case history (Column IV), and can examine, in some detail, the intervening variables between the two, as indicated in Columns II and III.

Assuming that this general notion is tenable, are there any empirical data which bear on this issue? We believe that there are and we shall turn, for such evidence, to a statistical study previously reported by Little and Shneidman in the *Journal of Personality* (24).

For this example we return to our acquaintance, John Doe. Little and Shneidman took the 17 essay-like interpretations written about John Doe's Thematic Apperception Test (TAT) and Make-A-Picture-Story (MAPS) test and, as previously indicated, reduced these essay-interpretations to 802 items of personality description. For each of the statements describing John Doe another statement contradictory to the original was constructed. (For example, the statement "He hates his mother" was paired with the contradictory "He has no strong feelings toward his mother.") Of this total item population (of 1604 items), 150 items were selected on a systematic sampling basis as representative of the personality attributes asserted about John Doe. These 150 items were sent to two groups of judges: (a) 17 *test* interpreters, who wrote the original essay-interpretations, and (b) 29 especially competent psychiatrists and psychologists, called *criterion* judges, who judged the 150 items on the basis of John Doe's complete *clinical report* (his case history, laboratory reports, social service reports, the psychotherapy notes, progress notes, etc.), and who did not see the psychological test protocols. All 46 judges had the same 150 items and all had the same *aufgabe*: to sort the 150 items into a forced normal distribution — using Stephenson's Q-Sort technique — by distributing the items along a "Most characteristic for John Doe" to "Least characteristic for John Doe" continuum.

To identify the criterion, factor scores (computed as the sum of the individual weighted scores assigned to it by the criterion judges), were obtained for each of the 150 items. The factor scores of the items were then ranked in order of magnitude and the upper and lower eight per cent were tabulated. The 12 identifying items of the criterion general factor with the highest ("most true") factor scores and the 12 items of the criterion general factor with the lowest ("most false") factor scores were computed. These items were largely dynamic-descriptive in type, but with a diagnostic flavor (e.g., "He has an enormous amount of hostility"). There was, by and large, little emphasis on either etiology or symptomatology, but rather on a cross-sectional picture of the individual's present psychological state.

The results of the analyses of the *test interpreter* data were as follows: Four groups of judges were isolated from a cluster analysis of the test interpreter intercorrelations: Cluster A included six judges, Cluster B included three judges, Cluster C

TABLE 3

IDENTIFYING ITEMS FOR CLUSTERS OF TEST INTERPRETERS (FROM LITTLE AND SHNEIDMAN) (24)

CLUSTER A

Most True	*Most False*
He has incestuous desires that have precipitated intense conflict in him.	He has little conflict over his incestuous sexual impulses.
One of the main factors in his personality development was an extremely hostile, dominant mother.	He has satisfactory interpersonal relationships.
He lacks positive interpersonal relations.	He has resolved the conflict between his sexual needs and his interpretation of his mother's standards.
His deep conflict in the sexual area is between sexual impulses and superego restraints.	He shows little guilt over his incestuous sexual impulses.
He feels deprived of the oral gratifications of childhood.	
His aggression is aroused by illicit sexuality.	
Sexuality is strongly rejected by him.	
He suffers from feelings of rejection.	

CLUSTER C

Most True	*Most False*
An acute break with reality has probably occurred.	His thought processes are orderly and well knit.
His thinking is characterized by highly symbolic autistic processes.	He has the well preserved mind of a person who is not psychotic.
His verbal peculiarities are many and rather striking.	His thinking processes are well preserved.
There is some straining for effect in his use of language.	He is not confused.
	There are no paranoid ideas of reference or malign influences.

included six judges, and the residual cluster included the two judges who could not properly be placed in any single cluster. For purposes of our exposition in the present context, only Clusters A and C will be discussed.

The cluster-defining items, for Clusters A and C, are indicated in Table 3. As can be seen, the judges of Cluster A are characterized by a preference for what is commonly called "dynamic" type items. These items are assertions about the nature of the intrapsychic conflicts, their genetic development, and the individual's affective response to them. A diagnosis for the subject appears only by implication. The judges of Cluster C, on the other hand, select items describing the subject's *patterns of thinking* — the idiosyncrasies presented by the subject vis-a-vis his characteristics of intellectual functioning.

What are the relationships between the two? The general results of the comparison of the test interpreters with the criterion may be anticipated from an examination of the items defining each. However, a more precise estimate of the extent of the agreement of each test interpreter with the criterion was made by inserting his correlations with the criterion judges' into the criterion matrix and computing his first centroid loading. These loadings may be considered as correlations with the criterion general factor. The test judges of Cluster A had an average correlation of .688 and the judges of Cluster C, .698 — a remarkable similarity. An analysis of variance of these coefficients indicated that there was no significant difference between the mean validity figures for Clusters A and C. A further finding from the statistical analysis was that there was no significant difference between the mean validity coefficients of Clusters A and C and the average general factor loading of the criterion judges and that the correlation between Cluster domains A and C was .93, a fairly high correlation.

What do these figures mean? They can be taken to indicate that, in the individual being investigated, *thinking* characteristics (Cluster C) and *general personality* characteristics (Cluster A) are indeed highly correlated aspects of that individual. For John Doe, we thus have an *empirical* demonstration that — based on the judgments of 17 test interpreters and 29 case material interpreters — *his ways of thinking are a reflection of his general ways of psychological being.*

IMPLICATIONS

In the sense that every essay constitutes an intellectual "projective technique," each reader will have, by the time he reaches this point, fantasied some implications from this paper for himself — as well as some rebuttals and defenses against those implications. For the writer the following implications seem to be contained within the letter and the spirit of the preceding text. These implications seem to be of three types that might, using broad labels, be termed theoretical, scientific, and (what might be heresy in a philosophic essay) practical.

The first kind of implication stems from the focus of the suggestion made in this paper, that is, that it is possible to translate thinking — aberrant or commonplace thinking — into forms of thought in such a way that the work that the theorist does in making this transformation illuminates the psychological process that the individual thinker traversed.

The second kind of implication is that this approach to logic and to ways of thinking is amenable to empirical verification. One might devise empirical tests of the different hypotheses that might yield quite interesting insights into the nature of thought processes; some work has already been done along these lines. Our criterion for belief might be that of statistical significance. It may not be unrealistic to aspire to the goal of metricizing philosophy.

The third kind of implication has to do with the practical power of such a scheme. Logicians have too long dealt with such irrelevancies — irrelevant to almost anything — as "Some cats have whiskers, all cats are fisheaters, some fish (namely catfish) who eat, have whiskers." The kinds of illogicalities and patterns of thinking that we would like to see investigated are those which have to do with man's meaningful problems such as the "logic" of prejudice, the "logic" of suicide (36), the "logic" of homosexuality, the "logic" of magical beliefs, the "logic" of delusions, the "logic" of neuroses, etc.

Perhaps the most important single implication of the above

general scheme is this: that there may not be one or two ways of thinking but a great *variety* of *ways* of thinking. Indeed, each individual may either have his own idiosyncratic ways of thinking or idiosyncratic aspects of his ways of thinking and these relate to (or are part of) other idiosyncratic aspects of his personality. Thus, what we are proposing is an *enthymematic* analysis, in the broad sense, of an individual's thought productions; a democratic attitude toward the ways of thinking of others (think and let think); and an attempt to understand the other's idiosyncratic psycho-logical involvement in his own world.

Resumé of the Argument. What has been discussed in this chapter is believed to be part-and-parcel of much of contemporary psychology; it is implied either directly or implicitly in topics such as "cognitive style," "Weltanschauung," "projective techniques," etc. What may be new in this presentation is that it possesses a somewhat different focus — the "logic" of the individual — and attempts to explicate some ideas in this direction. The development of the argument might be summarized as follows:

1. Thought is common to all. All individuals — possibly excluding neonates and unconscious persons — mentate, reason, cerebrate, deduce, induce, come to conclusions, etc. Thought (like sex) is not too good for common people.

2. Individuals think in various ways. There is not one "way" of thinking but many ways.[14] In this paper we are not talking about "correct" thinking, but just thinking. People think as they do often believing that they are thinking aright.

3. The concept of error in relation to modes of thinking has been applied somewhat narrowly, if not superciliously. "Error" has usually implied a departure from a particular (high) standard of thinking, usually that attributed to Aristotle (when he was thinking about thinking). Our position is that a madman's

---

[14]Dr. Reuben Fine, in a personal communication (December 7, 1959), wrote: "Traditionally, psychologists have assumed that people think in pretty much the same way, i.e., logically, or as close to it as they can come. This is clearly erroneous. Accurate logical thinking may turn out to be either (a) a sign of mental health, (b) a sign of high intelligence, or (c) a characteristic of certain individuals whom clinically we usually rate obsessional."

thinking or a feebleminded's thinking is as bona fide thinking as the thinking of a genius, and further, is as "correct" – given the thinker's premises and accepting his mode of thinking as a possible mode of thinking.[15] We are interested in how people *do* think, not in how they *ought* to think. "Reasoning," to quote William James, "is always for a subjective interest."

4. This non-evaluative point of view towards thinking provides a lever to understand (rather than to score or evaluate) the reasoning of the other individual. The main point of this approach is that the thinking of an individual is not best understood by labelling it as "illogical," but rather that our understanding of another person is better approached by assuming that the other person's thinking is logical for that person doing the thinking. Then one is in the position to cast about to see what logical assumptions – no matter how "illogical" from our point of view – would have to have been made for that individual to have thought as he did.

5. After one has identified the "idiosyncratic logical position" of the individual thinker, he may then proceed to inquire as to what kind of psychological state in that individual would be consistent with (or even, so to speak, force) that individual's adopting the logical position which he apparently assumed.

6. By supplying these intervening variables of idiosyncratic logical position and concomitant psychological status one could then better understand aberrant or unusual or idiosyncratic thinking in terms of psychological states, and aberrant or unusual or idiosyncratic psychological states in terms of ways of thinking. A bridge between these two might be a most interesting road to explore.

7. The way that a man thinks on occasion is not necessarily the way that he must think all the time. Specific idiosyncratic ways of thought need not be globally characteristic of an individual, but might occur only with specific content or in specific situations, so that there might well be intra-individual variations

---

[15]This statement is not meant to affirm that all thoughts are of equal value but just as some individuals are taller or brighter than others, some thoughts are more interesting, more reality-oriented, or more important than others.

in ways of thoughts which might account, within that individual, for the "logic of prejudice," the "logic of neurosis," the "logic of suicide," etc. Intensive idiographic (intra-personal) studies would be important in pursuing this approach.

8. It is believed that this approach, if consistently carried out, could clarify a number of problems in the psychology of thinking, which the purely logical or the purely (nomothetic) experimental approaches cannot handle. We would hope that data could be acquired about how people really do think — data which could be analyzed to obtain general principles and other conclusions about human psychology.

REFERENCES

1. Abelson, R. P., and Rosenberg, M. J.: Symbolic psycho-logic: A model of attitudinal cognition. *Behavioral Science, 3*:1-13. 1958.
2. Alekhine, A.: *My Best Games of Chess, 1924-1937*. New York, Harcourt, 1939.
3. Andrews, T. G.: The effect of benzedrine sulfate on syllogistic reasoning. *J. Exp. Psychol., 26*:423-431. 1940.
4. Arieti, S.: *Interpretation of Schizophrenia*. New York, Robert Bruner, 1955.
5. Bateson, G., Jackson, D. D., Haley, J., and Weakland, J.: Toward a theory of schizophrenia. *Behavioral Science, 1*:251-264. 1956.
6. Beier, E. G.: The effect of induced anxiety on flexibility of intellectual functioning. *Psychol. Monogr., 65*: No. 9. 1951.
7. Binswanger, L.: The case of Ellen West. In May, R. (Ed.), *Existtence*. New York, Basic Books, 1958.
8. Brown, R., and Lenneberg, E. H.: A study in language and cognition. *J. Abnorm. & Social Psychol., 49*:454-461. 1954.
9. Burnet, J.: *Early Greek Philosophers*. (Fourth Edition). New York, Macmillan, 1930.
10. Cameron, N.: Reasoning, regression and communication in schizophrenia. *Psychol. Monogr., 50*:1-33. 1938.
11. Cherry, C.: *On Human Communication*. New York, Wiley, 1957.
12. DeGroot, A.: *Het Denken van den Schaker*. Amsterdam, Noord-Hollandsche Uitgevers Maatschappij, 1946.
13. Dewey, J.: *Logic: The Theory of Inquiry*. New York, Holt, 1938.
14. Doyle, A. C.: The adventure of the copper beeches. In *The Adventures of Sherlock Holmes*. New York, Harper, 1920.
15. Fine, R.: Psychoanalytic observations on chess and chess masters.

Psychoanal. Monogr., No. *1:*1-80, 1956.
16. Fine, R.: The logic of psychology. *Psychoanalysis, 45*:15-41. 1958.
17. Fromm, E.: *Man for Himself.* New York, Rinehart, 1947.
18. Goldstein, K.: Methodological approach to the study of schizophrenic thought disorder. In Kasanin, J. S. (Ed.), *Language and Thought in Schizophrenia.* Berkeley, Univ. of California Press, 1944.
19. Gottesman, L., and Chapman, L. J.: Syllogistic reasoning errors in schizophrenia. *J. Consult. Psychol., 24:*250-255. 1960.
20. Greenson, R.: The mother tongue and the mother. *Internat. J. Psycho-Analysis, 31*:1-6. 1950.
21. James, W.: *Pragmatism.* New York, Longmans, 1907.
22. Kantor, J. R.: *Psychology and Logic.* Vol. I. Bloomington, Indiana, Principia Press, 1945.
23. Kasanin, J. S.: Disturbance of conceptual thinking in schizophrenia. In Kasanin, J. S. (Ed.), *Language and Thought in Schizophrenia.* Berkeley, Univ. of California Press, 1944.
24. Little, K. B., and Shneidman, E. S.: The validity of thematic projective technique interpretations. *J. Pers., 23:*285-294. 1955.
25. Matte-Blanco, I.: Expression in symbolic logic of the characteristics of the system ucs or the logic of the system ucs. *Internat. J. Psycho-Analysis, 40:*1-5. 1959.
26. Metfessel, M.: The all-or-none nature of emotional thinking. *J. Psychol., 9*:323-326. 1940.
27. Murray, H. A.: *Thematic Apperception Test Manual.* Cambridge, Harvard Univ. Press, 1943.
28. Orwell, G.: *Nineteen Eighty-Four.* New York, Harcourt, 1949.
29. Piaget, J.: *The Language and Thought of the Child.* (Second Edition). London, Routledge-Paul, 1932.
30. Piaget, J.: *Logic and Psychology.* New York, Basic Books, 1957.
31. Rapaport, D.: (Ed.) *Organization and Pathology of Thought.* New York, Columbia Univ. Press, 1951.
32. Ruesch, J., and Kees, W.: *Non-Verbal Communication.* Berkeley, Univ. of California Press, 1956.
33. Shneidman, E. S.: (Ed.) *Thematic Test Analysis.* New York, Grune & Stratton, 1951.
34. Shneidman, E. S.: (Ed.) The case of Jay. *J. Proj. Tech., 16*:297-345 & 444-475. 1952.
35. Shneidman, E. S.: A method for educing the present correlates of perception: An introduction to the method of successive covariation. *J. Gen. Psychol., 57*:113-120. 1959.

36. Shneidman, E. S., and Farberow, N. L.: (Ed.) *Clues to Suicide.* New York, McGraw-Hill, 1957.
37. Storch, A.: *The Primitive Archaic Forms of Inner Experience and Thought in Schizophrenia.* Washington, D. C., Nerv. and Ment. Dis. Monographs, 1924.
38. Sullivan, H. S.: Language of schizophrenia. In Kasanin, J. S. (Ed.), *Language and Thought in Schizophrenia.* Berkeley, Univ. of California Press, 1944.
39. Sullivan, H. S.: *Clinical Studies in Psychiatry.* New York, Norton, 1956.
40. Tomkins, S. S.: *The Thematic Apperception Test.* New York, Grune & Stratton, 1947.
41. Veatch, H. B.: *International Logic.* New Haven, Yale Univ. Press, 1952.
42. Vigotsky, L. S.: Thought in schizophrenia. *Arch. Neurol. & Psychiat., 31*:1063-1077. 1934.
43. Von Domarus, E.: The specific laws of logic in schizophrenia. In Kasanin, J. S. (Ed.), *Language and Thought in Schizophrenia.* Berkeley, Univ. of California Press, 1944.
44. Werner, H.: *Comparative Psychology of Mental Development.* (Revised Edition) New York, Internat. Univ. Press, 1957.
45. Wertheimer, M.: *Productive Thinking.* New York, Harper, 1945.
46. Wertheimer, M.: On discrimination experiments: I. Two logical structures. *Psychol. Rev., 66*:252-266. 1959.
47. Whorf, B. L.: (Edited by J. B. Carroll) *Language, Thought, and Reality.* New York, Wiley, 1956.
48. Witkin, H. A., et al.: *Personality Through Perception.* New York, Harper, 1954.
49. Woodworth, R. S., and Sells, S. B.: An atmosphere effect in formal syllogistic reasoning. *J. Exp. Psychol., 18*:451-460. 1935.

DISCUSSION OF DR. SHNEIDMAN'S PAPER

Julian D. Rotter, Ph.D.
Primary Discussant

Dr. Rotter: Dr. Shneidman has presented a stimulating analysis of the possibilities involved in analyzing the formal properties of the logical thought of individuals as evidenced in their verbal productions. Since his paper does not deal primarily with empirical data or an interpretation of empirical data, I have no recourse as a commentator but to follow his own example and make a logical analysis of his thinking.

In carrying out such a logical analysis I would have two aims. One of these is to discover both the explicit and hidden premises in his thinking. The second would be to make suggestions in regard to the kind of empirical data which would test or partially test these assumptions.

It seems to me that Dr. Shneidman is actually discussing two different, if related, propositions. One of these is that particular modes of arriving at deductive conclusions are characteristic of individuals and that these should be regarded either along a continuum or along characteristics other than those which deal merely with their truth or falsity. The second is that what might be called styles of thinking or styles of attack upon intellectual problems are characteristic of individuals, as exemplified by his discussion of the generality of behavior of chess masters. Here he introduces variables not usually thought of as pertaining to logic, i.e., aggressiveness, careful planning, etc. Since I do not feel that these are the same problem, I would like to restrict most of my comments to the first problem since this is the primary emphasis of the paper. This is the question of the significance or meaning that can be attached to errors in specific logical sequences verbally expressed by individuals. In making such an analysis I would like to go about the problem from what I would call a constructual point of view. That is, I would like to ask such questions as, what are the basic constructs which would be used in measurement of the logical properties of verbal productions? How reliably can such constructs be measured? What can be predicted from them? How do they tie into or relate to other constructs? What additional prediction or explanation is possible with the use of such constructs over other methods of abstracting from the same productions for the same or similar purposes? It is clear that there is an infinite number of ways in which abstractions can be made about verbal productions. The fact that such verbal abstractions can be made does not in itself provide any information as to their utility. With this introduction, then, I would like to go ahead and outline what I believe are the basic assumptions in Shneidman's logic.

These are as follows:

1. That when a series of statements, presumably deductive, does not follow common, conventional, or Aristotelian lines, it is possible to identify the nature of the deviation or the reason for the failure to follow the commonly accepted syllogistic lines.

2. That not only can a reason for the "error" be found but this may be arrived at reliably, that is, several experts can arrive at a similar reason. Otherwise, there will be little scientific gain in the procedure. For example, in selecting the missing premise, when it is assumed that there is such a missing premise, there are a great many possibilities and it may well be that if 20 psychologists were to supply what they thought the missing premise to be there would be 20 different premises.

3. That the kind of error in such logical sequences is characteristic of the individual, that is, that the error or type of error produced in one situation is predictive of the logical nature of his verbalizations in another situation. If this is not the case then obviously prediction would be extremely limited.

4. That if there is a characteristic mode of making deductions in a specific subject that this predicts other significant personality characteristics.

These then are, it seems to me, the basic assumptions underlying the major thesis of Shneidman's paper, i.e., that what are commonly thought of as errors of logic are predictive of significant generalized personality attributes of the individual. It is not possible without considerable data to evaluate the degree to which these assumptions are supportable. I can, of course, speculate on them.

That the nature of the error which is in many cases far from obvious can be reliably determined does in itself pose a considerable question. On the basis of other attempts to discover hidden meanings of verbal productions, it would appear that there is here, indeed, a tough nut to crack.

The degree of consistency of such logical processes is also a question. Consider the following thinking of a southern white: (a) some negroes are very intelligent, (b) negroes are inferior to whites, and (c) therefore all negroes are inferior intellectually. The type of error produced here is probably more a function of the needs of the individual present in a specific situation than they are characteristic of his formal logical processes in dealing with deductive sequences. If some consistency does exist in the type of error produced it appears to me that further specification will have to be made as to the kinds of situations in which such consistency may be expected.

Finally, I would like to remark on the relationship of such consistencies, if they could be found, to other major personality variables. It seems likely that they may have some relationship to gross diagnostic categorization when these categorizations are themselves based in part on the nature of the patients' logical thinking. This, of course, would not be either surprising or particularly useful. That they may relate to other broad personality characteristics is an open question.

Some comment should be made in regard to the latter implications of the paper. That is, that the styles of attack on intellectual problems is in itself generalized and predictive of other personality characteristics. I am referring here to styles of attack other than those which might traditionally be thought of as formal, logical characteristics. Such an interest has some history in psychology under the general topic of personality and problem solving and particular emphasis has been placed on such variables as rigidity and anxiety. We have done some research at Ohio State on dependency as a general characteristic related to problem solving behavior. Although these studies have not as yet produced any remarkably predictive generalizations they still seem to me to hold promise and the probabilities are greater that the same underlying assumptions discussed earlier can be met in regard to this hypothesis.

These comments are in themselves only speculations and the hidden assumptions in my logic perhaps need to be examined critically. In any case, it is to be hoped that the empirical findings that will result from Shneidman's provocative paper will relieve us of the infinite regress of further logical analyses.

Dr. Atkinson: Dr. Shneidman is dealing with cases where sometimes the observable conclusions do not appear to fit the scheme of Aristotelian logic, the scheme that you or I ordinarily use. We say, "This fellow is not thinking rationally, he is not thinking the way I do, he is not thinking in a way that would be described by the same conceptual scheme that describes my thought process." We can suggest, "Let's invent another scheme to account for his thought process." However, Dr. Shneidman is saying, "His thought process must appear 'logical to him,' " and I think Dr. Shneidman is assuming it must appear logical in the same sense that my thought process does. I think the heuristic methodological contribution is in asking this question, "Under what conditions would this conclusion appear logical to the individual?" Dr. Shneidman has proposed that we think of the psychological state of the individual as having a variety of parameters. These are usually unstated in the case of the normal or healthy individual. As one example, he suggested that "attention" might be one of these parameters. If attention is very limited, then the logical argument of this person would be different than for the normal person, and the consequences, though appearing logical to him, will appear illogical to me.

Dr. Holt: As I listened to Dr. Shneidman I kept looking for non-Aristotelian logics and not finding them.

If he is correct in assuming that by working with logical fallacies he can exhaustively deal with the logical features of thought encountered in this culture, then it seems to me this is really demonstrating that one logic will do. What I had hoped for, but realize is not very plausible to find in this culture, is that people have wholly different ways of approaching the problem of inference; ways that perhaps wouldn't even be syllogistic.

Judging by the work of Whorf, Sapir and others who have written about language in non-Western societies, the whole way of looking at the world and conceiving of things is organized in such a different way that the implicit logic there might require a truly non-Aristotelian logic. This scheme is non-Aristotelian only in turning Aristotle upside down, not in presenting a new logic. The thing that impresses me is that the Aristotelian logic is such an endemic and pervasive aspect of our culture that none of us can get away from it. We get away from it only by negating it in some way.

Dr. Kagan: An alternative point of view of behaviors such as slips of the tongue or statements of the type "I am Switzerland," is as follows. Cognitive associations are constantly going on. When a "slip" occurs, it means that for some reason one of the cues in the ongoing train of thought elicits, through association, not through any logical operation, another word or symbol.

Dr. Rotter: It is a question of whether all mental activity can be thought of as thinking, or whether you can make distinctions between associative mental activity, versus thinking as a method of arriving at statements about the order of nature. What Dr. Shneidman is treating as a thinking (logical) process is often considered to be an associative process.

STYLISTIC VARIABLES IN FANTASY BEHAVIOR: THE ASCRIPTION OF AFFECT STATES TO SOCIAL STIMULI[1]

Jerome Kagan, Ph.D.
Fels Research Institute
Yellow Springs, Ohio

THE HISTORY of projective methods in psychology revolves around two instruments — the Rorschach and the TAT — and each is in the midst of a change in emphasis with regard to its major variables. In the beginning, the Rorschach was advertised as an instrument that revealed structural properties of the personality, while the TAT was touted as an index of the content of the individual's values, motives, and attitudes. In the last few years, psychologists have reversed themselves and become interested in the content of ink blot imagery and the structure of the apperceptive story. This dichotomy between structural and content variables is also present in Gardner Lindzey's (12) recent classification of projective tests. Since these two terms are frequently used and rarely defined it seems profitable to attempt to spell out their definitions here.

Content Versus Structural Variables. Content variables refer to the semantic meaning of the fantasy response and, in practice, there is strong emphasis on attitudinal and motivational meaning. Semantic meaning is defined by Osgood, Suci, and Tannenbaum (16) as a representational, mediation process in which the sign (language label used) evokes in the S a mediation process which is a fractional part of the total behavior elicited by the significate (stimulus pattern to which the sign

[1]This research was supported, in part, by a research grant (M-1260) from the National Institutes of Mental Health, United States Public Health Service. The author acknowledges the collaborative effort of Dr. Howard A. Moss, who has been intimately associated with the research and theorizing presented in this paper.

applies). Thus, a content variable refers to a set of language responses which are assumed to be associated with specific situations, behaviors, and experiences. For example, the content variable "need aggression" assumes a relationship between words like "angry," "fight," "hit," and specific thoughts, situations, and behaviors in S's past experience that have been associated with that word. Content variables, therefore, refer to classes of words which denote or stand for specific stimulus situations.

Structural variables deal with the manner in which the individual interprets the fantasy stimulus; "how the response is given" as opposed to "what is given." The structural aspect of a response can refer to a variety of processes. First, a structural variable can include the syntax of the subject's verbal behavior and the ordering of language units in the verbal response.

A second class of structural variables is the preferred use of specific language forms over others. We are not concerned here with the semantic meaning of the labels used but with the fact that certain language forms are preferred or prepotently utilized, e.g., a high proportion of verbs to nouns, use of qualifying phrases, etc.

A third set of structural variables refers to the preferred perceptual organization of the stimulus. That is, for a given TAT picture, individuals differ with respect to those parts of the stimulus they initially describe. It is assumed that there is a correlation between the part first described and the stimulus aspect to which the S first attended. Some Ss characteristically describe the background of the scene first, others initially focus on the people illustrated, and still others initially describe the age and clothing of the illustrated figures.

A fourth variable is the coherence and logic of the fantasy production. A fifth is the tendency to "go beyond" what is given in the external stimulus. Some individuals tend to limit their story to what is obviously congruent with and supported by the external stimulus. Others habitually infer motives, feelings, and conflicts to the illustrated figures and make statements about the figures for which there is minimal validation in the stimulus. Thus, to Card 1 of the TAT, one subject will say, "That is a boy with a violin, the violin is on the table, he looks like he is staring at it and will probably play it." At the other extreme is the story, "That boy is disgusted, he loves the violin but can't play it well; so he is mad at himself for not being able to play." Aside from the differences in content, there is a striking difference with regard to the ascription of internal characteristics to the boy for which there is little confirmation in the external stimulus. The first story is descriptive of the stimulus; the second theme is inferential.

The structural variables described above deal only with the organization of the stimulus and the style of the language response. One might also include the nonthematic behavior of the subject (e.g., his resistance, or his subjective reaction to the examiner).

Other classifications of structural variables have sliced the pie somewhat differently and have often grouped together different psychological processes. Wyatt's (25) list of structural variables includes: (a) linguistic analysis (syntax plus language preferences), (b) manner of presentation (content emphasis of the story, quality of plot, introduction of new figures), (c) comprehension of the stimulus (perceptual organization), and (d) subjective reactions to the stimuli.

Henry's (6) four categories are somewhat different. They include (a) amount and kind of verbal production (productivity, variety of content, vividness of imagery), (b) organizational qualities (description of relations between people and parts of the story, coherence and logic of story, and imaginative elaboration), (c) acuity (acuity of concepts and observations), and (d) language usage.

Rapaport, Gill and Schafer (18), and Holt (8) prefer structural categories which are more closely tied to manifest aspects of pathological functioning in clinical syndromes. Rapaport's categories include (a) affect lability (exclamations, content shaped by affective response to the picture), (b) depression (sparse productivity, over-elaboration of a theme of happiness or sadness), (c) obsessiveness (intellectualizing, compulsive criticism of the picture, pedantry), (d) paranoid trends (deducing E's motives, perceptual distortions), (e) schizophrenia (over-elaborate symbolism; peculiar verbalization, disjointed organization).

Most of Rapaport's categories combine semantic variables, structural variables, and reactions to the examiner and are more multidimensional than the categories described earlier.

The major purpose of this paper is not to argue for a specific set of structural variables. This brief resumé was intended only as background material. However, in all classifications of structural variables there is an emphasis on "styles" of perceptual and conceptual organization. We will use the word "style" to refer to prepotent or preferred ways of organizing, labeling, and interpreting fantasy stimuli that (a) are not based primarily on the semantic meaning of the response and (b) show consistency across a variety of stimulus situations.

To illustrate, the consistent tendency to begin a story by describing the dress of the illustrated figures would be regarded as a style. This decision assumes that this response is more likely the result of a predilection for perceptual accentuation of details than a reflection of a motivational preoccupation with clothing as such. This assumption may be fallacious, but is subject to empirical test. The consistent reporting of aggressive actions, on the other hand, is usually regarded as a semantic variable because aggressive themes are assumed to be the consequent of preoccupation with aggressive action.

THE RESEARCH

The empirical data to be summarized have been gathered during the last three years and have focused on a variety of stylistic variables. However, this paper will deal with only one variable: "the tendency to use affect words in describing or conceptualizing social stimuli." We have selected this particular variable because at the present time it is the one to which we have devoted most of our energy and for which data analysis is most complete. Specifically, this variable refers to (a) the use of adjectives or verbs representing affect or feeling states in describing figures on TAT cards, (b) the tendency to group people together on the basis of similarity in affect state, and (c) the tendency to ascribe action to ink blot perceptions of human figures.

Affect words are adjectives or verbs which refer to internal emotional states which are neither meditative nor intellective, (thinking, dreaming, reflecting). Typical examples of affect words are mad, sorry, sad, love, hate, angry, exhaustion, fear, anxiety, grief, excitement. This response tendency seems to be on the border line between a content and a structural variable. The classifications of Rapaport, Wyatt, Henry, and Holt usually view this response as structural because it is related to the imaginative quality or richness of the story.

We feel that it has stylistic qualities for the following reasons. First, it usually requires a specific kind of perceptual organization. A TAT stimulus illustrates people in various backgrounds and offers the S a wide range of stimuli on which to focus his attention. The S who is likely to attribute affect states to the figures is apt to focus on the facial expression of the figure. Thus, use of affect language suggests a preferred perceptual organization. Second, this response represents a tendency to use descriptive labels which do not have clear cut, objective validation in the stimulus. The use of affect labels involves an inference about the figures; it involves "going beyond" what is given. This behavior does not refer to a specific affect state, such as anger or sorrow, but to a class of words with markedly different behavioral referents.

On the other hand, affect words do have some semantic meaning for these labels denote one type of psychic experience. It is possible, therefore, that Ss who ascribe affect states to TAT figures might have a prepotent tendency to conceptualize the social environment and their own experiences in terms of affect labels. We might expect such individuals to be introspective; to be both willing and able to discuss themselves in terms of their emotional and motivational states. It is acknowledged that there is not perfect congruence between the use of a class of verbal labels and the presence of the corresponding mental state that is denoted by the label. Thus, it would be foolish to assume that all Ss who use affect words tend to be aware of their affect states. However, since we have no available index of "awareness of affect states," we are using verbal behavior as an approximate measure of this variable.

The reader may feel at this point that the use of affect labels is not a stylistic variable. The significance of the empirical findings to be reported is not entirely dependent on the validity of that assumption.

The data deal with three related questions. First, to what degree is there intra-individual consistency in the tendency to apply affect labels to different kinds of social stimuli? Second, what is the relation between affect labeling and introspectiveness and related processes? Third, to what degree does this behavior show intra-individual stability over time?

STUDY A

The major study to be reported deals with the intra-individual consistency of the tendency to apply affect labels to four different classes of social stimuli. Three measures involve the direct use of affect labels to categorize "human-like" stimuli. These are the ascription of affect states to TAT and tachistoscopically presented figures and the grouping of human figures together on the basis of similarity in affect states. The fourth measure is the occurrence of human movement responses to ink blot stimuli. The rationale for the inclusion of the human movement score with the other three follows. Previous research (2, 11, 20, 22) suggests that human movement responses are produced by individuals who use affect language on the TAT, think about their psychological problems, and are introspective. Since human movement responses often involve the ascription of goal-related activity to human percepts, (people eating, people snuggling, people fighting, people dancing, people kissing) it is possible that the human movement response *reflects a prepotent tendency to interpret the environment in terms of human motives.* A motive is defined by McClelland (14) as "an anticipation of a change in affect state." This definition would suggest that there is an intimate connection between conceptualization of the social environment in terms of human motives on the one hand and affect states on the other. When an individual feels afraid, happy, sad, or mad, there are cognitive anticipations of incentive or goal states associated with these feelings. Similarly, when one anticipates certain goal states there is both the anticipation of a goal-related affect and the experiencing of any affect which is associated with deprivation of the goal. Thus, affect states and goal related action are psychologically linked. Since the nature of the ink blot stimulus precludes the frequent ascription of affect states to human percepts, it is suggested that ascription of action to ink blot humans is analogous to the use of affect labels on TAT-like stimuli. Thus, it was anticipated that (a) ascription of affect states to TAT and tachistoscopically presented figures, (b) sorting of human figures on an affect basis, and (c) ascription of activity to humanized ink blot percepts would all be positively intercorrelated, i.e., show intra-individual consistency. Since previous research suggested a relation between an introspective attitude and both human movement and use of affect language, (11, 22) it was predicted that each of these four measures would be positively related to independent interview based ratings of introspectiveness.

Method

Subjects and Procedure. The subjects (Ss) were 64 adults (34 males and 30 females) from the Fels research population. The age range of the group was between 19 and 29 with a median age of 25 years. The mean Wechsler-Bellevue IQ of the group was 123 and all IQ's were average or above (IQ range of 97-142). The Fels research population is predominantly a middle class sample residing in southwestern Ohio. Half of the Ss had some college training and the vocations of the Ss included professional, white collar, agricultural, and laboring groups. The data to be summarized were gathered as part of a larger, standardized assessment program. Initially, all Ss were interviewed for about five hours over two to three sessions. Following the interviews, the author rated each S on a series of 59 variables (7 point scale), one of which was called "introspectiveness." Introspectiveness was defined as the "ability to talk about motives, conflicts and sources of anxiety." The test material included a series of 32 ink blots derived from the standard Rorschach plates (hereafter called the modified Rorschach), a 13 card TAT, a figure sorting task, and a tachistoscopic experiment. The ink blots were administered in the first session, the TAT in the second session, and the last two tasks in the third session. The test sessions were separated by periods ranging from one day to six months with a modal intersession interval of one month.

Scoring and Administration: Modified Rorschach Movement Responses. For this research, the author devised a modified Rorschach stimulus in which part of the original Rorschach ink blot was covered with a template, leaving a common D or d area visible to the S (9). There were 32 stimuli in this ink blot series; each tended to be perceived as a unitary Gestalt and, with one exception, all the stimuli were either totally chromatic or achromatic.[2] Thus, over 90 per cent of the Ss produced 32 responses. The protocol was scored for occurrence of human movement which was defined as the ascription of action, motivation, affect, or postural stance to humans or "human-like" stimuli (elves, witches). Animal movement responses were also scored to determine if ascription of action to *human figures* was of special significance.

Scoring and Administration: Weighted TAT Affect. This score was based on the ascription of an affect state to TAT figures in a 13 card protocol. The males were administered Cards 4, 8 BM, 7 BM, 6 BM, 12 M, 17 BM, 13 MF, 14, 3 BM, 5, 1, 3 GF, and 18 GF. The females were administered Cards 4, 6 GF, 12 F, 2, 8 GF, 17 BM, 13 MF, 14, 3 BM, 5, 1, 3 GF, and 18 GF. All stories were electrically recorded and transcribed verbatim. The S was given a positive score for a picture if he attributed at least one affect state to any figure in the story. The most frequent affect labels used were mad, tired, happy, proud, excited, exhausted, angry, sad, unhappy, surprised, lonely, remorseful, grief-stricken, and afraid. No extra score was given if the S used more than one affect word in any one story. Some of the pictures had a greater tendency to elicit affect language than others and a separate weighting procedure was used for the male and female series of pictures. The four TAT pictures with the greatest tendency to elicit affect labels were given a score of "1," the four pictures with the least tendency to elicit affect labels were given a score of "3," and the five remaining pictures were given a weight of "2." The S's weighted affect score was the sum of his weights for all 13 pictures.

[2]Photostatic reproductions of the 32 stimuli are available upon request.

Scoring and Administration: Tachistoscopic Affect Score. This score was based on the ascription of affect states to tachistoscopically presented scenes. In this part of the experiment, the S was shown a series of 14 line drawings of people in various situations. The pictures were presented at seven different exposure speeds ranging from .01 to 1.0 seconds. The pictures were shown initially at the fastest exposure (.01 second) and each succeeding series was presented at a slower exposure speed. All exposures were above threshold and all Ss reported seeing something at each exposure. The S sat in a light-proof room 22 inches from a flash-opal, glass screen. The image was projected from the back of the screen and the field was constantly illuminated by a 35 mm. projector (30 foot candles at the screen). The S was not told to make up a story, but was asked to state for each picture (a) the sex of the figures, (b) their approximate ages, and (c) what each person in the picture was doing. The instructions were intended to orient the S to report objective facts about the picture rather than inferences about the affect states of the figures. The S was given three practice pictures to adapt him to the task and its requirements, and the entire protocol was electrically recorded and transcribed verbatim. The tachistoscopic affect score was the number of pictures (98 in all) in which an affect state was ascribed to a figure.

Scoring and Administration: Figure Sorting Affect. The third affect labeling measure was derived from a figure sorting task. Three arrays of cardboard figures (similar in size and stimulus quality to Shneidman's Make-a-Picture-Story Test stimuli (21), were constructed with 22 figures in each stimulus array.[3] In the third test session, the S was presented initially with Array 1 and given the following instructions:

> We are now going to show you a group of human figures that are arranged in *no* special order. We would like you to pick out one group of figures that go together on some common basis, any basis you like. The number of figures in the group can be any size you like. Just pick out a group of figures that go together on some common basis and tell us the basis upon which you grouped these figures.

[3]Photostatic reproductions of these stimuli are also available.

After the first sort, the figures S had selected were replaced in the original array and S was asked to produce another group that went together on a different basis. This procedure was repeated until the subject produced six different sorts. Following an interpolated task (the French Insight Test), the S was presented with Array 2 and asked to produce six more sorts. The S was then administered the tachistoscopic experiment described above and this was followed by a coffee break. Then the S was presented with Array 3. For Array 3, S was instructed to divide the group of 22 figures into two piles on the basis of one concept. After the S repeated this task four times, the Wechsler-Bellevue Scale and Hanfmann-Kasanin tests were administered. The S was then presented with Array 1 again and asked to produce six more conceptual groupings. Finally, Arrays 1 and 2 were pooled, and the examiner selected one figure from the pooled group. The examiner then asked the S to select all the figures that he would classify with the one the E had selected. This procedure was repeated for ten different figures. The entire figure sorting procedure resulted in a total of 32 conceptual responses and these responses were scored for a variety of conceptual and content categories. The score we are primarily concerned with here is the number of abstract concepts in which the grouping of figures was based on similarity in affect state. Typical examples include, "These are all happy," "These are all mad," "These are all remorseful."

The inter-rater reliability for these variables was satisfactory. For each of the four affect labeling scores, percentage of agreement was in the nineties. The inter-rater reliability (product moment correlation) for the interview rating of "introspectiveness" was +.81.

The four affect labeling scores (TAT weighted affect, tachistoscopic affect, figure sorting affect, and human movement) were intercorrelated. The distributions for human movement and figure sorting affect were not perfectly normal and we computed phi coefficients. The distribution for each of the four scores was divided at the median and chi square (with Yates' correction) and phi coefficients were computed for the males and females separately. Since the results were in the same direction for both sexes, the male and female data were pooled and new phi coefficients were computed for the total population.

Results

The only variable for which there was a sex difference in mean score was TAT affect, with the females having a higher weighted affect score than the males ($p < .05$). This was the only instrument in which different stimuli were presented to males and females and more of the female pictures elicited affect language than the male pictures. Table 1 presents the six intercorrelations among the four scores.

TABLE 1

INTERCORRELATIONS AMONG FOUR AFFECT LABELING MEASURES (PHI COEFFICIENTS)

Variable	*Tachistoscope*	*Figure Sorting*	*Human Movement*
TAT Affect	.31‡	.34‡	.44‡
Tachistoscope Affect	—	.34‡	.26†
Figure Sorting Affect		—	.22†

†p < .05; one tail
‡p < .01; one tail

Although the phi coefficients were not extremely high, all six correlations were statistically significant. The correlations between animal movement and each of these four affect scores were all very low, for the phi coefficients ranged from −.07 to +.14. Thus, ascription of action to *human figures* is of psychological significance for this conceptual tendency. The fact that the human movement response was positively related to the three direct, affect labeling scores supports the original hypothesis relating the use of affect words in describing people and the ascription of action to ink blot perceptions of humans. There are marked differences in stimulus material between a figure on a TAT card and an ink blot. The significant associations among TAT affect labels, human movement, and figure sorting affect indicate that the tendency to infer affect states to social stimuli has generality across a variety of conceptual tasks.

As discussed earlier, previous research and theory point to an association between an introspective attitude on the one hand and human movement response and use of affect language on the other. It will be recalled that each of these Ss was interviewed prior to the administration of the tests and rated (7 point scale) for the degree to which the S talked about his motives, conflicts, and sources of anxiety during the interview. The relation between this rating and each of the independent affect scores was assessed by comparing the mean introspectiveness rating for Ss above and below the median on each affect variable. The results were in the same direction for both males and females, and the sexes were pooled to arrive at an over-all difference score. Table 2 shows the difference on mean introspective rating for Ss above and below the median on each of the tests and the biserial correlation relating each of the dichotomized variables to introspectiveness.

TABLE 2

MEAN INTROSPECTIVENESS RATING FOR SS ABOVE AND BELOW MEDIAN ON AFFECT SCORES AND BISERIAL CORRELATION BETWEEN AFFECT SCORE AND INTROSPECTIVENESS

	Introspectiveness Rating		
Variable	*Above Median*	*Below Median*	*Biserial r*
TAT Affect	4.5	2.9	.62+
Tachistoscope Affect	4.4	3.0	.54+
Figure Sorting Affect	4.0	3.3	.28‡
Human Movement	4.5	2.9	.62+

+$p < .005$; one tail
‡$p < .05$; one tail

The results indicate that the Ss who were above the median on each of the four affect scores were significantly more introspective than Ss below the median. The biserial correlations were also quite high with TAT affect and human movement being the best predictors of introspectiveness.

The results of this first study suggest that the tendency to apply affect labels to pictures of people does have a significant degree of intra-individual consistency and is associated both with the ascription of action to ink blot human percepts and to interview ratings of introspectiveness. Thus, we have the empirical beginnings of a construct which has objective operations for its measurement and a criterion behavior that can be predicted from each of the measures.

STUDY B

Since the tendency to apply affect labels to social stimuli showed consistency across instruments, we inquired next into the long-term stability of two of the measures for which we had earlier longitudinal data, the TAT weighted affect score and the human movement response. In addition, we tested the ability of each of these scores to predict the rating of introspectiveness in adulthood.

Method

Of the 64 Ss in Study A, 34 had TAT protocols administered at a median age of 17-6 and 53 had standard Rorschach protocols administered at a median age of 16-2. The eleven TAT stimuli were identical for both sexes and included Cards 1, 5, 14, 6 BM, 7 GF, 3 BM, 3 GF, 17 BM, 13 B, 12 F, and 12 M. The stories were scored for ascription of affect states to the figures and a weighting procedure was followed similar to the one used in Study A. The distribution of weighted affect scores for each sex was split at the median. Phi coefficients were then computed relating the weighted affect score on the adolescent protocol with the score obtained in adulthood approximately eight years later. The Rorschach protocols were scored for human movement and the distribution of human movement was split at the median. Chi square and phi coefficients were then computed relating occurrence of movement on the adolescent protocol with occurrence on the modified Rorschach stimuli. Finally, the Ss above and below the median on each score were compared with respect to mean rating on introspectiveness in the adult interview.

Results

Stability of Affect Scores. The human movement response showed moderate stability with the female data reaching a significant degree of reliability and the male data just falling short of significance. When the sexes were pooled, the resulting phi coefficient was +.42 ($p < .01$; two tails). The TAT weighted affect score was not as stable as human movement but was in the expected direction. The phi coefficient for the total sample of males and females was +.24 ($p = .16$; two tails).

Both human movement and weighted TAT affect scores obtained in adolescence predicted the adult rating of introspectiveness. For Ss above and below the median on human movement, the mean introspectiveness ratings were 4.1 versus 3.0 ($t = 2.44$; $p < .05$; two tails). For Ss above and below the median on TAT weighted affect, the mean ratings were 4.2 versus 2.8 ($t = 2.98$; $p < .01$; two tails). Thus, both human movement and TAT affect scores gathered in late adolescence were predictive of an introspective attitude eight years later in early adulthood.

Although it may seem surprising, occurrence of human movement responses during very early adolescence was also predictive of the adult rating of introspectiveness. For 49 of the 64 Ss in Study A (28 males and 21 females), there were two standard Rorschachs administered at 10½ and 13½ years of age. The number of human movement responses for these two early adolescent protocols was summed and the resulting distributions partitioned into low, medium, and high movement groups. The mean introspectiveness rating in adulthood was then computed for each of the three groups. The mean ratings for the low, medium, and high groups were 2.7, 3.5, and 4.5 for the boys and 3.4, 3.0, and 4.1 for the girls. The difference between the low and high groups was significant for the boys ($p < .01$; two tails) and short of statistical significance for the girls. When the sexes were pooled the difference between the lows and highs was statistically significant ($p < .05$; two tails). Thus, adolescent human movement responses were able to predict an S's ability to talk about motives, conflicts, and sources of anxiety over a dozen years later.

STUDY C

The results of the first two studies indicate that the tendency to conceptualize social stimuli in terms of affect states shows consistency across tests, stability over time, and validity correlates with an introspective attitude. The association between this response tendency and introspectiveness suggests an additional hypothesis regarding the significance of this conceptual style. The Ss rated as introspective were individuals who had conflictful thoughts available to verbal report. These people recognized sexual, aggressive, and dependent motivation in themselves and were able to accurately label these motives and related conflicts. Thus, they had available to consciousness concepts which dealt with conflictful ideas and events. In order to test the validity of this last statement we devised a concept formation task and related two of the affect measures (human movement and figure sorting affect) to ease of concept attainment where the content of the concepts included both conflictful and nonconflictful stimulus material. It was hypothesized that Ss high on the affect measures would learn the conflictful concepts earlier than Ss low on the affect scores, while ease of attainment of the neutral concepts would show no relation to the affect indices.

Method

The Ss were thirty female undergraduates who were tested individually by a female student approximately five years older than the subject. Each S was administered four tests in one ninety-minute session but we will only be concerned with the first three tests. The instructions were tape recorded and played back to each S with the author's voice as the source of instructions. The tests in order of administration were:

Modified Ink Blot Stimuli. An ink blot series consisting of 40 ink blots was administered to each S. This series included 23 of the stimuli used in Study A, four stimuli from the Behn-Rorschach, and thirteen from a new series of ink blots recently devised by Wayne Holtzmann of the University of Texas. The protocol was scored for number of human movement responses.

Concept Formation Task. Five concepts were selected for the learning task. Two of them dealt with a conflictful motive (sexual excitement and anger), two were neutral (number and texture), and one was neutral in content but dealt with an affect state (happiness or contentment). For each of the five concepts, ten stimuli were selected which were illustrative of the concept. For each concept five of the stimuli were words and five were pictures. For example, for the concept "anger" the words used were threaten, mad, jealous, violent, and hate. The five pictures illustrated people with angry expressions or fighting. For "texture," the five words were scaly, soft, crusts, gravel surface, and smooth. The five pictures illustrated various textured surfaces. For "sexual excitement" the five words were crave, exciting, desire, passion, and romantic. The five pictures depicted couples in a romantic embrace and women with seductive facial expressions. The language stimuli for "number" were greater, first, mile, second, and number, and the pictures illustrated a clock, a graph, a table of numbers, the number "2," and the stimulus "3rd." Finally, the concept of "happy" included the words enjoy, glad, laugh, happy, and satisfied. The pictures illustrated people in happy or pleasant situations, e.g., a woman smiling, family around a TV set. The S was seated in front of a milk glass screen and the stimuli were projected from the rear. The S indicated his response by pressing one of five buttons placed before him. The instructions were as follows:

> You will now be shown a series of stimuli on this screen. The series of stimuli is constructed so that each stimulus belongs to one of five concepts. As you know, a concept is a word or phrase which represents a group of similar things. In this experiment each concept will be named by a nonsense syllable and you see before you the five syllables. LAG, BIK, CEV, MUR, KAM. When the stimulus is shown on the screen you have to guess which concept it belongs to, that is, whether it's a LAG, a BIK, a CEV, a MUR, or a KAM. You will have ten seconds to decide which concept fits the stimulus, then whenever you are ready, press one of these five buttons corresponding to the concept you believe is correct. After you have pressed the button for your answer, the experimenter will tell you if you are right or wrong. She will say "that is correct" if your answer was right and "that is wrong" if your answer was incorrect. You will know after each stimulus whether you were right or wrong. At first, you can only guess at the correct concept, but with time you should be able to anticipate the correct concept.

The experimenter then administered some practice concepts to orient the S to the task and then administered the series of 50 test stimuli twice. If at the end of the 100 presentations the S had guessed the last 15 stimuli correctly the task was completed. If the S had not guessed the last 15 stimuli correctly, the E continued to present the stimuli until S responded correctly to 15 successive stimuli, or until the third presentation of 50 stimuli was completed. Each S was then asked to verbalize his concept for each of the five nonsense syllables. The measure of concept attainment was the trial number at which the S made his last error for that concept, i.e., the trial following which all successive presentations of an instance of a concept were correctly guessed and no incorrect use of the concept occurred to nonrelevant stimuli.

Figure Sorting Affect. Following the concept formation test, the S was successively presented with two arrays of cardboard figures (similar but not identical to those used in Study A) and asked to sort them on a conceptual basis. The S was asked to produce six sorts from each array. The protocols were scored for number of sorts in which figures were grouped together on the basis of similarity in affect state.

Results

The distributions for the trial of concept attainment were rectangular and the range of scores was very large. The median trial of attainment for the sex, anger, number, texture, and happy concepts were 78, 78, 62, 61, and 62 respectively. The sex and anger concepts were, therefore, more difficult to attain.

Since the distribution for trial of concept attainment and figure sorting affect were not normal, chi square was first applied to the data to test the relation between human movement, figure sorting affect, and ease of concept attainment. The three distributions were each divided at the median and chi squares (with Yates' correction) computed. There was a significant and positive relation between number of human movement responses and ease of attainment of the sex concept ($p < .05$; one tail) and the anger concept ($p < .05$; one tail). However, there was a completely chance relationship between human movement and attainment of each of the three nonconflictful concepts. Since the human movement distribution was normal, biserial correlation coefficients were also computed. The correlations between human movement and attainment of the sex, anger, number, texture, and happy concepts were +.69, +.50, +.05, .00, and .00 respectively with the first two coefficients reaching statistical significance.

Thus, ascription of action to humanized ink blot perceptions was associated with early acquisition of a concept which required the grouping of conflictful stimuli under a common label. The number of affect sorts in the figure sorting task showed no relationship to ease of concept attainment for any of the five concepts. This lack of relation could have been due to the fact that the figure sorting followed the concept formation task. Thus, the sorting responses could have been influenced by the concept task. In addition, the range of affect sorting responses was very narrow (0-7) in comparison to the range of human movement responses (4-21).

The above results are in agreement with data obtained from an earlier, less elaborate, group administered experiment in which human movement responses were related to ease of concept attainment of neutral and affectively laden concepts.

Method: Group Experiment

Subjects and Procedure. The Ss were 30 male and 33 female college undergraduates. The Ss were divided into two groups of 31 and 32 each (males and females in both groups) and each group was administered the modified Rorschach and a concept formation test in one session.

Scoring and Administration: Modified Rorschach. Colored slides of the 32 modified Rorschach stimuli used in Study A were flashed on a screen in front of the group and the Ss were instructed to write down what the stimulus "looked like to them." Each stimulus was on the screen for 20 seconds and the Ss were allowed ten extra seconds to write down their responses. The protocols were scored for human movement responses.

Concept Formation Test. Following the administration of the modified Rorschach, the Ss were presented with a pamphlet which contained six separate lists of words. The lists varied from 15 to 17 words in length and there was one list on each page. The Ss were given the following instructions:

> On the following sheets there are six concept formation tasks. There will be one practice list followed by the six test ones. In each test there will be listed a series of words on the left side of the page. Your job is to fit these words into four concepts: that is, to group all of the words into four different groups with each group of words going together on some common basis. After you have done the grouping, write the definition or basis for each concept in the space provided. The number of words in each of

> the concept groups does not have to be equal. Beside each word in the list, write the letter A, B, C, or D, indicating the concept to which the word belongs. You will be allowed three minutes for each list.

Each list was devised so that one of the concepts in each of the lists was an affect or feeling state and five of the affect concepts were potentially anxiety arousing. The six affectively laden concepts were: unpleasant internal feelings, anger, ambitious striving, loneliness, love, and general affect. The remaining three concepts in each of the lists did not involve affect states. The data were scored for number of correct lists. A correct list was defined as the grouping of all the words involving the affect state and the use of a conceptual label which described a feeling, mood, or affect.

Results

The Rorschach human movement distribution was divided into low, middle, and high groups and the mean number of correct lists was computed for these three groups. The results revealed a positive and linear relation between human movement and the number of correct lists for both sexes, and when the low movement ($N=22$) was compared with the high ($N=20$), there was a moderately significant difference between the number of correct lists ($p < .05$; one tail). There was no significant difference between Ss high or low on human movement with respect to number of lists finished or number of correct groupings of the nonaffect concepts.

Discussion

The Concept of Repression. One of the major implications of these studies is the possibility of developing measures of a construct closely related to repression. Repression is defined as the "nonavailability of thought material to verbal report." Since repressed material is usually anxiety arousing, we commonly assume that conflictful thoughts are most apt to be repressed. The measures utilized here, especially TAT affect and human movement, are predictive of (a) the tendency to think about the self and others in concepts dealing with motives and conflicts and (b) the ease with which conflictful stimuli can be accurately conceptualized. These two behaviors should be characteristic of the S who does *not* use repression as a primary defense against conflictful ideas.

Current research supports these conclusions. Cox and Sarason (4) found that male Ss scoring high on a test anxiety questionnaire, as compared with those scoring low, produced significantly more Rorschach movement responses. The test anxiety questionnaire was composed primarily of items tapping the degree to which an S admitted feeling worried and tense. Thus, movement responses were correlated with the tendency to report awareness of unpleasant affect.

Bieri and Blacker (2) reported that male college subjects who perceived people in a highly differentiated fashion on the Kelly Repertory Test (10) gave more human movement responses than subjects who did not see people in a differentiated fashion. Thus, males who were able to apply a wide variety of personality related labels to other people were more likely to produce human movement responses than Ss unable to differentiate people on personality dimensions. It would seem plausible to assume that the latter group, with a stereotyped perception of people, have either a minimal availability or weak behavioral tendency to use labels describing human motives and affect states.

Singer *et al.* (22) intercorrelated both Rorschach scores and a variety of other variables derived from the protocols of 100 male schizophrenics. Four factors were extracted from the intercorrelations, one of which was called introspectiveness. This introspective factor had high loadings on human movement, the attribution of affect and motive states to TAT figures, and admission of anxiety following failure.

Additional support for the current hypothesis comes from a study (11) in which neuropsychiatric patients were administered Rorschachs and then interviewed and rated on a variety of variables. The Ss high on human movement, as compared with those low, were more likely to (a) attribute their problems to interpersonal relations, (b) associate past childhood events with their problems, and (c) utilize interpersonal fantasy of the problem solving type in dealing with their emotional problems, i.e., think about their motives, conflicts, and feelings.

It is obvious that this construct, i.e., conceptualization of self and others in terms of affect and motive states, has relevance for prognosis in therapy. Therapists agree that when the patient has language symbols available to describe his feelings and conflicts, prognosis for therapy is enhanced. Affleck and Mednick (1) have recently reported that occurrence of human movement responses can be used to predict those individuals who stay in therapy as opposed to those who are early terminators.

Lorr, Katz, and Rubinstein (13) reported a significant, positive association between Taylor Manifest Anxiety Scale scores and length of stay in psychotherapy. The authors write . . .

> The remainder (in therapy) is seen as an anxious, self dissatisfied individual with some psychological insight who is willing to explore his personal problems with others (13, p. 327).

Studies by Frank *et al.* (5), Hiler (7), and Taulbee (23) found essentially similar results. The person who remains in therapy is one who reports experiencing anxiety and readily reports socially undesirable characteristics. Thus eagerness to work out one's problems in therapy, admission of anxiety, and the reporting of conflictful and undesirable thoughts appear to be positively intercorrelated.

I would like to suggest that this dimension of repression-nonrepression of anxiety arousing material influences the responses obtained on every instrument that gathers verbal responses — be it questionnaire, interview, or projective stimulus. That is, degree of repression of anxious material is a parameter that must be recognized as potentially operative in all situations where the content of verbal statements is being assessed, especially when that content refers to thoughts and behavior believed to be associated with anxiety. This means, for example, that a high score on a test anxiety scale may be produced by a person who is aware of and ready to admit conflictful ideas. Recent research supports this conclusion. Schonbar (19) has reported that subjects high on the Cattell IPAT Manifest Anxiety Scale recalled their dreams more frequently than Ss low in manifest anxiety. There were no differences between high and low anxious Ss on independent indices of unresolved tensions.

Trapp and Kausler (24) found that Ss high on the Taylor Manifest Anxiety Scale, as compared with those low, produced a greater number of negatively toned associations to nonsense syllables.

Finally, Chance (3) has reported that adults who report anxious and dysphoric feelings on a questionnaire are those who recall unpleasant rather than pleasant childhood memories.

It is urged that psychologists evaluating the presence of motivational and conflictful content on projective tests and questionnaires consider the possibility that the score obtained is a measure of the S's willingness or ability to produce this material rather than an index of his "hostile motivation" or "level of anxiety."

Affect Scores and Intelligence. Two final questions which seem relevant in evaluating the present results are: (a) to what degree is affect labeling a function of mere verbosity, and (b) what is the relation between these affect variables and measured intelligence? The affect measures derived from the TAT, figure sorting, and tachistoscope tasks in Study A showed no systematic relationship to length of verbal response. Further, over 90 per cent of the Ss gave thirty-two responses to the modified Rorschach stimuli and protocol length was constant on this test. Thus, mere verbal productivity is not sufficient to explain the consistency of these findings.

As far as intelligence is concerned, the results were more complicated. In Study A, TAT affect, tachistoscopic affect, and human movement showed positive correlations with Wechsler-Bellevue Verbal Scale IQ for both sexes (correlations in the low forties). Performance Scale IQ was correlated with these affect measures for men, but not for women. However, the correlations among most of these measures remained significantly positive when the variance due to IQ was controlled. Introspectiveness also showed a positive relation to IQ and one might posit that intelligence was the main determinant of the relationship between the affect scores and introspectiveness. However, the partial correlation coefficient between TAT affect and introspectiveness (both of which showed normal distributions) remained significant (partial $r = .33$ and $.47$ for males and females; $p < .05$; two tails), when the variance associated with Verbal Scale IQ was held constant. Thus, for this sample of subjects with average or above IQ, the tendency to apply affect labels or be introspective is not simply a consequent of high intelligence.

SUMMARY

This paper summarized some data on one type of fantasy response which has both structural and content qualities. The variable in question was the tendency to infer affect states to human figures. The four measures used were ascription of affect states to figures in TAT and tachistoscopically presented pictures, grouping of figures together on the basis of similarity in affect state, and the ascription of action to ink blot percepts of human figures. The data indicated that:

(a) This conceptual response tendency shows a significant degree of intra-individual consistency across a variety of stimulus situations, for all four variables were intercorrelated to a significant degree.

(b) Ascription of affect states to TAT figures and action to ink blot humans showed a moderate degree of stability from late adolescence to adulthood.

(c) Each of the four affect variables was significantly related to an interview based rating of introspectiveness, i.e., ability to talk of motives, conflicts and sources of anxiety. In addition, two of these indices (TAT affect and ink blot human movement) obtained in adolescence were able to predict degree of introspectiveness in adulthood.

(d) Finally, ascription of action to ink blot percepts of humans was correlated with ease of attainment of two conflictful concepts (sexuality and anger) but showed no relationship to ease of attainment of neutral, nonconflictful concepts.

It was suggested that the data formed the beginnings of a construct related to the process of repression versus nonrepression of conflictful thoughts. Subjects who have a prepotent tendency to infer affect states to TAT figures and action to ink blot human percepts tend to be aware of their own motives and conflicts.

The present results, together with the findings of other investigations, point to the usefulness of these measures for the early prognosis of progress in psychotherapy.

REFERENCES

1. Affleck, D. C., and Mednick, S. A.: The use of the Rorschach test in the prediction of the abrupt terminator in individual psychotherapy. *J. Consult. Psychol., 23*:125-128. 1959.
2. Bieri, J., and Blacker, E.: The generality of cognitive complexity in the perception of people and ink blots. *J. Abnorm. Social Psychol., 53*:112-117. 1956.
3. Chance, June E.: Some correlates of affective tone of early memories. *J. Consult. Psychol., 21*:203-205. 1957.
4. Cox, F. N., and Sarason, S. B.: Test Anxiety and Rorschach performance. *J. Abnorm. Social Psychol., 49*:371-377. 1954.
5. Frank, J. D., Gliedman, L. H., Imber, A. D., Nash, E. H. Jr., and Stone, A. R.: Why patients leave psychotherapy. *Arch. Neurol. Psychiat., 77*:283-299. 1957.
6. Henry, W. E.: *The Analysis of Fantasy.* New York, Wiley, 1956.
7. Hiler, E. W.: Psychological factors associated with premature termination of psychotherapy. Unpublished doctoral dissertation. Univ. of Michigan, 1954.
8. Holt, R. R.: Formal aspects of the TAT—a neglected resource. *J. Proj. Tech., 22*:163-172. 1958.
9. Kagan, J.: The long term stability of selected Rorschach responses. *J. Consult. Psychol., 24*:67-73. 1960.
10. Kelly, G. A.: *The Psychology of Personal Constructs: Vol. I. A Theory of Personality.* New York, Norton, 1955.
11. King, G. F.: A theoretical and experimental consideration of the Rorschach human movement response. *Psychol. Monogr., 72:* Whole No. 458. 1958.
12. Lindzey, G.: On the classification of projective techniques. *Psychol. Bull., 56*:156-168. 1959.
13. Lorr, M., Katz, M. M., and Rubinstein, E. A.: The prediction of length of stay in psychotherapy. *J. Consult. Psychol., 22*:321-327. 1958.
14. McClelland, D. C.: *Personality.* New York, Sloane, 1951.
15. Moss, H. A.: The generality of cautiousness as a defense behavior. Unpublished doctoral dissertation. The Ohio State Univer., 1958.
16. Osgood, C. E., Suci, G. H., and Tannenbaum, P. H.: *The Measurement of Meaning.* Urbana, Univ. of Illinois Press, 1957.

17. Rapaport, D.: Cognitive structures. In *Contemporary Approaches to Cognition*. Cambridge, Harvard Univ. Press, 1957, pp. 157-200.
18. Rapaport, D., Gill., M. R., and Schafer, R.: *Diagnostic Psychological Testing: Vol. II*. Chicago, Yr. Bk. Pub., 1946.
19. Schonbar, Rosalea A.: Some manifest characteristics of recallers and nonrecallers of dreams. *J. Consult. Psychol., 23*:387-389. 1959.
20. Shatin, L.: The constriction-dilation dimension in Rorschach and TAT. *J. Clin. Psychol., 14*:150-154. 1958.
21. Shneidman, E. S.: *The Make-a-Picture-Story Test*. New York, The Psychol. Corp., 1949.
22. Singer, J. L., Wilensky, H., and McCraven, Vivian G.: Delaying capacity, fantasy, and planning ability: A factorial study of some basic ego functions. *J. Consult. Psychol., 20*:375-383. 1956.
23. Taulbee, E. S.: Relationship between certain personality variables and continuation in psychotherapy. *J. Consult. Psychol., 22*:83-89. 1958.
24. Trapp., E. P., and Kausler, D. H.: Association tendencies of groups differentiated on the Taylor Manifest Anxiety Scale. *J. Consult. Psychol., 23*:387-389. 1959.
25. Wyatt, F.: The scoring and analysis of the Thematic Apperception Test. *J. Psychol., 24*:319-330. 1947.

DISCUSSION OF DR. KAGAN'S PAPER

Irving E. Sigel, Ph.D.
Primary Discussant

Dr. *Sigel:* Dr. Kagan's paper is an illuminating set of empirical facts, but it is not embedded in a conceptual framework. He reports the inter-relationships among response tendencies on various types of stimulus situation and finds very exciting and important relationships.

He has not developed the significance of these findings nor pointed to some of the issues arising from his methodology. In discussing this paper, I should like to focus on two problems: (a) conceptual (b) methodological.

All of us are familiar with the complexity of problems involved in the study of cognitive behavior. The term cognitive itself is fraught with many difficulties. Its definition is not consistent among all users. There is no need here to elaborate all the problems except to mention that, aside from the problem of definition, there is also the problem of conception. Granting even that we can define cognitive functioning to everyone's satisfaction, can we come to agreement conceptually? By this is meant the relevance and significance for cognitive function in psychology. Judging from recent publications, there is increased interest and admission that, after all, man does have some rational components. How he thinks, organizes his world, and judges it are therefore of some import to psychologists. The danger, however, is that this increased interest in cognitive function can lead to an artificial isolation of cognitive operations, ignoring the conative dimensions of man.

Dr. Kagan's paper is a good illustration of reasonable interdependence – he demonstrates the connection between affect and thought, or shall we say between conation and cognition.

The basic hypothesis in this research seems to be that individuals will organize stimulus material in a consistent way. The implications of this are tremendous. Numerous interesting and important research questions arise regarding antecedents for particular cognitive styles.

The finding that introspectiveness correlates positively and significantly with an affective approach is of particular interest today. In Dr. Kagan's scoring, affective sorts are also inferential ones. This indicates that inferential approaches and introspectiveness are related. Further elaboration of this point is important and should be made. It follows that individuals who organize material in inferential ways are psychologically different from those using a noninferential approach. Dr. Kagan did not emphasize the difference on a formal basis. Rather he tended to emphasize the content connotation of affective labelling and minimize the formal aspects here. For example, one question arises. Is introspectiveness a necessary condition for inferential thought regardless of the content of the inference? Or does using inferential sorts depend on the available stimuli; e.g., inferential when opportunities for using affect are available, but not necessarily under other stimulus conditions. Yet we should ask what predictions could be made regarding consistency of affect labelling when dealing with mathematical or other material where affective content is not available? This is one type of implication that seems fruitful to explore.

A further question is how to account for the relationship. Can the paradigm of a defense system be applied to help explain the findings? Are people who are introspective sensitized toward self and project their feelings, or does it mean they are inhibited or defensive in their identification of feelings in others? They do see significantly more M on the Rorschach and they are consistently sensitive to affective features of the environment. Time does not permit developing a number of other similar questions. I am sure Dr. Kagan is aware of the need for increased conceptualization here.

Let us turn to some methodological issues. One is the nature of the stimuli employed. The figures used in the sorting tests have built-in ambiguity. The Rorschach has ambiguity too. Thus, one correlation obtained between M and affect may be due to the similarity in task demands — the labelling of ambiguous or unstructured stimuli. If this is so, the stylistic consistency is not so surprising. The TAT poses the same problem.

For Dr. Kagan the question resolves itself to this: When style or consistency is being examined, how varied and divergent can the stimuli be? Are individuals consistent in cognitive style essentially within situations making similar demands: TAT figures and sorting-task figures? Are there critical dimensions within the stimuli that may predetermine consistency? Or, the other side of the argument, how diverse can situations be and still show the stylistic consistency presented? Does the person who manifests affective orientation with a TAT react affectively to music, to preferences in reading, while on the job, etc? Only by more extensive laboratory testing and life history examination can the data be obtained to answer such questions. My point is that cognitive style must be carefully described in terms of stimuli of the situation, and then how pervasive particular styles are become the empirical questions.

In studying this phenomenon, extreme care must be taken to consider task demands, e.g., sorting as compared to free association or showing language preferences, etc., as well as the content of the stimuli employed. One can almost artificially induce consistency of cognitive style if the test materials lend themselves to similar orientations.

Another methodological question refers to the use of the concept formation (I prefer the term concept attainment) task employed by Dr. Kagan. Why not have the concepts learned by the subjects be of equal difficulty in order to test for the predominance of a particular orientation? One is not sure whether the difficulty question confounds the results. In such experimentation the problem of difficulty as well as the problem of content of concept to be attained creates a dual problem for the subject. Is it legitimate to assume that one learns the concept more readily if it is consistent with his cognitive orientation? It first must be established how facile the subject is in attaining new concepts and then determine variations in learning efficiency when the content of the concept varies.

Finally, the order of presentation of a variety of tasks is an important factor to consider when examining such questions as cognitive style. When a subject is given a large battery of tests in which there is content overlap, one must determine the effect of the order of presentation of the tests. Set, perseveration, fatigue, individual perception of tasks, are among the factors that come into play to influence performance. When under such testing conditions the subject doesn't even know when he is right or wrong, he may proceed in a consistent fashion believing that this is what is expected.

All of the preceding point to a host of conceptual and methodological problems which must be attacked in order to clarify the issues in research in cognitive functioning. Experimentation with various stimuli, modes of presentation, and ranges of content are called for.

Dr. Kagan's paper poses many provocative questions and a number of fruitful problems for further research. Above all it is an exciting venture into a challenging area, the interaction between cognitive and conative aspects of human behavior.

Dr. Atkinson: Let me give you some data that may be relevant. I don't yet want to label the variable involved. We did an experiment once with variable X in a study of perceptual sensitivity. We used Blackwell's technique of putting a picture in each of four quadrants on a slide and flashing the slide on the screen. In three of the quadrants there was an inanimate object or a book having the same figural properties as the human face and the fourth quadrant contained a human face. We then projected these stimuli at a level that was below the threshold of conscious awareness and asked the subjects only one question: Which of the four quadrants is clearest or brightest? We did not ask, "What's there?" since they couldn't report that; but which stands out the most? This was a technique that Blum had used in some of his research on perceptual defense. We found that a group that was high on variable X frequently chose the quadrant which had the human face even though they couldn't see it. Another researcher has reported a correlation of plus .45 between this variable X and test anxiety scores. Would this fit into your matrix?

Dr. Kagan: What is X?

Dr. Atkinson: Need for affiliation, which is a score based on imagery having to do with establishing, maintaining, and restoring positive affective relations with people. What you are calling a cognitive style may be a very generalized instrumental tendency of persons who are moving toward people. I think you might develop the argument that seeing human movement in the Rorschach and being sensitive to human affects could reasonably be construed as a behavior that a person who moves toward people would show.

One of the defining behavioral symptoms of need for affiliation is that fraternity brothers who are high in need for affiliation are more frequently reported by their peers as approval-seeking. Affiliation is a motive that expresses itself in behavior and what you are calling a style may not be the screen through which motivation expresses itself as much as something in the service of particular needs.

Dr. Tomkins: I was helping Dr. Donald McKinnon do some assessment of creative and noncreative female mathematicians this year and I was supposed to find out something about the dynamics of the development of their interest in mathematics. What I actually did was to conduct what I call an affect interview and I asked them, among other things, "When was the last time you felt very ashamed, very angry, very afraid," and so on. If a person could talk about one affect, she could talk about another one. But more interesting was the fact that the creative female mathematician was quite able to talk about her affects. The others I interviewed were quite unable to in a way that really floored me.

It was my impression that there was a strong positive relationship here between the ability to communicate affect and the freedom of the individual to do creative mathematics. Of course, there are a number of differences I could talk about. The creative ones happened to be much younger, which introduced an additional factor.

Dr. Holt: Some years ago when Dr. Lester Luborsky and I were working on the selection of psychiatric residents we were facing a number of the same problems. In going over the literature, largely the statement about the kind of personal variables to be sought in people who were in training for this kind of work, we found many references to things like empathy, sensitivity, psychological-mindedness, psychological gift, or talent. These terms were used in a number of cases more or less interchangeably. They all seemed to have something to do with awareness of, specifically, a psychological dimension of experience, an interest in people's motives, a capacity for feeling them, etc.

Dr. Rotter: There is no need, is there, to talk about motive and style as different kinds of things? If you think of the stylistic variable as having any kind of behavioral references, style is really descriptive of the nature of behavior, whether you think of it in terms of the organizing, or thinking level, or whether you prefer to think of it in terms of test responses. At the same time this behavior, like all behaviors, has motivational characteristics. I just don't understand your setting up a dichotomy between a motivational variable and a stylistic variable.

Dr. Holt: The aim is to get at an aspect of behavior that is different from motivation, that is, independent of it, that cuts across different kinds of motives. Now, certainly in any concrete act you can't separate motivation from ability, from style, from defenses. There are all kinds of variables that go into any particular concrete act, but conceptually we can and must separate them and see the extent to which they are independent dimensions that we need to hypothesize and measure if we are to cope with human personality.

Dr. Rotter: You are asserting that some behaviors have motivational characteristics and some behaviors don't have motivational characteristics?

Dr. Holt: I am saying all behaviors have stylistic characteristics, some have motivational characteristics. That doesn't mean that motivation is style. The stylistic aspect of a behavior is a qualitative how-it-is-done aspect. I feel style is orthogonal to motive.

Dr. Lazarus: I am not objecting to the use of the term "style." I think I am objecting, however, to saying that there is style which somehow is independent of or orthogonal to a concept called motivation. Even if you talk about rate of talking as a style, you can always think of these as choices which have become acquired, that is, habitual behavior patterns which have become acquired as choices on the part of the individual.

Dr. Holt: But with a style in talking, you don't have to assume that the person has a *need* to talk fast or a *need* to talk slowly.

Dr. Sigel: If you do observations of children you can see clear-cut stylistic differences in the motor area. You don't know anything about why the child climbs or to what end, but you can discriminate among the children who climb in certain ways — the way in which he climbs is independent of the goal sought.

Dr. Atkinson: I would be willing to accept two possibilities. One possibility is a complete independence between what kinds of goals a person is trying to attain, which we will call motivation, and how he goes about doing it. I think that is the distinction that Klein makes. "What?" is the goal question, and "How?" is the style question. If motive and style turned out to be completely independent, it would pose serious methodological problems for the assessment of motives. If we had this kind of independence, many of our cognitive methods of assessing motivation would be seriously questioned.

The other possibility is that particular cognitive styles develop in the service of particular motives. Today there is a suggestion that the attribution of affect to people, which may be a style, might have developed in the service of a need for affiliation. This cognitive style might, nevertheless, characterize the behavior of the person in a great variety of situations, even when the need for affiiliation is not the important thing. That is, if we argue that cognitive style develops early but develops early in the service of particular motives, it is conceivable to me that we might turn up correlations between cognitive style measures and particular motives. If it made good sense we might think of an historical connection. Nevertheless, the cognitive style might characterize the person in every situation, particularly if the particular motive is a dominant one, if this is the salient aspect of his personality.

When you go at projectives the way some of us have, looking only at isolated motives, you lose contact with the whole person. It seems to me the cognitive style-motive issue might have in it the beginning of a way to integrate the total person, the type of person who has a dominant motive, and who develops a particular style that characterizes him in a wide variety of situations. That, of course, is arguing one hypothesis. The other one, and again I think equally plausible, is that cognitive styles are completely independent of motives. If that turns out to be true we will have to examine seriously the way we are measuring motives. If we have a complete confounding, then what I call high need for achievement may not be that at all, but a kind of cognitive style.

Dr. Tomkins: The word "style" is being used for an invariance of some kind. You look at certain variables and if they are invariant with respect to different needs, you suggest they are styles. I would argue that we can't afford to overlook any large structuring principle that works. That is to say, human beings move around in space, they think, they perceive, they feel, they remember. These are different response domains and it is an empirical question: Which of these domains begins to assume a monopolistic and organizing influence? If a psychologist can discover a set of invariances in any domain, more power to him. But let him not polarize us into the situation where we can't look for relationships any place else.

THE ROLE OF THE STIMULUS IN THE MANIFESTATION OF FANTASY

Bernard I. Murstein, Ph.D.
University of Portland

THE CONCEPTUAL model utilized herein is that a projective response is the result of the pooled interaction of the "stimulus," "background" and "organismic" variables in the behavioral situation (60). The projective response is thus analogous to the concept of adaptation level (AL) expounded by Helson (34, 35). According to this concept variation in any of the variables may change the adaptation level (i.e., the projective response). This fact will be readily observable if we utilize the general equation derived from Helson (35), but modified for our purposes. Projective Response = $S^aB^bO^c$ where *a, b,* and *c* are weighting factors showing the importance attributed to *S* the stimulus, *B* the background, and *O* the organismic factor.

Helson has found it helpful to expand his equation into logarithmic form. Not enough is known of the projective test situation at present however to warrant much speculation as to the best mathematical form to utilize. The multiplicative form utilized represents a "first" guess.

In adapting the above equation to fantasy responses it may be of benefit to spell out in some detail the referents of each of the above variables.

STIMULUS PROPERTIES

It is important to distinguish between two often confounded variables, *structure* and *ambiguity*. *Structure* will be used in the physical sense, i.e., "The arrangement and organic union of parts in a body or object (27, p. 2401). *Ambiguity* is defined by the same dictionary (p. 86) as "The quality of being ambiguous, obscure, or *uncertain in meaning,* especially where either of two interpretations is possible." When, therefore, a projective technique is said to possess little structure, the reference will be to its physical stimulus properties. When ambiguity is alluded to, the reference will be to the *meaning* of the situation. Some examples may clarify the matter. Card 13MF on the TAT, which depicts a nude woman beneath the covers of a bed and a man standing with his arms across his face is highly *structured*. It is also *ambiguous* since the scene is capable of multiple interpretation. Accordingly, many *Ss* see the scene as depicting illicit love, while others state that the woman is ill or has died.

Certain of the projective techniques such as the Draw-A-Person Test possess no stimulus structure and are completely unstructured since the materials consist usually of an 8 x 11 sheet of white paper and a pencil. The Rorschach strictly speaking possesses form ranging from moderately structured to fairly unstructured depending upon the card and the section of the blot referred to. It is also, objectively speaking, non-ambiguous since it is obviously an inkblot. When, however, the *S* is requested to state what the blot looks like it becomes much more ambiguous since the response "ink blot" is not allowed or certainly not encouraged. The TAT, which is more heterogeneous in makeup, contains some unstructured cards in which the characters are difficult to distinguish and some in which the characters are readily distinguished but their actions are ambiguous since their feelings or the actions they engage in are not readily apparent.

BACKGROUND CHARACTERISTICS

Here, reference is made to all factors determining the projective response which are not part of the *S's* behavioral pattern nor part of the stimulus properties of the test. "Background characteristics" refer to the environment in which the test is administered. Of concern is the locale of the test: college classroom, guidance clinic, state hospital, or penal institution. Other pertinent variables are the instructions, actions of the examiner, including his reaction to the *S* and to the testing situation. Not to be overlooked is the stimulus value of the examiner insofar as this can be objectively ascertained. Is the examiner attractive, young, easy-going, insecure, or ugly, old, stern and confident?

ORGANISMIC CHARACTERISTICS

The organismic variable is itself a function of other variables. It includes the objective traits possessed by the individual, his self-concept with regard to these traits and the totality of his experiences apropos of these traits. The first two of these variables, objective trait possession and self-concept, are easier to assess than "past experience."

It may be of interest to compare this schema with that of Rotter (67, 68), whose equation is

$$B. P. = + (E. \& R. V.)$$

where B. P. = behavior potential, E. = expectancy of reinforcement, and R. V. = reinforcement value of the behavior.

This view is similar to that of Atkinson (3) although the latter spells out the meaning of these variables in the projective technique situation in somewhat greater detail. Rotter's equation may be compared with the equation formulated herein if we understand that E is itself primarily dependent on the "stimulus" and "background" variables, while R. V. is a function of the "organismic" variable. There are, however, some important differences. First, when Rotter refers to "expectancy" he is referring to *subjective* expectancy. The paradigm employed in this paper when referring to "stimulus" and "background" variables has reference to their *objective properties.* The subjective influence on behavior in the AL concept is accounted for in the "organismic" variable. The possible advantages of the AL approach in comparison to the Rotter and Atkinson approaches are twofold:

1. The nature of "expectancy" is spelled out in directing attention to the stimulus and background factors which largely comprise expectancy.

2. By making behavior a function of both objective and subjective factors greater precision of measurement is possible. It is easier for example to record the objective value of TAT cards on the dimension of hostility (stimulus variable) and to record the objective background data (kind of instructions, lo-

cale of test, characteristics of the examiner) than it would be to determine the subjective value of "expectancy" of reinforcement.

Having stressed the importance of the stimulus variables in my conceptual framework I shall attempt to indicate the progress in clarifying the role of the stimulus in thematic techniques.

THE ZEITGEIST

The first systemizer of projective techniques was Frank, who advanced the belief that projective techniques evoke responses tapping the "private world of the individual comprising as it does the feelings, urges, beliefs, attitudes, and desires of which he may be dimly aware and which he is often reluctant to admit to himself much less to others. . . ." (25, p. 66). This belief is continued in the war years and typified by the rationale utilized for the TAT by Murray (57).

"The procedure is merely that of presenting a series of pictures to a subject and encouraging him to tell stories about them, invented on the spur of the moment. The fact that stories collected in this way often reveal significant components of personality is dependent on the prevalence of two psychological tendencies: the tendency of people to interpret an ambiguous human situation in conformity with their past experiences and present wants, and the tendency of those who write stories to do likewise: draw on the fund of their experiences and express their sentiments and needs, whether conscious or unconscious.

"If the pictures are presented as a test of imagination, the subject's interest, together with his need for approval, can be so involved in the task that he forgets his sensitive self and the necessity of defending it against the probings of the examiner, and before he knows it he has said things about an invented character that apply to himself, things which he would have been reluctant to confess in response to a direct question. As a rule the subject leaves the test happily unaware that he has presented the psychologist with what amounts to an x-ray picture of his inner self" (57, p. 1).

The advent of the "new look" in psychology, around 1947, further tarnished the value of the objective properties of stimuli as determiners of perception. Even the perception of such clearly defined objects as coins and swastikas was held not to be independent of personality. By 1951 we find Rosenzweig asserting that "The stimulus was dethroned . . . the stimulus is often merely a trigger, sometimes only an 'excuse' for evoking prepared reactions that have already been set in motion by the inner stimulation of an impulse" (66, p. 215).

The key to analysis, Rosenzweig goes on to state, is in an R-R approach rather than an S-R one. The R-R approach means that the response to a projective technique is correlated with responses to other behavioral situations. Since each person has the same overt stimulus (for example, the 10 "male" series of cards in the TAT) the effect of the stimulus is standard for each person and therefore is cancelled out. The reader familiar with Rosenzweig's article will note a certain paradox here. On the one hand Rosenzweig views projective techniques as instruments designed for tapping the idioverse (*the population of feelings and behaviorisms in a given individual*) as compared to the nomothetic nature of most paper and pencil tests which are designed to ferret out differences between people. On the other hand, his description of the importance of the stimulus as a standard indicates that the data he obtains are most meaningfully interpreted as *differences between persons.* Moreover, these differences are meaningless unless anchored down by a knowledge of the stimulus value of the projective technique. By way of illustration, suppose individual "A" obtains a hostility score three times as high as individual "B" in response to a series of thematic cards. Does this indicate that he is three times as hostile as "B"? We could also adapt "A" as our standard and say that "B" perceives *far less hostility than he ought to.* In the absence of information about the stimulus value of the cards (as well as "background" factors) we are, to use an analogy, in the position of trying to decide whether it is a warm or cold day, knowing only that the temperature is several degrees higher today than yesterday.

Suppose now we bring individual "C" into the picture, noting that he has the same hostility score as "A." Are they equally hostile in their fantasy perceptions? One would be loathe to answer affirmatively, particularly if we add that "A" follows the stimulus pull of the cards, whereas "C" derives his score by giving stories involving hostility to ambiguous cards, and non-hostile stories to "hostile" cards. In truth, there is no evidence currently to conclude that "C" is in reality more hostile than "A," nor even that he is more deviant. The task of determining the behavioral correlates of deviancy in perception and story-telling from the stimulus properties of thematic techniques, however, appears to be promising, and capable of attainment in the immediate future. It is apparent then that it would be much more meaningful from an idiopathic point of view to assess the *absolute* rather than the *relative* effect of the stimulus on the response. To accomplish this task, however, requires an investigation of the absolute properties of the stimulus and it is to this problem that we now turn.

THE IMPORTANCE OF THE STIMULUS IN THEMATIC TYPE TESTS

It is one thing to assert that the stimulus properties of thematic pictures are important and quite another to determine the objective properties of the cards. There are three common methods of procedure:

1. ***Define the Stimulus by the Response.*** Beck (5) has used this method in arriving at his good (F+) and poor (F–) ratings in the Rorschach. His "mail order house" *S*s were considered the "normal" group and their Rorschach protocols were compared with those of a schizophrenic population. If a particular section of a blot was seen as a bat by more normal people than by schizophrenics, the "bat" was called F+. If more schizophrenics than normals saw a "mouse" then mouse was scored F–. The responses of the group thus determined the objective value of the card.

2. ***The Experimenter and/or a Few of His Colleagues Judge the Pictures and Assign Ratings.*** The Klopfer "form level" approach (43) uses this method. The rationale is that the examiner familiar with the blots and population he deals with is best qualified to appraise the objective qualities of the blot.

3. ***A Third Possibility is to Have Judges Composed of a***

Large Number of People Who are More or Less Representative of the Population on Which the Established Norms are to be Utilized. These persons judge the pictures in a manner analogous to the construction of attitude scales, each picture being treated as an attitude item. TAT-type pictures have been scaled by Auld, Eron, and Laffal (4), Lesser (51), and Murstein, Coulter, Bowdish, David, Fisher, Furth and Hanson (61). Ranking or rating procedures have been followed by Jacobs (37), Birney (12), and Haber and Alpert (33).

Each of these methods has its limitations. Defining a stimulus by its response necessitates the assumption that the response is not influenced by factors other than the "official" stimulus. If S *does not* evince hostility in a story told to the card, does this mean that the card contains no hostile characteristics? Is it not possible that the arousal of another motive than that depicted by the stimulus may determine the response? Moreover, do not the "background" and examiner influence the character of the response?

The objection to the use of an expert opinion in determining the stimulus value is twofold. First the expert has usually heard so many stories to the card that it is probable that his own perception now reflects a rough summary of the responses he has collected to the picture. Secondly, we must face the fact that there are differences of opinion as to what constitutes the objective properties of the picture, these opinions perhaps varying with age, sex, and personality. Under these circumstances the stimulus value assigned should be as representative of the measured group as possible and as reliable as possible. A large number of representative persons should more readily meet both of these requirements than the judgments of one or two clinicians.

It should not be assumed, however, that the use of such a group precludes distortion. *Au contraire*! The large group may account for representativeness of population but almost never is the representativeness of the environment in which the testing takes place considered (15). Thus, scaling a group of pictures for degree of "sexuality" would undoubtedly yield different values at Ye Olde Bar & Grille than on the campus of Podunk

University. Still, all in all, the use of a large available group such as a sophomore class seems justifiable if *the characteristics to be judged are not likely to be affected by the campus locale nor the academic position of the experimenter.*

An even more stringent approach was utilized by Haber and Alpert in selecting their pictures. Not only did the pictures used have to be high in the motive examined (achievement) as derived from the judges' cognitive rankings, but the pictures had to be high in achievement imagery obtained via the stories and be low in the elicitation of motives other than the one examined.

At this point, a review of the studies relating to the importance of the stimulus in the TAT will be undertaken. The first part will deal with the TAT cards themselves and the second with the effect of stimulus variations.

STIMULUS VALUES IN THE TAT

Murray (57) in the manual for the Thematic Apperception Test, describes the male series TAT as ". . . divided into two series of ten pictures each, the pictures of the second series (numbers 11 through 20) being purposely more unusual, dramatic, and bizarre than those of the first" (p. 2).

Among the first to stress the crucial role of the stimulus in the TAT was Eron (21, 22, 23, 24). He gave the "male" series to a group of college males and neuropsychiatric patients. The patients were matched and their stories were evaluated by his "emotional tone" and "emotional outcome" ratings. He found that the first ten or "everyday" series, which in the main contained humans in everyday social situations, elicited the greater part of the themes of aggression, hostility, conflict and occasional aspiration, while the second ten or "fairy tale" series containing few instances of social situations, provoked stories of a descriptive, impersonal and symbolic nature. Moreover, considered as a whole, the cards produced far more themes of disequilibrium than of equilibrium. This finding is corroborated by Lebo (47) who found that his college students found most of the cards to be "sad." Newbigging (62), however, found most of the stories elicited from his London college population were rated "happy." It is not known whether the differences are due to the greater structuring in Eron's scoring system, to cultural differences in the population studied, or to the fact that different TAT cards were utilized (Newbigging's cards were selected by virtue of their being spaced evenly along a happiness-sadness continuum). The median response time and median number of words per story correlated negatively with the happiness of the pictures. This finding unfortunately is confounded, as recognized by Newbigging, because the pictures had been given in the order "most happy" to "least happy." Ideally each *S* should have received the pictures either randomized or in a Latin Square sequence.

As might be expected, attempts to predict psychiatric classification and overt behavior via the content of the stories has suffered because of the structuring of the pictures. Thus, Eron's diagnostic groups (college males, neuropsychiatric males, schizophrenic males) were not separated by the ratings derived from the stories (23).

Similarly Jensen (38) was unable to separate overtly aggressive boys from passive ones on the basis of content although he could do so by virtue of *the language used to tell the stories.*

Weisskopf (81) found that college students, when asked to describe both sets, projected significantly more fantasy material to the first "everyday" series than to the latter "fairy tale" one. A heterosexual group of college students were asked by Bijou and Kenny (9) to rank 21 "male" series TAT cards according to their ambiguity (estimated number of interpretations that might be derived from each card). The authors computed a *t* test between the mean ambiguity level for the first Murray series as compared to the second one. The second "fairy tale" series proved to be more ambiguous, at the .05 level of confidence, although the authors did not reject the null hypothesis in post-adopting an .01 level. They also compared the "personality revealingness" value of the first series as compared to the second one by analyzing the themes of the TAT stories (42). The mean "personality revealingness" value of the "everyday" series proved to be somewhat higher than the "fairy tale" series, but the *t* test of .92 was not statistically significant.

Dividing fifteen cards, selected from the twenty-one, into three groups of five cards each, according to their high, medium, or low ambiguity, they found that the medium-ambiguous series yielded themes of greater "personality revealingness" than either the low or highly ambiguous series. The difference in "revealingness" was not a function of the length of the story told. Dividing the fifteen cards into the dichotomy used by Murray, eight were found to belong to the "everyday" series, while seven were assigned to the "fairy tale" series. No significant difference in "transcendence" (mean number of responses going beyond pure description) was found between the two groups of cards. The interaction between ambiguity, "transcendence," and exposure time showed that the medium-ambiguity pictures yielded a greater amount of "transcendence" than the high-ambiguity ones under long exposure time (2 minutes) but not under short exposure time (5 seconds). The medium-ambiguity group of pictures did, however, show a higher "transcendence" than the least ambiguous pictures under both long and short exposure time.

Ullmann (77) and Gurel and Ullmann (32) in a series of studies showed that the entire "male" series of twenty cards is sufficiently structured as to differ significantly in number of "emotional words" elicited as well as in "transcendence." Moreover, clinicians have gravitated perhaps unknowingly towards the use of cards eliciting greater emotional depth in that the correlation between median number of "emotional words" per card and frequency of use by thirty-five clinicians was found to be .62. Noting also that Gurel and Ullmann found a correlation of .85 between "transcendence" and median number of "emotional words" and that Bijou and Kenny earlier found that medium-ambiguous cards elicited the greatest amount of "transcendence," it seems quite probable that medium-ambiguous cards also elicit the greatest number of "emotional words." In a later study (78) Ullmann reported that "externalizers" (projectors) and "acter-outers" (impulsive behavior) produced more "emotional words" to cards that ranked high in the production of these words than did "internalizers" (defense characterized by denial) who produced most of their "emotional words" to cards low in the hierarchy of emotional word arousal. These findings seem to indicate that "internalizers" are less influenced by the cue properties of the cards in the production of stories than are "externalizers" and "acter-outers."

Murstein (59), using Bijou and Kenny's (9) rankings of ambiguity of a "male" series of cards with some modifications, found significant curvilinear correlations with the number of themes elicited from an all-male population composed of both college students and psychiatric patients used by Eron (22). The moderately ambiguous cards produced the most themes, while the high- and low-ambiguous cards were less productive. While the curvilinear correlation involving the heterogeneous group and male-only group proved to be highly significant, the use of the female rankings of ambiguity did not yield a significant difference between eta and the Pearson *r*. The range of etas was from .43 to .95, the Pearson *r*'s ranging from .03 to .09.

In another study, Murstein (58) had twelve female *S*s rank a "female" series of twenty cards for "pleasantness" as well as for "physiological ambiguity." When compared to the "emotional tone" scores obtained by Eron (24) from a similar female population, the following average correlations were obtained: ambiguity vs. emotional tone .56; ambiguity vs. pleasantness .40; pleasantness vs. emotional tone .59. Thus, the results indicated that the more ambiguous the TAT card, the more "pleasant" the "emotional tone" of the story; the more "pleasant" the stimulus properties of the card, the more "pleasant" the "emotional tone" of the stories.

The stability of fantasy as a function of stimulus ambiguity was investigated by Kagan (40). The TAT protocols administered to a group of normal boys and girls on three separate occasions when the median ages were 8-9, 11-6, and 14-6 were culled from the files. While generally speaking the content dimensions were not stable over time, the only two motives showing stability over time, n-Achievement and n-Physical Aggression, were obtained to pictures whose stimulus properties are highly suggestive of these needs. These were one (boy with violin), 17BM (man on rope) for n-Achievement, and 3BM (slouched figure with object nearby usually seen as a gun) for n-Physical Aggression. Kagan concludes that long term stability of a fantasy motive is dependent upon the structure of the TAT cards.

Making the assumption that the presence of a motive in a fantasy story reflects the motive and response tendencies of an individual, he further states that a theme told to an ambiguous stimulus may be a less sensitive indicator of a motivational predisposition than a theme told to a non-ambiguous stimulus. There is some experimental support for this statement. Kagan (39) earlier found that boys rated as non-aggressive were differentiated from boys rated as aggressive via stories told to highly structured hostile pictures but not differentiated by ambiguous pictures. Murray (56) found sleep-deprived *Ss* were similarly differentiated from non-deprived *Ss* by pictures suggesting sleep but were not so differentiated by ambiguous pictures. Rosenstein (mentioned in Atkinson, 3, p. 611) separated chemistry majors from physical education majors by the use of pictures portraying laboratory scenes. Scenes depicting athletic competition did not separate the group. The reason for this failure presumably is that athletic prowess is a fairly universal motive for college males.

It is perhaps too much to expect such unanimity in the field of psychology, and sure enough Atkinson (2) reports a study which strikes a contrary note, though not concerned with TAT cards. He classified students as high and low achievers on the basis of stories to eight pictures. He then computed the differences between the groups for the three high-cue pictures and for two low-cue pictures. The mean differences were almost identical. He thereby concluded that: "The effect of suggesting achievement situations in pictures containing adult characters is equivalent to the addition of a constant value to what the n-Ach (-ievement, i.e., achievement motive) score would be in response to pictures having comparable adult characters but an unstructured or unrelated situation" (2, p. 33).

Epstein and Smith (20) found that hungry *Ss* perceived fewer food responses to high-pull pictures for hunger than to low-pull pictures. The authors employ an approach-avoidance paradigm to explain their results. It would seem that the contrary results stress the fact that the "background" and "organismic" variables must be considered as well as the stimulus variables if behavior is to be accurately predicted.

DIFFERENCES BETWEEN MEN AND WOMEN

Bijou and Kenny (9) had twenty-eight men and twenty-three women college students rank the "male" series of twenty-one cards for ambiguity, and achieved a rho correlation of .75 between the sexes. Since the multi-judge reliability was .80, there appeared to be little sex difference with regard to the judgment of ambiguity. A similar correlation for judgments of the continuum happy-sad resulted in a r of .96 between male and female college students in London (62). Lastly, Murstein and associates (61) report a correlation of .93 for the dimension of hostility in their studies of fifty men and fifty women students at Portland University.

Differences between the sexes, however, appear in the process of telling stories if not in perceptual judgments. Weisskopf (81) found that women tended to have significantly higher "transcendence" indices than men for *both* the "male" ($p < .02$) and "female" ($p < .05$) series. Women used significantly more words in stories told to relatively "unhappy" pictures as compared to "happier" ones in the study by Newbigging. This behavior was not found for men. The response time for the men increased significantly as the happiness of the pictures decreased, but this was not true for women. Men also tended to tell significantly happier stories than the women irrespective of the picture concerned. Overall, the response time of women as well as total number of words used per story was significantly shorter than for men.

The results of Newbigging indicate that women are more stimulus-bound in their perceptions than are men. These results accord nicely with the findings by Witkin and Asch (86) as well as Ford and Beach (26). The former, drawing from a wide range of perceptual experiments, conclude that women are more dependent than men in the dependence of their perceptual process upon the stimulus field. The latter indicate that the sexual behavior of higher-order mammals including man indicates likewise that female sexual behavior is more rigidly structured by the stimulus field than is the case for men. It will be noted, however, that Weisskopf's results are contrary to this conclusion and indicate that a good deal more evidence is necessary before our conclusions harden.

CONCLUSIONS DERIVED FROM THE TAT

1. The twenty cards from the "male" series are sufficiently structured as to differ significantly in "transcendence" and number of "emotional" words elicited. Generally speaking, clinicians are aware of these differences and tend to utilize cards high in "emotional" impact more frequently than cards low in this regard. Moreover, certain personality groupings ("externalizers" and "acter-outers") are maximally prone to produce "emotional" words to these high-cue cards, while other persons ("internalizers") produce more "emotional" words than the other group to low-cue cards.

2. Increasing the "psychological" ambiguity of a picture does not result in an increased response to the picture. Rather, the relationship is curvilinear with an increased response productivity being followed by a decrease as the gestalt of the picture begins to disappear.

3. The meaningfulness of stories for personality evaluation seems to follow a similar curvilinear relationship with ambiguity, with the medium-ambiguous pictures facilitating the expression of the most revealing stories.

4. The "pleasantness" of stories seems to increase as ambiguity increases. This occurrence may be a function of the fact that most highly structured cards on the TAT are negatively structured. Another factor may be that as the stimulus "pull" becomes weaker, the personality needs of the *S*, as well as the background factors such as the personality of the examiner, the reason the test is being given, and the locale of the test, become increasingly important. It seems reasonable to assume that most persons for cultural reasons prefer to see "good" rather than "bad." Also of importance for college students who form the hard core of *Ss* used in these experiments is the need of impressing and favorably influencing the examiner who may

well be perceived as a teacher-surrogate. Under these conditions, the exceedingly ambiguous pictures may act as a cue to set the *S* on his guard to put his best perceptual foot forward.

5. The effect of varying the time of exposure is minimal providing the *S* may perceive the cards for at least a few seconds. Presenting the card for only a fraction of a second seriously affects the productivity of response. Allowing the picture to be exposed for two minutes has little if any advantage over showing it for five seconds.

6. There is little difference between men and women in the cognitive judgment of such personality dimensions as "ambiguity," "happiness" and "hostility." There is considerable difference between the sexes in story-telling approach, but the evidence is contradictory and adequate conclusions await further research.

7. The stability of fantasy needs and presses is low, and appears to vary inversely with stimulus structure. The diagnosis of psychiatric groupings via TAT protocols would not seem to be profitable using *content* as a basis for diagnosis. Elsewhere Holt (36) and Schafer (69) present arguments for the possibilities of *formal analysis.*

THEMATIC MODIFICATIONS

In the effort to ferret out the importance of different aspects of the stimulus, investigators have turned to TAT-type cards, modifying the cards to suit the particular question under investigation. In this section we shall consider variations in lighting, exposure time, structure of the card, and variations of the central figure.

Variations in Lighting

Weisskopf (81) had college students write descriptions of several TAT cards which were presented either in an unaltered form, or as pictures taken under reduced exposure, giving the pictures a hazy effect. No significant differences in "transcendence" were obtained. More recently, Bradley and Lysaker (14), using a life-like TAT type picture, varied the illumination from normal to three successive darker stages of illumination, as well as three lighter ones. The *S*s were several hundred housewives (range 122 to 171 for each stage) with each *S* seeing the picture in only one stage. Similar to Weisskopf's (81) finding, no difference in productivity of response was noted. In analyzing the content of associations with regard to the picture, however, a clear positive linear relationship was found between increasing degree of darkness and pleasantness of association. When the picture was used with a varying degree of increasing light, the picture slightly lighter than the control elicited the most favorable association, followed by the next lighter picture, the lightest picture, and the control picture. The effect of light was apparently not a linear function, with a moderate amount of supranormal illumination considered most pleasant, and either more or less illumination considered less pleasant.

It seems clear that with the absence of light, the stimulus properties of the picture became increasingly vague, thus resulting in an increasing "internal" perception on the part of the *S*. In the relative absence of sensory stimulation, a person finds it easier to introspect and to relate personal material with considerably less inhibition than under normal circumstances. The soothing, yet fantasy enriching, effect of darkness is what makes a motion picture more enjoyable in a "movie" house than under the semi-lighted atmosphere of a television room. Moreover, many psychotherapists have their seating arranged so as to be out of the patient's direct gaze on the assumption that there is less interference with the patient's private thoughts. Here, too, the darkened room is often more likely to educe free association than is the normally lighted one.

The supra-illumination effects are more difficult to interpret. Possibly a limited amount of extra light obscures the picture and permits pleasant fantasies to be evoked. An increasing amount of light may be irritating to the nervous system and accordingly elicit less pleasant associations. The relative lack of "pleasantness" occurring under normal illumination may have stemmed from the stimulus properties being most clear at this stage, and hence the *Ss* having been more likely to respect the neutral emotional tone of the pictures (woman baking a cake).

The question may arise as to why an association elicited under less than optimal sensory conditions should be pleasant rather than unpleasant. Two factors may be suspected of playing a part here. In the first place, fantasy often occurs as a temporary vicarious means of satisfying needs and tensions which are as yet unsatisfied in the outer world. The teen-age girl dreams of a prince charming, the young executive imagines himself as a junior vice-president. Many of our fantasies are thus related to a need to succeed in a variety of activities, the attainment of which would be associated with pleasant feelings. It is, of course, sure that unpleasant, even hostile, tensions may also be present. The young girl may be annoyed because a rival seems to have currently won her prince charming; the young executive may chafe under the imposition of being a "yes-man" to the "boss." Nevertheless, militating against the appearance of hostility on the TAT would be the fact that the *S* would probably deem the testing situation as inappropriate for the expression of hostility. The inhibitory effect of the "background" might be due to a weak generalization gradient from hostility to the "boss" to hostility in an ambiguous situation, or the *S* might simply inhibit all expression of hostility because he felt he was being judged and he wanted to make a good impression. Since it is socially acceptable to perceive pleasant things and not as acceptable to perceive hostility in others, it is more than likely that when the stimulus properties of the object being perceived are weak enough, the *S* will be apt to fantasize publicly only over a narrow band of ideation, namely those topics which do not conflict with what the *S* perceives to be the ego demands of the social situation in which he is involved.

Variations in Time Exposure

Weisskopf (81) presented college *S*s with two sets of TAT pictures exposed for .2 of a second and for five seconds. The latter group manifested a higher number of fantasy scores ("transcendence"). Kenny (41) exposed the TAT pictures to college *S*s for five seconds and two minutes, respectively. The correlation between "personality revealingness" of the themes elicited and "transcendence" was .62 and .64 for the five-second and two-minute conditions of exposure.

Apparently, the individual fantasizes with greater personal involvement as well as greater productivity when he has sufficient time to appraise the stimulus qualities of the card. After a sufficient time has elapsed (optimally, perhaps, a few seconds), added length of exposure has little effect.

Variations in the "Ground"

Completely traced line drawings proved to be more effective in evincing fantasy than incompletely traced ones, in two studies by Weisskopf (82) and Weisskopf-Joelson and Lynn (84). Bradley and Lysaker (14) reported that varying the background of a picture, when the figure (woman baking a cake) remained constant, had no effect insofar as altering the productivity of responses to the pictures. These studies seem to indicate that ambiguity of the figure affects fantasy production, but alteration of the background has little effect provided the figure remains clear.

The Picture-less TAT

The novel idea of simply reading the descriptions of the TAT cards as provided by Murray, (57), to the *S*s instead of presenting the cards themselves was hit upon by Lebo and Harrigan (48). Their justification in so doing was the possibility that verbal descriptions might be easier to translate than redrawing a TAT picture to conform to another cultural milieu; it might be easier to administer to a group, and might be valuable as a projective test for the blind. A counterbalanced order of presentation of TAT cards and their spoken descriptions was utilized, the *S*s being college women. Over-all analysis of word count, idea count, story mood, outcome mood, level of response and dynamic content indicated little difference between the presentations. Comparison of the normative data of Eron (22), Eron, Terry and Callahan (23), and Terry (74) with the responses to the pictures, and to the spoken description was made. The correlations on the aforementioned variables were only negligibly lower for spoken description vs. the norm than for the TAT pictures vs. the norm. In another study Lebo and Sherry (49) compared the spoken descriptions with the written descriptions (i.e., Murray's description was typed out one description per page and presented to the *S*s who also were college women). Comparison of the two versions yielded no significant differences for the variables "number of words," "number of ideas," "emotional tone of story," "emotional tone of outcome," "response level," "dynamic content," and "perceptual range," though the written description was either equal or superior in each variable. Both measures correlated significantly with the normative data for the variables "story mood" and "common themes." The correlation did not quite reach significance for "level of response" and "outcome mood."

The results are a bit trying for the TAT. Apparently, many of the TAT pictures are so unambiguous that it matters little whether visual or verbal description of the card is presented. It would be interesting to see whether these results would hold if a series of the more highly ambiguous TAT cards had been utilized. The Lebo studies, rather than necessarily stressing the utility of non-picture forms of the TAT, may well have indicated why the highly unambiguous TAT has repeatedly failed to differentiate varying psychiatric groups. Perhaps, what is needed for accurate personality diagnosis is a new set of highly structured yet highly ambiguous cards.

Variations of Central Figures

Thompson Modification: Murray (57) suggested that at least one card should be chosen showing a figure of approximately the same age and sex as the subject. Tomkins (76), on the other hand, has proposed that the TAT may be interpreted most meaningfully by taking into account the psychological distance of the stimulus from the *S*. Moreover, the meaningfulness of the responses elicited by the TAT should be a function of the "remoteness" of the thematic material presented.

Thompson (75), adhering to Murray's suggestion, believes that the closer the stimulus resembles the actual *S*, the more the *S* will identify with the figure, and accordingly, be likely to produce more meaningful material. To test this hypothesis, he constructed a set of TAT cards similar to the original TAT, except that Negro characters were substituted for white ones. Using twenty-six Negro college students from a Negro school, the Thompson TAT was group-administered by a Negro examiner who flashed the cards on a screen by means of a projector. The *Ss* were instructed to write stories to the projected pictures. In order to compare the Murray and Thompson versions, the *Ss* were divided into two groups of thirteen each, with half receiving the Thompson series first and the Murray version second, while the other half received both series with the order of presentation reversed. Thompson found a significant increase ($p < .01$) in story length to the Thompson TAT for each of the ten cards used.

More recent studies, however, have been highly critical of the value of the Thompson modification. Riess, Schwartz, and Cottingham (65) used thirty Negroes and thirty white females from Hunter College in New York City. The usual AB, BA order for the two TAT tests was followed, using a Negro examiner for half of both the Negro and white group, and a white examiner for the other half. The results were:

"Negroes and whites in the North produce stories that differ insignificantly in length regardless of whether the stimulus material is Negro or not, and regardless of the color of the examiner, with the exception of a tendency for northern whites to increase story length on Negro stimulus material with a Negro examiner" (65, p. 708).

In another article using the same data (70), the authors investigated the number of ideas appearing in the stories rather than merely the story length. Their data showed that (a) Negroes expressed the most ideas when given the cards by a white examiner. The set of cards used was of little consequence. (b) Whites gave more ideas when the Thompson set was used. This result was not a function of whether the examiner was white or Negro. (c) The production of ideas was quite low when the stimulus, examiner, and *Ss* were of the same race.

Korchin, Mitchell, and Meltzoff (44) used two groups of eighty Negro and eighty white male *Ss* from Philadelphia, half of each group being "middle class" while the other half was of "low" socioeconomic status. The examiner was white. An analysis of variance showed no significant effects due to race, nor any significant interaction between race and status for story length. Only the "class" differences were significant ($p < .01$), with the "middle class" telling the longer stories.

In still another experiment, Light (53) divided twenty-six white students into two groups of thirteen each, one-half receiving the Murray TAT, while the other received the Thompson version. No significant differences in story length were found, although Light found certain themes to be more frequent with the Thompson set. These themes were crime, poverty, occupational inferiority, witchcraft, and prostitution.

Cook (16) used sixty male college students (30 Negro, 30 white), divided into four groups of fifteen each. One-half of the Negro and white groups each received the Thompson TAT, while the remaining two groups received the Murray TAT. The latter group was composed of the remaining Negro and white *S*s, respectively. The examiner here also was white, and most of the *S*s had spent at least fifteen years in the South. Cook wished to examine the relationship between the *S* and the stimuli used. The measures of ego-defensiveness used were word count, compliance with instructions given, vagueness of stories, number of words indicating uncertainty, number of alternatives offered, number of references to the pictures (i.e., excessive use of description), and number of different themes offered. No significant differences solely attributable to the two sets of pictures were found. Both the Negroes and whites were interviewed with regard to their perception of the test. It was found that the great majority of the Negroes perceived both the Murray and Thompson TATs as dealing with "people in general." On the other hand, the whites perceived the Thompson TAT as dealing with Negroes rather than "people in general." Hence, it would be expected that the chief differences between the Negro and white *S*s would be found with regard to the Thompson TAT. This was precisely what happened. The Murray TAT yielded only two significant findings at the .05 level. Negroes used more words indicating uncertainty and made more references to the pictures.

On the Thompson TAT, however, the protocols of the whites had a significantly higher word count. The Negroes had a greater number of alternatives, uncertainty, vagueness, and references to the pictures. All measures were significant beyond the .01 level. Cook believed his findings indicated that the more remote the relationship between the stimulus and the *S*, the less the ego-defensiveness.

The foregoing studies lead to a consideration of the following:

1. Are Negroes to be treated as a homogeneous class? The data hardly suggests that such a treatment is warranted. Apparently, it would be more justifiable if anything to use a "socio-economic class" approach to interpretation.

2. The degree of similarity between stimulus and *S* is of itself insufficient as an explanation of the type of response elicited because it does not take cognizance of the background characteristics. Thus, in Schwartz's (70) work, Negro *S*s who were administered Negro cards by a Negro examiner manifested a smaller number of ideas in their stories than any other grouping. Negro *S*s receiving the same cards from a white examiner expressed the greatest number of ideas. For the white *S*s, however, the Negro cards seemed to educe the greatest number of ideas regardless of the race of the examiner.

3. In view of the fact that the Stimulus X Background X Person interaction seems to be of considerable importance in determining the nature of the response, the *t* test favored by previous investigators would appear to be a relatively insensitive statistic. The analysis of variance would appear to be more powerful in this regard.

4. The question arises as to whether story length or number of ideas expressed is an adequate measure of the *S*'s involvement in the TAT. Is it not conceivable that sophisticated *S*s (college students) might manifest an excessive superficial verboseness to mask the projection of manifest or covert needs? What is needed is a quantitative scale measuring the personality meaningfulness of the stories rather than indirect and unproven correlates such as "word-count" and "number of ideas."

5. The influence of the stimulus is not a simple function of its similarity to subject. The culture plays a crucial role in the interpretation of perception. Negroes tended to perceive the Murray TAT characters not as "whites" but as "people in general." Whites, however, perceived the Thompson cards as

dealing with "Negroes." Thus, majority populations are far more apt to perceive minorities as "different" than vice versa. They also are less apt to have had contact with them. Minority groups such as Negroes, however, must constantly live in a "white" world. Although certainly aware of the special privileges whites possess which they do not have, they must adapt perceptually to the majority white culture, if they are to be maximally adjusted to their environment. Thus, the finding that Negro girls preferred white dolls to Negro ones (30) should come as no surprise. When, however, Negroes are confronted with the Thompson figures, particularly in the presence of a white examiner, it is apparent to them that something unusual and different is involved, and they tend to be cautious and vague.

Projection to Same Sex Figures vs. Opposite Sex Figures: McIntyre (55) used short film strips as projective instruments and congruity of answers to MMPI items between the self and predictions for the character depicted in the film as an index of projection. His results indicate that the chief determinant of projection was *the scene depicted.* No evidence was found that *Ss* projected more onto same sex figures. In fact, it is noteworthy that while all of the *Ss* were young college men and women, the most effective scenes for producing projection had as their chief protagonists an old man an an old woman, respectively. A subsequent study by Silverstein (71) employed parallel sets of male and female pictures of approximately the same age and sex as his students. The Edwards Personal Preference Schedule (EPPS) also was administered. The correlations between nine needs as assessed by Murray's TAT system and the EPPS were quite low and did not differentiate same sex identification via projection from opposite sex projection, the findings thus agreeing with those of McIntyre.

There is, however, some evidence hinting at greater facilitation for opposite sex projection for women. DeCharms, Morrison, Reitman and McClelland (17) report a study by Morrison, who found in testing college women who held office, that n-Achievement scores derived from stories written to pictures of career women would *not predict* performance in an achievement situation. In order to manifest performance, the picture cues had to be of men or of women in non-achievement situations.

Even more explicit evidence is forthcoming from Veroff, Wilcox, and Atkinson (79). Under both "relaxed" and "achievement-oriented" conditions, women students produced significantly more achievement themes to pictures of males than females. Both sexes were comparable in the situation depicted, differing essentially only in the sex of the figure. The authors suspected that background cues, the classroom situation, male examiner, etc., may have influenced the women to strive harder. Consequently, a second experiment stressing low motivation to achieve was undertaken in which the presence of males was omitted. The results were identical to those of the first experiment.

It would seem then that "women" as a class behave similarly to Negroes in following certain prescribed cultural rules. The prototype of achievement in our society "the male" is much more important in stimulating themes of fantasy achievement than is the presence of a figure of the same sex as the perceiver. It appears likely that "culture" exceeds "narcissism" as a motivating agent for other needs also, but here the experimental evidence is largely lacking.

Other Modifications: Lasaga y Travieso and Martinez-Arango (45), in working with nuns, found no improvement in the diagnostic value of the TAT stories when they substituted nuns for the usual TAT central figures. Weisskopf and Dunlevy (83) used three groups of ten each of normal, crippled, and obese male undergraduates. Each *Ss* received three sets of TAT cards, one of which was unmodified, the other sets being modified so that the central figure was obese in one set and crippled in the other. The *Ss* were asked to describe the cards rather than to tell a story. The results indicated that the mean transcendental index (number of elements in the stories going beyond pure description) was significantly less for the obese figures than for the normal and crippled ones. This trend was consistent among all three groups.

In a related study, Greenbaum, Qualtere, Carruth, and Cruickshank (31) administered several TAT pictures and modified versions which were generally similar except that the figures were depicted as physically handicapped. The method of assessment was a rating for depth of projection. The authors concluded that the original TAT series encouraged a greater level of productivity than the modified series ($p < .04$). They state that "...in pictures where the child is forced to perceive a handicap his main preoccupation is with this barrier and he only cursorily treats the nature of the goal region from which the handicap is barring him. On the other hand, pictures which do not force a response to a handicap seem to encourage the production of fantasy material in which the child tells about the nature of his wishes in regard to interpersonal goals" (31, p. 43).

In another study, Weisskopf-Joelson and Money (85) modified the TAT with somewhat crude approximations of the original drawings. In the first series, the head of the central character was a more or less neutral face. In the second session, the same cards had actual photos of the *S*s' heads instead of the original neutral heads. A control group was used to account for the effect of repetition. No significant increase in projection was found for the "photo" set over the neutral set as measured by the transcendence index and word content. In addition, the diagnostic value of the "photo" set when judged by two judges was not found to be any higher than the other set.

In a recent study by Edgar and Shneidman (18) a group composed of psychotics, psychoneurotics, and persons suffering from personality disorders was used. Material obtained from "patient government" discussions was compared with that obtained from the MAPS technique, and a variation of this technique, in which full-length cut-out photos of every person in residence on the ward at the time as well as all staff members, was used. Using Bales Interaction Process Method to analyze the data, the authors found as much reluctance to show antagonism to photos of peer figures as to peers in face-to-face contact, such as occasioned by the group meetings. They suggest that one use of the "photo" technique may be in measuring the feelings of need for evaluation from others and feelings of need for direction. Nevertheless, the authors concluded that "photos, in general, seem to elicit more positive feeling than fantasy figures did, the latter calling forth more overt aggression" (18, p. 11).

It would appear then that similarity of the central character to the *S* is not only non-effectual in furthering projection but actually may be detrimental. Since obesity is the butt of jokes in our society, it is unlikely that fat persons derive any satisfying tension reduction in identifying with obese characters. Crippled individuals also would prefer to forget about their handicap. Before concluding, however, that similarity *per se* inhibits projection, it may be of value to recall that the background characteristics (purpose of the experiment) are much more readily apparent to the *S* under these conditions. Thus, while the *S* is taking the TAT under the usual nomothetic experimental procedure, he may not suspect that his responses as an individual will be noteworthy. The *S* who, as in Weisskopf-Joelson and Lynn's study (84) sees a photo of his head planted somewhat out of context on a crude sketch may not suffer this delusion.

It may be that under non-social conditions similarity might well stimulate projection. Indeed, the mirror probably does richly stimulate fantasies in teen-agers as they carefully preen themselves before going out on a "heavy date." Some support for this statement comes from the data of Beier, Izard, Smock, and Tougas (6) who gave young adults sets of photos of younger, peer, and older persons having them signify the ones liked and disliked. Male *Ss* most frequently "liked" peer males, while female *Ss* preferred peer females.

In sum, however, as far as the usual testing procedure is concerned, it seems clear that similarity to the point of idiosyncratic identification promotes ego-defensiveness and a reduction in the degree of projection.

Variations in Stimulus Dimensions: Relatively little is known in this area. Solkoff (72) used two sets of pictures selected from magazines, one set representing the dimension of hostility, the other the dimension of sexuality. The *Ss* were Iowa undergraduate college students. Half of the *Ss* were told to give their stories in the first person, the other half in the third person. The cards consisted of six pictures from each stimulus dimension. Analysis of the stories indicated a significant interaction between instructions and stimulus dimension. Thus, initial reaction time was significantly increased from third to first person instructions only for the hostility pictures. Inhibition ratings were increased under first person instructions only for the sexual pictures. Verbal productivity was greatest for the hostile cards and least for the sexual series. The only consistent finding was that inhibition ratings were highest for the cards within each dimension which were highest on the dimension characteristic. The author concluded that "verbal output as a response measure does not in fact operate in a consistent fashion in various 'socially' inhibiting situations" (72, p. 81).

The Use of Animals Instead of Humans: Bellak and Bellak (7), believing that children identify more readily with pictures containing animal figures than with human ones, created the Children's Apperception Test. Bills (10) compared a series of pictures of rabbits with several TAT cards using as *Ss* children (both male and female) aged five through ten. Significantly longer stories were obtained with the "rabbit" pictures. In another study (11), a new group of third-grade *Ss* had six play-therapy sessions and then took the "rabbit" pictures test and TAT. Both tests correlated only slightly with the material obtained from play therapy using Murray's rating approach for manifest needs. Their correlations with each other also were rather low, ranging from –.09 to .58.

Biersdorf and Marcuse (8) used a broad approach to the problem employing CAT cards and cards especially constructed, which were almost identical to the CAT cards except that humans were substituted for the animals while keeping the same emotional expressions. The *Ss* were thirty first graders, the group containing both sexes. Not only were no significant differences found between numbers of words used in both tests, but further analysis revealed no difference in length of time before response, length of response time, number of words used, number of ideas used, number of characters mentioned in the pictures, and the number mentioned who were not in the pictures. Mainord and Marcuse (54), using the same set of cards, tested emotionally disturbed boys and girls (mean age, seven years) and found similar nonsignificant differences for the aforementioned quantitative measures. They, however, also asked five clinicians to rate the protocols as to "clinical usefulness," the judges being ignorant of the hypotheses of the authors and the stimulus properties of the cards eliciting the protocols. The human figure cards were found to be more "clinically useful" at better than an .001 level of confidence.

In yet another study comparing the CAT with its "humanized" analogue, Furuya (28) studied the protocols of seventy-two children ranging in age from six to twelve. He was interested in answers to the following two questions:

1. With different criteria and age-groups — from those of Biersdorf and Marcuse (8) and Mainord and Marcuse (54) — what kind of difference will be found between the productivity to animal pictures and human pictures, equivalent in scenes and situations?

2. Is there any tendency toward relative decrease of productivity to animal pictures compared with human pictures as the children grow older? (28, p. 248).

The results are confounded with methods of presentation in that the youngest children received the cards individually, while the older ones received the cards as a group. Nevertheless, the results are consistent with earlier studies in indicating the superiority of the human pictures. Of the twenty *t* tests, four proved to be significant at the .05 level or better. These indicated that the percentage of stories containing expressions of feeling, significant conflict, and having a definite outcome, was significantly higher for the human pictures as compared to the animal ones.

No tendency was found for any increase or decrease in the relative productivity of the animal or human pictures from the youngest to the oldest age range.

Lastly, the author implies that the results might have been even more extensive but for the fact that "most of the animal pictures that have been used were 'personified or human-like' animal pictures" (28, p. 252).

Light (52) working with nine- and ten-year-olds, found significant differences between the CAT and TAT. The TAT was found to elicit more feelings, different kind of feelings, conflicts, number and kinds of outcomes, number and kinds of themes, and number of figures. Only the number of words was not significantly different from test to test. Light believed that this result may have been due to the imposed time limit of seven minutes to write the stories after the pictures had been flashed on a screen.

Armstrong (1), working with intellectually superior first, second, and third graders, also found no difference in number of words used between the CAT and a set of pictures corresponding in style and composition but containing humans instead of animals. The Weisskopf transcendence index, however, indicated that the children gave significantly more nondescriptive statements to the human series.

The effect of both stories and pictures was examined by Boyd and Mandler (13) in a study of eight-year-olds. All *S*s were first told a story containing either animals or humans as the central characters, followed by a similar set of pictures. A 2X2X2 factorial design was employed based on the variables (a) type of stimulus story (animal or human), (b) content of stimulus story ("good" or socially approved behavior vs. "bad" or socially disapproved behavior), and (c) type of stimulus picture (animal or human). The majority of the *S*s preferred the animal stories but tended to be more involved in the human ones. Contrary to the aforementioned studies the animal pictures tended to elicit more emotional material.

The results of the foregoing studies point at two issues — one theoretical, the other practical. The theoretical issue is whether children do or do not project more meaningful responses to animal pictures as compared to human ones. The evidence is contradictory here. The question is, however, were these findings due to the *nature of the situation portrayed rather than simply to the presence of animals or humans*? The answer to our theoretical question will not be solved by *any* crucial experiment, but by a *series* of crucial experiments. Only if a *representative sample* of behavioral situations is examined can the supremacy of animals or humans as stimulus figures be determined. It may be that no clear-cut supremacy will ever be demonstrated. Even if the majority of experiments favor one type of figure, however, it will always be conceivable that given another type of stimulus situation, the inferior figure might prove to be the superior one.

The second issue, the practical one, is much more definitive. Is the CAT the best thematic technique available for children? The evidence clearly indicates that it is inferior to a "humanized" analogue and to the TAT. Is the cause of this inferiority the animals themselves or the situation depicted? Only further research can provide an answer.

Conclusions derived from TAT Modifications. 1. A lack of visual stimulation (darkness) seems to enhance the occurrence of pleasant association to TAT-type cards. The effect of supranormal illumination is more complex with a slight increase resulting in a manifestation of more pleasant responses than under normal lighting. As the intensity of illumination is further increased, however, the pleasantness of association diminishes.

2. Mere similarity between the *S* and the central figure in the stimulus cards is insufficient to expedite the projection of meaningful responses. Projection is most readily elicited when the stimulus figure is culturally high in status and yet not so similar to the *S* as to arouse his suspicion as to the purpose of testing. It is not similarity *per se* that accounts for the censoring of responses, but the new awareness of the background characteristics (i.e., purpose of the testing) which causes the *S* to filter his responses. Other background factors such as the race of the examiner may also play a part in determining the nature of the response elicited.

3. The fact that Negro *Ss* when tested by white examiners tend to be superficial in approach, hewing closely to mere description of the thematic cards, hardly means that they do not have tensions which could be perceptually expressed. Rather, the lack of involvement may have been a function of a low expectancy of satisfying these needs even to the extent of verbalizing them, because of the inhibiting presence of the examiner. With a Negro examiner, however, the stories told by Negroes would probably be more meaningful, though this particular comparison has not as yet been made.

The tendency of whites to give richer stories to the Thompson stories rather than to the Murray TAT would seem to be a way of expressing either a need for verbalization of tolerance or a feeling of freedom in talking about a socially subservient group. Presumably, the Northern *S*s would be most prone to strive for tolerance in their stories, while Southern students (Light's group?) might be more apt to play upon the social and economic inferiority of Negroes.

4. Racial differences as determiners of projection have been overestimated while socioeconomic factors have been underplayed. Middle-class Negroes may have more in common with middle-class whites with regard to perceived needs, than have middle-class Negroes with lower-class Negroes.

5. The CAT has been shown to be somewhat less effective than human pictures in eliciting meaningful projective responses from children. The theoretical issue of human vs. animal pictures is at present unresolved.

SCALING OF THEMATIC CARDS

One of the first researchers to report measurement of the stimulus properties of cards was Symonds (73). He had judges rate a series of cards and stories told to the cards on a five-point scale in which adolescents were the central characters. The dimensions rated included goodness of story, genuineness of story, emotion expressed in picture, and lack of detail in the picture. The ten variables were intercorrelated, and the results indicated that the best pictures were those having a minimum of detail, vague in theme, incomplete in content, and yet suggesting characters who were readily identified with by the adolescents.

Jacobs (37) used average intercorrelation of judges' rankings for various personality dimensions. For fourteen "goal concerns" the *r*'s ranged from .20 to .60 over twelve pictures. The pictures with high *r*'s may be conceived of as the most unambiguous, the ones with the lower *r*'s as the most ambiguous.

The rank method has been employed also by Birney (12) on a series of "achievement" pictures. The ranks were found to correlate with a percentage of achievement imagery in the stories of $r = .41$, despite the fact that most of the pictures were high in achievement-pull.

A possible difficulty with this method resides in the heterogeneity of the pictures. Where the pictures tend to be fairly similar, the rankings are bound to contain a good deal of error variance and the intercorrelations will be spuriously low. The result might be that the pictures would be erroneously described as more ambiguous than they actually are. This objection is overcome through the use of more absolute measures such as the Thurstone scales. More will be said about these scales shortly.

A multi-criterion method of selecting pictures having high stimulus pull for "achievement" was employed by Haber and Alpert (33). Their three criteria were (1) In pre-tests at least 75 per cent of the *Ss* had to write stories containing achievement imagery. (2) A paired-comparison method was employed to obtain values in achievement for each of the cards. (3) Each picture was rated for several concerns. To be selected, the first three concerns ranked by every *S* for a picture must have been achievement-related. Of a total of twelve pictures initially selected, forty met all these criteria. For these pictures the correlation between cue-rank and achievement imagery was .71.

Scaling Methods. The first actual scaling of thematic cards resulted from a study of Auld, Eron and Laffal (4). They felt that a scaling technique might supply the answer to two pressing problems:

1. "When should one consider two responses as indicative of a single underlying trait (habit or motive of the subject)? and 2. Conceding that two or more responses both reveal the strength of the habit or motive, how can one combine the ratings obtained from the two responses into a single rating of the habit or motive?" (4, p. 423)

The authors felt that the solution to both problems lay in a method which would order the subjects unequivocally regardless of the weights that might be assigned. An approximation to such a scale might be achieved with the Guttman technique providing that the coefficient of reproducibility was greater than .90.

The *Ss* were 100 sailors at a submarine school; the test was the Navy Group TAT, an amalgam of especially drawn pictures and selected TAT cards. The task was to scale the cards for the dimensions of *aggression* and *sex*. The rationale underlying the construction of scales was that the pictures differed in "stimulus pull" for any given dimension (sex, for example). *Ss* also differ in their need to tell stories with sexual themes. Moreover, the greater the need the less strong the stimulus pull required to elicit a sexual theme. *Ss* with little need to express sexual themes should react only, if at all, to blatantly sexual pictures. It should then be possible to order each person's "sexual story expression" once the stimulus properties of the cards are known. One measure of the stimulus pull is the percentage of *Ss* giving "sex stories" to each of the cards. Starting out with ten cards, only three cards evoked stories indicating aggression from any appreciable number of *Ss*. The small number of cards as well as the fact that they were not evenly spaced (78%, 22%, 21%) led to an abandonment of the construction of an aggression scale. Four cards were extracted for the sex scale however, the coefficient of reproducibility being .93.

The ordering of *Ss* by the test-retest method yielded a product moment correlation of .13. This finding, however, is highly equivocal since the *Ss* on the first occasion were applying for participation in an experiment and on the second occasion were just emerging from a submarine after having been submerged for thirty days. The authors do, however, give some important advice with regard to scale construction. First they advise that the probability of achieving a scale is enhanced by having a large number of cards to start with. Further, one should select cards which are specifically designed to elicit the motive in question. Moreover, the picture should, if possible, tap *no other motive*. One possible weakness of the Guttman scale, however, is the fact that it fails to take into account the inhibitory forces acting on the *S*. It has already been demonstrated in the work of Pittluck (63). Kagan (39) and Lesser (50) show that consideration of these inhibitory factors greatly enhances predictive ability with regard to overt behavior.

Using seventy-two boys aged ten to thirteen, Lesser (51) also attempted to construct a Guttman scale of aggression. A special set of pictures was drawn, each of which contained two boys, and an attempt was made to minimize motives other than aggression. The scale achieved contained seven pictures and had a coefficient of reproducibility of .91. Lesser suggests that scaling procedures which take account of inhibitory factors would improve prediction. If fantasy aggression and fantasy aggression anxiety could both be scaled simultaneously, we might possess a very powerful predicter of overt behavior. To date such a "double scaling" has not been attempted.

In a recent study, Murstein and co-workers (61) had slides of the thirty-one TAT cards scaled for hostility by the Thurstone Equal Appearing Interval, Thurstone Successive Categories, Likert, Edwards Scale Discrimination, Guttman and H-Technique methods. The subjects were 100 students (fifty men and fifty women) obtained from a beginning psychology course at the University of Portland. The results of the two Thurstone methods indicate that most of the cards fell below the midpoint of hostility. Whether this result was due to haziness over the meaning of "average," or represented the type of student body (middle class Catholic) can only be checked by future studies with a more representative population.

The Likert results, however, indicated that the mean rating fell somewhat towards the hostile end of the continuum. Since the same students participated in the construction of both scales, it is possible that the discrepancy was contaminated by practice and/or position effects (the Likert followed the Thurstone procedure). On the other hand, the discrepancy might have been due to genuine differences in orientation due to the different judgments required in each scale. The Thurstone procedure consisted of sorting the cards in one of nine categories, with the fifth category described as the midpoint of hostility. The Likert procedure called for one of five judgments per card: very hostile, somewhat hostile, undecided, probably not hostile, definitely not hostile. Possibly, the inclusion of the "undecided" category accounted for the disparity. It might be omitted from future scaling since as Edwards (19) points out, neutral categories contain a good deal more error variance than positive or negative categories.

The successive category judgments of the men and women revealed no significant difference except for 17GF, which was seen as significantly more hostile by women than by men. By and large, however, the judgments of the two sexes are very close as attested by the correlation of .93 between the successive category judgments of both sexes.

The Q values of most of the cards are comparable to values found when scaling attitudes. This would tend to confirm the suspicion that the cards are highly structured. Along the same vein of thinking it is possible to conceive of Q, the interquartile deviation, as an index of projection. The rationale for this belief would be that one of the signs of a good projective card is the fact that a great disparity of opinion exists as to whether the card is hostile or non-hostile. The occurrence of such a disparity well might be due to the fact that the objective stimulus offers little clue as to what is happening, resulting in a wide range of sorting judgments which reflect projection on the part of the judges.

There is, however, a fly in the ointment. *For the above to be true it must follow that each card can be judged by the vast majority of the judges for the given dimension.* It is possible that a card cannot be meaningfully located on a dimension. Accordingly, individuals considered as a group might tend to randomly sort these cards thus ensuring a high Q value. This possibility might be forestalled in the future by having the cards evaluated for relevance to the dimension under consideration, and non-relevance to the dimensions not under consideration.

The Likert item analyses consisted of taking the twenty-five persons whose ratings were the highest of the total group and comparing them card for card with the twenty-five persons whose scores were lowest in hostility for the total judgments. The computation of thirty-one t tests (one-tailed test) for the entire series of cards yielded three non-significant ts, ten significant beyond the .05 point and eighteen significant beyond the .01 point. The card least differentiating was Card 16, the blank card. This finding confirms the earlier work of Murstein (58, 59, 60) concerning the ineffectuality of this card due to its lack of ambiguity. Although this card is structured, *it is not ambiguous.* There is simply "nothing to see" and the vast majority of judges perceive it as non-hostile. The second most undifferentiating card, 18GF, was highest in hostility according to the equal appearing interval method. This card is described by Murray as follows:

"A woman has her hands squeezed around the throat of another woman whom she appears to be pushing backwards across the banister of a stairway" (57, p. 20). This card can hardly be called structureless. It is highly structured and highly unambiguous.

In general, the least and most hostile ends of the continuum contain the greatest number of non-differentiating cards. This is only a trend, however, for there are several exceptions. Thus, Card 10 whose equal appearing interval scale value was 1.27 and would thus be considered very low on the hostility continuum, had a t value of 11.20. This card is described as "A young woman's head against a man's shoulder" (57, p. 19). Clinical experience has shown that many persons see the figures as elderly people who are embracing. The explanations for this embrace are varied. Some see them as happily married for many years; others see them as joyfully reuniting after a long separation; still others perceive the card as a scene where they are trying to comfort each other after the death of a child. It is apparent then that the *action engaged in by the figures is quite structured* although the lack of structure of the faces makes the ages of the figures somewhat ambiguous. In any event there is no clue as to the cause of their embracing and hence the *interpretation of the picture also is ambiguous.*

Card 13MF is almost as hostile as 18GF (equal appearing interval value 8.15 as compared to 8.32). Nevertheless, the t value for this card is 3.79 ($p < .01$) as compared to the t value of 1.06 ($p < .05$) for 18GF. It will be recalled that 13MF is described by Murray as "A young man is standing with downcast head buried in his arm. Behind him is the figure of a woman lying in bed" (57, p. 20). This picture is quite highly structured but also very ambiguous as has been mentioned earlier.

The results of the Likert procedure help to emphasize the earlier confounding of the concepts of *structure* and *ambiguity*. It appears that the most differentiating cards with regard to this study were those highly structured and yet highly ambiguous.

Cards low in structure as well as those high in structure have drawbacks for use in differentiating individuals on a perceptual basis. The former probably tend to induce "sets" to be on guard since little can be distinguished from the card itself. The *S* is most likely, therefore, to be aware that his response is a function of his perceptual world rather than of the stimulus properties of the card. Under these circumstances, the depth of the response may well be a function of the motivation of the *S* towards exhibiting his "private world" to the examiner. In the case of the highly structured highly unambiguous Card (18GF), the stimulus pull is so strong and the choice of explanations so narrow that to oppose this pull is to deny objective reality itself. This is not to deny that some individuals do perceive this card as non-hostile. The card would thus be of value in detecting those individuals with a strong need to avoid the objective properties of the card. For most people, however, the stimulus nature of such a card precludes the possibility of injecting personal values into the judgment.

In constructing the Guttman scale, the advice of Edwards (19) was followed in utilizing an item analysis prior to testing the scale for uni-dimensionality. First, the cards had to be more or less evenly spaced throughout the hostility continuum. Secondly, they had to possess low *Q* values, and thirdly they had to differentiate very significantly with regard to *t* values as determined by the Likert method. The result of this analysis was the selection of eight cards. These cards, in order of least to most hostility, are 10, 17BM, 7GF, 9GF, 3GF, 18BM, and 13MF. The method used to obtain the coefficient of reproducibility is the one proposed by Goodenough (29). The method used by Guttman is spuriously high due to the fact that the experimenter takes advantage of sampling bias in selecting the cutting point of the statement or card. Goodenough's method gives an unbiased representation of the degree of accuracy with which the responses to the cards can be reproduced from a knowledge of the total scores alone. The obtained coefficient was .88 which is sufficiently high to meet one of Guttman's standards for a "perfect scale." Guttman's criterion is actually .90, but this figure is an inflated one due to the aforementioned spurious factor. The coefficient of marginal reproducibility tells us what our accuracy of reproduction would have been had we just used our marginal totals as a basis for cutting points. It was found to be .74 indicating that we were able to improve our predictions considerably from knowledge of the total scores.

Lastly, the eight cards were combined into three "contrived cards" following the H-technique procedure (19). By this means, the coefficient of reproducibility was elevated to .96.

In reviewing the data on scaling, several conclusions seem pertinent:

1. Generally speaking, adequate success has been attained in scaling the cards by conventional scaling procedures. This fact would seem to confirm the suspicion, if it is still a suspicion, that the TAT is as a whole quite structured. It is hardly conceivable that an instrument which professes to "tap the private worlds" of individuals would tap such a concordant note with regard to the dimensions of *sex, aggression,* and *hostility* as to result in coefficients of reproducibility exceeding .90 in each case. It would seem that a change is required both in the selection of cards for future thematic series and in the procedure utilized in measurement. As Lazarus has well pointed out, "to depend upon only the most ambiguous kinds of stimuli in projective procedures results in uncertainty as to when an interpretation is avoided because of repressive defenses and when it is ignored because of lack of tension" (46, p. 444). The solution then should be a series of graded stimuli for a given dimension ranging from highly ambiguous to highly unambiguous. To distinguish between what is ambiguous and what is unambiguous it is helpful to employ scaling methods. Once we have a card scaled for a dimension we can proceed to investigate the meaning of conformity or deviancy from the stimulus value. There is extremely little information on this matter, since heretofore scaling methodology has been used for demonstrative purposes rather than in the investigation of perception and personality. It is no secret that our so-called perceptual tests are really verbal tests as Webb and Hilden (80) indicate rather neatly. Thematic cards, however, can be used as non-verbal perceptual judgment tasks by having *S* sort the cards into a number

of categories for a given personality dimension. The sort can then be compared with the scaled values obtained from a population similar to the *S* in age, socio-economic background and other important variables. The sum of the squared discrepancies over all the pictures might represent the *S*'s perceptual deviancy scores. The same could be done if desired for the *S*'s stories. These deviancy scores could then be compared with other behavior to see whether they contribute anything to the measurement of personality.

There are still other possibilities as Jacobs has indicated (37). If the experimenter wishes to determine whether certain perceptual responses are independent of the stimulus properties of the cards, cards very high on the ambiguity continuum may be selected. An ambiguous group of pictures also would be suitable for investigating "background" variables. *Ss* might be given varying instructions or exposed to different kinds of "arousal" stimuli. The responses to the pictures before and after the introduction of the experimental "background" factor could then be compared. The use of ambiguous pictures would insure a minimum of response determination due to the stimulus, and a maximum due to the "background" factor, "organismic" factor and their interaction.

Non-ambiguous pictures are, however, not without use. For one thing they insure a good spread of scores for almost every *S*. In addition, they are ideally suited for detecting "sets" on the part of the *S*. One may speculate, for example, that adequately adjusted persons from a personality standpoint are apt to respect the stimulus properties of thematic pictures more than are maladjusted persons. If then a series of fairly non-ambiguous "hostile" pictures are presented to a mixed group of "normal" and "ego-defensive" *Ss* we might expect the "normal" group to perceive the cards as "hostile," while the ego-defensive group might be less prone to acknowledge the stimulus properties of the cards in an effort to maintain a good impression before the examiner.

In emphasizing the importance of stimulus properties, it has not been my intention to slight the importance of "background" and "organismic" variables. It is because the stimulus properties are more readily determined and quantified than the other two, that I have concentrated on them. Once determined they can be used to advantage in the assessment of the other variables, as I have illustrated above.

If we are to understand and successfully predict human behavior, the "stimulus," "background" and "organismic" variables, or if you prefer, the "motives," "expectancies" and "reinforcement values" relating to the testee, must be adequately quantified. Perhaps in the quantification of our clinical instruments we shall achieve the long-sought rapprochement between the emphatic specialists of the "idioverse" and the numerical "nomotheticists."

REFERENCES

1. Armstrong, Mary A. S.: Children's responses to animal and human figures in thematic pictures. *J. Consult. Psychol., 18*:67-70. 1954.
2. Atkinson, J. W.: Studies in projective measurement of achievement motivation. Unpublished doctoral dissertation, Univ. of Michigan, 1950.
3. Atkinson, J. W.: Thematic apperceptive measurement of motives within the context of a theory of motivation. In *Motives in Fantasy, Action, and Society.* John W. Atkinson (Ed.) Princeton, Van Nostrand, 1958, pp. 596-616.
4. Auld, F., Eron, L. D., and Laffal, J.: Application of Guttman's scaling method to the TAT. *Educ. Psychol. Measmt., 15:*422-435. 1955.
5. Beck, S. J.: *Rorschach's test.* New York, Grune & Stratton, 1949.
6. Beier, E. G., Izard, C. E., Smock, C. D., and Tougas, R. R.: Response to the human face as a standard stimulus: a re-examination. *J. Consult. Psychol., 21*:165-170. 1957.
7. Bellak, L., and Bellak, Sonya S.: *Manual of Instruction for the Children's Apperception Test.* New York, C. P. S. Co., 1949.
8. Biersdorf, Kathryn R., and Marcuse, F. L.: Response of children to human and to animal pictures. *J. Proj. Tech., 17*:455-459. 1953.
9. Bijou, S. W., and Kenny, D. T.: The ambiguity of TAT cards. *J. Consult. Psychol., 15*:203-209. 1951.
10. Bills, R. E.: Animal pictures for obtaining children's projections. *J. Clin. Psychol., 6*:291-293. 1950.
11. Bills, R. E., Leiman, C. J., and Thomas, R. W.: A study of the validity of the TAT and a set of animal pictures. *J. Clin. Psychol., 6*:293-295. 1950.

12. Birney, R. C.: Thematic content and the cue characteristics of pictures. In *Motives in Fantasy, Action, and Society.* John W. Atkinson (Ed.) Princeton, Van Nostrand, 1958, pp. 630-643.
13. Boyd, Nancy A., and Mandler, G.: Children's responses to human and animal stories and pictures. *J. Consult. Psychol., 19*:367-371. 1955.
14. Bradley, J. E., and Lysaker, R. L.: Ambiguity as a variable in the use of a projective technique. Pillsbury Mills, Inc., Minneapolis, Minn., 1957 (Mimeographed).
15. Brunswick, E.: Representative design and probabilistic theory in a functional psychology. *Psychol. Rev., 62:*236-242. 1955.
16. Cook, R. A.: Identification and ego defensiveness in thematic apperception. *J. Proj. Tech.,* 312-319. 1953.
17. de Charms, R., Morrison, H. W., et al.: Behavorial correlates of directly and indirectly measured achievement motivation. In *Studies in Motivation.* D. C. McClelland (Ed.) New York, Appleton, 1955, pp. 414-423.
18. Edgar, Clara L., and Shneidman, E. S.: Some relationships among thematic projective tests of various degrees of structuredness and behavior in a group situation. *J. Proj. Tech., 22*:3-12. 1958.
19. Edwards, A. L.: *Techniques of Attitude Scale Construction.* New York, Appleton, 1957.
20. Epstein, S., and Smith, R.: Thematic apperception as a measure of the hunger drive. *J. Proj. Tech., 20*:372-384. 1956.
21. Eron, L. D.: Frequencies of themes and identification in stories of patients and non-hospitalized college students. *J. Consult. Psychol., 12*:387-395. 1948.
22. Eron, L. D.: A normative study of the Thematic Apperception Test. *Psychol. Monogr.,* 1950, *64*:No. 9 (Whole No. 315).
23. Erol, L. D., Terry, Dorothy, and Callahan, R.: The use of rating scales for emotional tone of TAT stories. *J. Consult. Psychol., 14*:473-478. 1950.
24. Eron, L. D.: Responses of women to the Thematic Apperception Test. *J. Consult. Psychol., 17*:269-282. 1953.
25. Frank, L. K.: *Projective Methods.* Springfield, Ill., Charles C Thomas, 1948.
26. Ford, C. S., and Beach, F. A.: *Patterns of Sexual Behavior.* New York, Harper, 1951.
27. *Funk and Wagnalls New Standard Dictionary of the English Language.* New York, Funk, 1955.

28. Furuya, K.: Responses of school children to human and animal pictures. *J. Proj. Tech., 21*:248-252. 1957.
29. Goodenough, W. H.: A technique for scale analysis. *Educ. Psychol. Measmt., 4*:179-190. 1944.
30. Goodman, Mary E.: *Race Awareness in Young Children*. Cambridge, Mass., Addison-Wesley, 1952.
31. Greenbaum, M., Qualtere, T., Carruth, B., and Cruickshank, W.: Evaluation of a modification of the thematic apperception test for use with physically handicapped children. *J. Clin. Psychol., 9*:40-44. 1953.
32. Gurel, L., and Ullmann, L. P.: Quantitative differences in response to TAT cards: The relationship between transcendence score and number of emotional words. *J. Proj. Tech., 22*:432-439. 1958.
33. Haber, R. N., and Alpert, R.: The role of situation and picture cues in projective measurement of the achievement motive. In *Motives in Fantasy, Action, and Society*. John W. Atkinson (Ed.) Princeton, Van Nostrand, 1958, pp. 644-663.
34. Helson, H.: Adaptation-level as a basis for a quantitative theory of frames of reference. *Psychol. Rev., 55*:297-313. 1948.
35. Helson, H.: An experimental approach to personality. *Psychiat. Res. Rep., 2*:89-99. 1955.
36. Holt, R. R.: Formal aspects of the TAT—a neglected resource. *J. Proj. Tech., 22*:163-172. 1958.
37. Jacobs, B.: A method for investigating the cue characteristics of pictures. In *Motives in Fantasy, Action, and Society*. John W. Atkinson (Ed.) Princeton, Van Nostrand, 1958, pp. 617-629.
38. Jensen, A. R.: Aggression in fantasy and overt behavior. *Psychol. Monogr., 71*: (Whole No. 445). 1957.
39. Kagan, J. The measurement of overt aggression from fantasy. *J. Abnorm & Social Psychol., 52*:390-393. 1956.
40. Kagan, J.: The stability of TAT fantasy and stimulus ambiguity. *J. Consult. Psychol., 23*:266-271. 1959.
41. Kenny, D. T.: Transcendence indices, extent of personality factors in fantasy responses, and the ambiguity of TAT cards. *J. Consult. Psychol., 18*:345-348. 1954.
42. Kenny, D. T., and Bijou, S. W.: Ambiguity of pictures and extent of personality factors in fantasy responses. *J. Consult. Psychol., 17*:283-288. 1953.
43. Klopfer, B., *et al.*: *Developments in the Rorschach Technique: Vol. I*. Yonkers, New York, World Bk. Co., 1954.

44. Korchin, S. J., Mitchell, H. E., and Meltzoff, J.: A critical evaluation of the Thompson Thematic Apperception Test. *J. Proj. Tech., 14*:445-452. 1950.
45. Lasaga y Travieso, J. E., and Martinez-Arango, C.: Some suggestions concerning the administration and interpretation of the TAT. *J. Psychol., 22*:117-163. 1946.
46. Lazarus, R. S.: Ambiguity and non-ambiguity in projective testing. *J. Abnorm. & Social Psychol., 48*:443-445, 1953.
47. Lebo, D.: Immediate affective reaction to TAT cards. *J. Clin. Psychol., 11*:297-299. 1955.
48. Lebo, D., and Harrigan, Margaret.: Visual and verbal presentation of TAT stimuli, *J. Consult. Psychol. 21*:339-342. 1957.
49. Lebo, D., and Sherry, P. J.: Visua and vocal presentation of TAT descriptions. *J. Proj. Tech., 23*:59-63. 1959.
50. Lesser, G. S.: Conflict analysis of fantasy aggression. *J. Pers., 26*:29-41. 1958.
51. Lesser, G. S.: Application of Guttman's scaling method to aggressive fantasy in children. *Educ. Psychol. Measmt., 18*:543-550. 1958.
52. Light, B. H.: Comparative study of a series of TAT and CAT cards. *J. Clin. Psychol. 10*:179-181. 1954.
53. Light, B. H.: A further test of the Thompson TAT rationale. *J. Abnorm. & Social Psychol. 51*:148-150. 1955.
54. Mainord, Florence R., and Marcuse, F. L.: Responses of disturbed children to human and to animal pictures. *J. Proj. Tech., 18*:475-477. 1954.
55. McIntyre, C. J.: Sex, age, and iconicity as factors in projective film tests. *J. Consult. Psychol., 18*:475-477. 1954.
56. Murray, E. J.: Thematic apperception during sleep deprivation. Paper read at meeting of Eastern Psychological Assn., Philadelphia, 1958.
57. Murray, H. A.: *Thematic Apperception Test Manual.* Cambridge, Harvard Univ. Press. 1943.
58. Murstein, B. I.: Nonprojective determinants of perception on the TAT. *J. Consult. Psychol., 22*:195-198. 1958.
59. Murstein, B. I.: The relationship of stimulus ambiguity on the TAT to productivity of themes. *J. Consult. Psychol., 22*:348. 1958.
60. Murstein, B. I.: A conceptual model of projective techniques applied to stimulus variations with thematic techniques. *J. Consult. Psychol., 23*:3-14. 1959.
61. Murstein, B. I., Coulter, W., Bowdish, Carol, David, Charlotte, Fisher, D., Furth, H., and Hansen, I.: A study of scaling methods

applied to the TAT for the dimension of hostility. Univ. of Portland, 1959. (Mimeographed)

62. Newbigging, P. L.: Influence of a stimulus variable on stories told to certain TAT pictures. *Canad. J. Psychol., 9*:195-206. 1955.
63. Pittluck, Patricia: The relationship between aggressive fantasy and overt behavior. Unpublished doctoral dissertation, Yale Univ., 1950.
64. Reitman, W. R., and Atkinson, J. W.: Some methodological problems in the use of thematic apperceptive measures of human motives. In *Motives in Fantasy, Action, and Society.* John W. Atkinson (Ed.). Princeton, Van Nostrand, 1958, pp. 664-683.
65. Riess, B. F., Schwartz, E. K., and Cottingham, Alice.: An experimental critique of assumptions underlying the Negro version of the TAT. *J. Abnorm. & Social Psychol., 45*:700-709. 1950.
66. Rosenzweig, S.: Idiodynamics in personality theory with special reference to projective methods. *Psychol. Rev., 58*:213-223. 1951.
67. Rotter, J.: *Social Learning and Clinical Psychology,* New York, Prentice-Hall, 1954.
68. Rotter, J.: The role of the psychological situation in determining the direction of human behavior. In *Nebraska Symposium on Motivation, 1955.* Marshall R. Jones (Ed.). Lincoln, Univ. of Nebraska Press, 1955, pp. 245-268.
69. Schafer, R.: How was this story told? *J. Proj. Tech., 22*:181-210. 1958.
70. Schwartz, E. K., Riess, B. F., and Cottingham, Alice: Further critical evaluation of the Negro version of the TAT. *J. Proj. Tech., 15*:394-400, 1951.
71. Silverstein, A. B.: Identification with same-sex and opposite-sex figures in thematic apperception. *J. Proj. Tech., 23*:73-75. 1959.
72. Solkoff, Norman: Effects of a variation in instructions and pictorial stimuli on responses to TAT-like cards. *J. Proj. Tech., 23*:76-82. 1959.
73. Symonds, P. M.: Criteria for the selection of pictures for the investigation of adolescent phantasies. *J. Abnorm. & Social Psychol., 34*:271-274. 1939.
74. Terry, Dorothy: The use of a rating scale of level of response in TAT stories. *J. Abnorm. & Social Psychol., 47*:507-511. 1952.
75. Thompson, C. E.: The Thompson modification of the Thematic Apperception Test. *Rorschach Res. Exch., 13*:469-478. 1949.
76. Tomkins, S. S.: *The Thematic Apperception Test.* New York, Grune & Stratton, 1947.

77. Ullmann, L. P.: Productivity and the clinical use of TAT cards. *J. Proj. Tech., 21*:399-403. 1957.
78. Ullmann, L. P.: Clinical correlates of facilitation and inhibition of response to emotional stimuli. *J. Proj. Tech., 22*:341-347. 1958.
79. Veroff, J., Wilcox, S., and Atkinson, J. W.: The achievement motive in high school and college age women. *J. Abnorm. & Social Psychol., 48*:108-119. 1953.
80. Webb, W. B., and Hilden, A. H.: Verbal and intellectual ability as factors in projective test results. *J. Proj. Tech., 17*:102-103. 1953.
81. Weisskopf, Edith A.: A transcendence index as a proposed measure in the TAT. *J. Psychol., 29*:379-390. 1950.
82. Weisskopf, Edith A.: An experimental study of the effect of brightness and ambiguity on projection in the TAT. *J. Psychol., 29*:407-416. 1950.
83. Weisskopf, Edith A., and Dunlevy, G. P.: Bodily similarity between subject and central figure in the TAT as an influence on projection. *J. Abnorm. & Social Psychol., 47*:441-445. 1957.
84. Weisskopf-Joelson, Edith A., and Lynn, D. B.: The effect of variations in ambiguity on projection in the Children's Apperception Test. *J. Consult. Psychol., 17*:67-70. 1953.
85. Weisskopf-Joelson, Edith A., and Money, L.: Facial similarity between subject and central figure in the TAT as an influence on projection. *J. Abnorm. & Social Psychol., 48*:341-344. 1953.
86. Witkin, H. A., and Asch., S. E.: Studies in space orientation: IV. Further experiments on perception of the upright with displaced visual fields. *J. Exp. Psychol., 38*:762-782. 1948.

DISCUSSION OF DR. MURSTEIN'S PAPER

Gerald S. Lesser, Ph.D.
Primary Discussant

D*r. Lesser:* Dr. Murstein has covered a great deal of ground in his review of stimulus factors in the evaluation of personality by apperceptive techniques. This discussion will focus only upon a few of the issues raised. The following areas appear to pose either especially promising or especially puzzling problems: (1) the relative importance of the stimulus, (2) definition of stimulus ambiguity, (3) reliability, validity, and stimulus ambiguity, (4) scaling of thematic responses and stimulus ambiguity.

With regard to the relative importance of the stimulus in apperceptive tests, Dr. Murstein organizes the variables contributing to a thematic response into the categories of (1) variables associated with the properties of the stimulus, (2) background variables, and (3) organismic variables. He then proceeds to make quite a convincing case for the importance of stimulus properties in determining projective responses.

Without devaluating the importance of stimulus properties, it is, however, perhaps even easier to present a convincing case for the crucial influence of "background" and "organismic" variables in determining the nature of thematic responses. For example, Dr. Murstein includes the following variables under the heading of "background" variables: (1) the nature of the examiner's approach to the *S*; (2) the *S*'s attitudes toward the *E*'s sex, age, role, etc.; (3) *S*'s hypotheses regarding the purpose of the test; (4) *S*'s interpretation of the instructions; and (5) the environment in which the test is administered. Dr. Murstein cites as *"organismic"* variables: (1) the objective traits of the *S*, (2) the *S*'s self concept with regard to these traits, and (3) the totality of the *S*'s past and present experience apropos of these traits. This is only a partial listing of specific "organismic" variables.

Since these variables, subsumed by the headings of "background" and "organismic" characteristics, are precisely those variables that most psychologists are attempting to assess in using thematic tests for clinical or research purposes, their importance is obvious.

It is not my intention to minimize the role of the stimulus in determining thematic material. It seems clear, however, that we know very little about the empirical problem of estimating the relative proportions of the variance contributed by stimulus, background, and organismic variables (and their complex interactions) to the psychological meaningfulness of thematic responses.

These statements are not intended to correct anything that Dr. Murstein has said. He states himself that his emphasis has been upon the stimulus properties because they are "more readily determined and quantified," and that "the stimulus x background x organism interaction is of considerable importance in determining the nature of the response." The present state of affairs seems to be that we can have only opinions about what variables are crucial in determining the nature of projective responses; we have little empirical information which allows us to estimate their relative contributions.

With regard to the definition of stimulus ambiguity, Dr. Murstein draws a distinction between the concepts of "structure" and "ambiguity." As defined, "structure" refers to sensory input, to the objective physical characteristics of the stimulus presented, to the "who and what is in the picture." By contrast, "ambiguity" denotes perceptual response, "what the *S* experiences when seeing the picture and constructing a story." The distinctive property of an ambiguous stimulus is that it is uncertain in perceptual meaning, that it is "capable of multiple interpretation." According to these definitions, there is little basis for anticipating overlap between these concepts; a "structured" stimulus may be ambiguous or unambiguous; an "unstructured" stimulus may also be ambiguous or unambiguous.

This distinction may clarify certain matters. For example, it may help in setting criteria for the selection of TAT-type pictures to be included in a scaled series; this will be elaborated later. But the definition of "ambiguity" also raises certain questions.

When an ambiguous stimulus is viewed operationally as "capable of multiple interpretation," is this in an intra-individual sense, an inter-individual sense, or both? That is, does "ambiguity" refer to reliability or stability of intra-individual perceptual meanings, to variability of inter-individual perceptual responses, or both? These criteria are not identical (and as a matter of fact may be somewhat incompatible) and the definition of ambiguity must specify which is its observational referent.

Not only must intra-individual ambiguity be distinguished from inter-individual ambiguity, but when the term "ambiguity" is used in its inter-individual meaning, the group or groups for which a stimulus is "capable of multiple interpretation" must be carefully designated. A Japanese psychologist describes the following characteristics of the sets of TAT cards most commonly used in Japan and contrasts these cards to the Murray series:

> When you compare Japanese pictures, of whatever version, with Murray's there is one thing that impresses one. It is: that Japanese pictures are, generally speaking, more beautiful—I am not speaking in the artistic sense—more "soft," less powerful, less horrible, less fear-provoking, less "stirring" than Murray's version, so that some psychologists here are skeptical about the possibility of the Japanese pictures drawing out what lies at the innermost depth of the hardened human heart. Thus there are many Japanese psychologists who are using Murray instead of Japanese versions of TAT. The Japanese artist who was asked to draw pictures for the Nagoya TAT is reported, when he was shown Murray pictures, to have been remarkably impressed with the latter and observed that no Japanese artist might be able to draw pictures of Murray's power. Contrary to the opinion expressed above, however, the softened tone of the Japanese pictures might, it is argued, appeal better to Japanese sentiment, and serve the purpose of the test better. (*Psychologia, I,* No. 2, p. 95, 1957.)

We know that the Murray TAT series produces wide individual differences in response for the variable of aggression among American *Ss* and is "capable of multiple interpretation" for this population; the Murray series therefore possesses some degree of ambiguity for American *Ss*. A Japanese psychologist (personal communication) reports that the Murray cards are either rarely perceived or rarely reported as aggressive by Japanese *Ss;* that is, the Murray cards do not seem to Japanese *Ss* to be "capable of multiple interpretations" for aggression. For the Japanese samples, the Murray series is therefore unambiguous for the absence of aggressive content.

The point here is that the same stimulus may be ambiguous for population A and unambiguous for population B. The psychological or cultural differences between the populations must be exactly specified.

In addition to asking "ambiguity for whom?" it is also important to ask "ambiguity for what?" This is a truism, but the same stimulus for the same population will be ambiguous for certain variables and unambiguous for others. Exact identification and definition of the variables must also be provided.

Incidentally, apart from the definition of stimulus ambiguity for a moment, the quotation from the article by the Japanese psychologist raises a series of questions, some more facetious than others:

(1) What would the history and present status of TAT research be had Henry Murray been Japanese?

(2) What is it possible to do methodologically about the discrepancy between what an *S* "sees" and what he "reports"?

(3) What stimuli do different psychologists choose to present to their clinical or research *Ss* and why?

(4) The sociology of the TAT and TAT research may involve many valuable explorations, such as

- (a) What social class differences in TAT response exist for a variety of variables?
- (b) Do the results of TAT research (like Rorschach research) vary as a function of where (e.g., academic vs. clinic) the research is done?

(5) Cross-cultural comparisons in TAT response for a variety of variables have been rare and are significant sources of research evidence.

I am certain that you all recognize that the only unfacetious issue I have mentioned is that concerning Henry Murray being Japanese.

The next issue provoked by Dr. Murstein's paper concerns the possible relationships between reliability and validity of apperceptive measures and level of stimulus ambiguity. Dr. Murstein has reviewed the relationships between stimulus ambiguity and variables such as "transcendence," "personality revealingness," "pleasantness" of response, "preference" for the stimulus, "productivity," etc. In addition, it may be useful to focus selectively on the small amount of research evidence relating stimulus ambiguity to reliability and validity of thematic responses.

Regarding reliability, I'll restrict myself to test-retest reliability in order to make some general points most rapidly.

Most of the evidence supports the general conclusion that test-retest reliability of TAT measures is very low, far below levels of reliability demanded by constructors of tests of mental ability, social attitudes, etc. Many clinicians may see this as a virtue instead of a weakness, but for the research use of the TAT it is a formidable obstacle.

However, there is some evidence that thematic responses may show higher test-retest reliability when the pictures used unambiguously present a particular content area. Kagan (8), for example, reports that only two of eight variables showed statistically significant test-retest reliability over the course of a six-year period, but indicates that these two relatively stable variables were elicited primarily by pictures which unambiguously portrayed these variables. Two studies (10, 14) report low but significant test-retest reliability data for achievement measures when the stimuli used were relatively clear for this variable. The word "evidence" is far too strong a term to use in this context, but there are at least some additional suggestions in the literature (e.g., 3, 4, 6, 12, 13) that test-retest reliability can be improved by using less ambiguous pictures, when this is appropriate to the research objective.

Two questions summarize this section of test-retest reliability of projective responses as a function of stimulus ambiguity: Do less ambiguous stimuli really improve test-retest reliability of projective tests? If so, why so?

Dr. Kenny: I don't agree with you in your summarization of the studies of "test-retest" reliability. The intervals used in these studies do not correspond to a definition of "test-retest" reliability from the psychometric viewpoint. Some people on test-retest have used something like Gardner Lindzey did, that is, an interval of two months. This is not test-retest in the psychometric sense; that is something else. My understanding of test-retest reliability is that it involves an interval of about one to two days.

Dr. Lesser: You are right. I agree that I have employed a special usage of the term "test-retest."

Dr. Kenny: In other words, we don't have any evidence of test-retest reliability.

Dr. Lesser: That's correct; we have very little. What evidence we have is a longer-interval evidence, and it shows extremely low "reliability."

Dr. Atkinson: I would like to suggest that the kind of test-retest reliability that Dr. Kenny suggests is probably impossible to obtain.

Dr. Kenny: It might be. I think the only way you could get test-retest is to instruct the subjects to give a different story.

Dr. Tomkins: Assuming that we can accurately estimate the test-retest reliability of fantasy responses is like assuming that we can measure the reliability of a response to a joke. If I tell it to you twice in a row, or even separated by two days, and you don't laugh as much the second time, I say this is no measure of the reliability of that first response.

The problem, I think, in measuring test-retest reliability is that the researcher does not know what to instruct the *S* to do. There is no meaning to the concept of reliability when the *S* says, "You want me to give the same story or a different one?" and you, the examiner, don't know what to say.

Dr. Kenny: This is the point I am raising. It is probably impossible to estimate the test-retest reliability in the psychometric sense.

Dr. Lesser: If you give no instructions, some subjects will say, "I have already said that. Now I will say something different."

They have this alternating interpretation in the absence of instructions on the retest. Dr. Atkinson has discussed this earlier in this conference. There is no doubt that defining test-retest reliability as applied to apperceptive tests and obtaining empirical evidence for this kind of reliability are extremely complex problems.

Concerning the possible relationship between the validity of apperceptive tests and their level of stimulus ambiguity, I shall mention only a few studies that have related thematic responses to the construct validity criteria of the *Ss'* overt behavior in the drive area investigated.

Some of the evidence (e.g., 5, 7, 15) suggests that the less ambiguous the stimulus employed, the stronger the relationships between fantasy elicited by the stimulus and overt behavioral criteria. Other studies (e.g., 9, 16, 17), however, report apparently greater construct validity of themes produced in response to pictures of medium ambiguity. Just to complete the circle, there is at least one study (1) that suggests that construct validity is greater for responses to highly ambiguous stimuli.

Adding the results of all these studies together, we may perhaps assume that we have some beginning evidence of greater construct validity of fantasy responses to unambiguous stimuli. However, the question still remains: what psychological significance can be assigned to this observation? Does it have any theoretical significance? Is it a methodologically significant finding? Or is it a methodological artifact?

There are at least a few methodological interpretations which are readily apparent. Perhaps low validity coefficients to ambiguous stimuli are a function of the restriction in range of scores for any single variable. Or, perhaps the ambiguous stimuli (and this may be a strength in the clinical setting), by evoking different variables in different *Ss*, do not allow clear assessment of a single variable, unconfounded by many other variables. With high ambiguity, a projective test may not measure a lot of one variable but a very little of any of the many variables evoked simultaneously, thereby reducing a relationship between any one variable and a validating criterion.

The general questions posed concerning validity and stimulus ambiguity are: Do less ambiguous cards really produce greater construct validity of the thematic response? If so, so what? That is, what does it mean?

Dr. Atkinson: I think that many of the studies concerning validity and stimulus ambiguity can probably be integrated. We use terms like "high," "low," "modal," "intermediate" ambiguity. If we ever get to use the same scale of strengths, we can perhaps tie the studies together. What was "high" ambiguity for one researcher might have been "intermediate" for another.

Dr. Lesser: With regard to the application of scaling procedures to projective responses, Dr. Murstein has described some attempts to scale projective responses in order to obtain greater precision of measurement for research purposes. I think this development is of great interest and would like to extend Dr. Murstein's remarks along the following lines: (1) advantages of scaling, (2) conditions for scaling, (3) problems in scaling, and (4) research uses of scaled projective material.

As you know, there are many varieties of scaling approaches: judgment methods, methods of summated ratings, latent structure analysis, unfolding techniques, etc. My remarks will be limited to scalogram analysis, which Louis Guttman originally formulated to increase precision in attitude measurement.

This cumulative item technique was formalized by Guttman in scalogram analysis, and when applied to projective responses of, for example, aggression, would take the following form:

		Pictures			
		Ambiguous			*Unambiguous*
		1	2	3	4
	A	+	+	+	+
	B	—	+	+	+
Ss	C	—	—	+	+
	D	—	—	—	+
	E	—	—	—	—

where aggression is scored as either present (+) or absent (—) for each theme from each *S*, and where the pictures are ordered on a stimulus ambiguity dimension. The premise upon which this procedure is based when applied to projective responses is that when a need is strong, it will be expressed in response to stimuli of high ambiguity for that need and to all stimuli of lesser ambiguity, while a weaker need will be expressed only in response to stimuli of low ambiguity. Thus, subject D manifests relatively weak aggressive need by responding aggressively only to the most unambiguous picture, while subject B manifests relatively strong aggressive need by responding aggressively to all except the most ambiguous stimulus.

There are two major advantages to scale construction as applied to thematic responses. Guttman states, "If an area is scalable, this indicates that there is but one dominant variable in the area along which to order persons" (2, p. 78). Such information about the degree of unity or unidimensionality of variables would seem especially crucial where experimenters are forced pretty much to take on faith the fact that they are dealing with unitary variables at all. For example, a measure of "fantasy aggression" used recently (11) included, in order to approach the diversity of behaviors subsumed clinically by the label of aggression, such widely disparate themes as torturing, repudiating, expressing disdain, and killing. It was of great utility to know that this "fantasy aggression" measure does primarily represent a single dominant variable.

Dr. Kenny: There is some evidence that it is not particularly sound to assume that Guttman's scalogram method will yield only one factor. In other words, you can factor analyze the items in the Guttman scale and you are likely to pull out more than one factor. We do not know how wide this is likely to be. We do need further research before we could safely assume you are tapping one and only one factor, because at least in the attitude field there are some findings to indicate that if you factor analyze the items you are likely to get more than one factor.

Dr. Lesser: I was not aware of those findings in the area of research on attitudes. They would certainly lead one to be cautious, then, in assuming unidimensionality in a variable, even when the items form a close approximation to a perfect scale.

The second major advantage of scaling thematic material centers upon the complex problems psychologists have encountered in the differential weighting of projective responses for research purposes. Does one explosively intense aggressive response to an ambiguous picture equal ten weakly aggressive responses to unambiguous stimuli (not when it comes to judging pathology or bizarreness) when it comes to measuring a *S*'s aggressiveness? Conceding that two responses both are related to the strength of a motive, how can one combine the ratings obtained from these two responses into a single score? Ordering pictures according to the degree of ambiguity with which they represent a single motive will circumvent certain problems in weighting projective responses.

Dr. Murstein: I think scaling can also be used not only for achieving scale types, but the very fact that we do obtain non-scale types can in itself be very interesting. We want to study not only the scale types but those people who deviated. So, in the first onslaught on the problem of scaling, I think we would not want to throw away anything; we would use everything, and only later, when we had refined our procedures somewhat, could we then proceed to be more selective.

Dr. Lesser: An extended discussion of the conditions necessary for scaling a series of apperceptive stimuli would include a long list of specific methodological considerations. This would take more time than we have available. In the general sense, however, scaling a series of TAT stimuli forces you to take as much of the hodgepodge as possible out of both the definition of the variable to be assessed and the properties of the stimuli used to assess the variables.

With regard to definition of variables, Guttman, in discussing the scaling of attitude items, stresses the care necessary in defining (in his terms) the "universe" of which the items are a sample. In other words, creating the necessary conditions for scaling forces the *E* to purify both his definitions of variables and his measuring instruments if his pictures are to meet the criteria of useful approximations of perfect scales.

There are, of course, a number of problems involved in attempts to scale projective material. One serious limitation is that it will probably be enormously difficult to scale one series of pictures to assess many drive areas simultaneously. Thus, scaled pictures in clinical use would probably arouse the objection by clinicians that the interactions among various drives cannot be observed when a series of scaled pictures represents only one fairly unitary drive area. You may lose information concerning, for example, the interaction between the sexual and aggressive needs of an individual.

It is probably true that, in order to obtain more precise quantification through scaling, some degree of the range of generality of the thematic responses may be sacrificed. If you have a scaled series of "aggression" stimuli, you will not be able to draw conclusions about the strength of sexual, dependent, achievement, and other drives, nor about the interactions among them.

There are probably solutions for this problem, such as multivariable scaling or, at least, the construction of a number of graded scales, but these developments are far in the future.

Dr. Murstein has indicated another problem in scaling projective responses. At one point in his paper, Dr. Murstein distinguishes between two hypothetical *Ss* who have obtained the same hostility score. In asking whether they are equally hostile in fantasy perceptions, Dr. Murstein suggests that we examine the degree to which they adhere to the stimulus pull of the cards. He states that subject A may follow the stimulus pull of the cards, while subject C may derive his score by giving stories involving hostility to ambiguous cards and non-hostile stories to "hostile" cards. Although Dr. Murstein questions the conclusion that subject C is therefore more deviant, this kind of data is nonetheless unavailable when scaled series of pictures are used. If there are enough Subject C types ("non-scale types") in the standardization population, the series would not have been scaled in the first place.

This does not say, however, that once the series of pictures is scaled on a sample of "normal" *Ss* (which, we assume, does not contain many "non-scale types"), then the degree of divergence of "disturbed" responses from the scaled series may be ascertained. Dr. Murstein has already referred to this application in his earlier comment during this discussion.

Thus, scaled pictures may not only allow for increased precision in the determination of need strength, but scaling may eventually provide an approach relevant to assessing "deviancy" of behavior through the criterion of non-scalable responses. This suggested method of evaluating "disturbance" will, of course, demand careful validation.

There are a great many potential research uses of such scaled projective material. We have discussed certain aspects of using scaled pictures to measure strength of need. The importance of estimating the strength of anxiety over the expression of need as well as need strength itself has been demonstrated empirically (e.g., 11), and we have frequently stressed the value of measuring avoidance variables at this conference. If measures of both aggression and aggression-anxiety emerged as simultaneously scalable, we would possess extremely powerful instruments for understanding and predicting behavior.

This raises the broader issue of how to measure anxiety over the expression of needs at all, much less how to scale measures of anxiety. One approach may be to employ a series of pictures starting with extremely unambiguous cards and increasing in ambiguity. Another approach to developing scaled series of aggression-anxiety pictures might follow a familiar procedure in this research area by creating experimental conditions which would arouse varying degrees of anxiety over the expression of aggression and measuring the effects produced on fantasy aggression-anxiety indices. These are tentative suggestions; the simultaneous measurement of needs and defenses, of approach as well as avoidance variables, is a formidable methodological problem for scaling techniques and for measurement in general.

Once in possession of even a crude series of stimuli scaled for anxiety or control responses, the investigation of a number of problems would help to refine the measure as well as answer some substantive problems:

(1) What developmental pattern does the emergence of anxiety variables take?

(2) What parental attitudes and practices are related to the nature and degree of anxiety manifestations in children?

(3) What are the relationships between various anxiety manifestations and various pathological conditions?

(4) How are certain natural variables (e.g., hospitalism, traumatic incidents, school experiences, etc.) related to the development of anxiety responses?

(5) To what extent do defenses (or anxiety manifestations) operate across drives?

REFERENCES

1. Epstein, S., and Smith, R.: Thematic apperception as a measure of the hunger drive. *J. Proj. Tech., 20*:372-384. 1956.
2. Guttman, L.: The basis for scalogram analysis. In S. A. Stouffer et al., *Studies in Social Psychology in World War II, Vol. IV, Measurement and Prediction.* Princeton Univ., 1950, pp. 60-90.
3. Haber, R. N., and Alpert, R.: The role of situation and picture cues in projective measurement of the achievement motive. In J. W. Atkinson (Ed.), *Motives in Fantasy, Action, and Society.* New York, Van Nostrand, 1958, pp. 644-663.
4. Hurley, J. R.: The Iowa picture interpretation test: a multiple choice variation of the TAT. *J. Consult. Psychol., 19*:372-376. 1955.
5. Jacobs, B.: A method for investigating the cue characteristics of pictures. In J. W. Atkinson (Ed.), *Motives in Fantasy, Action, and Society.* New York, Van Nostrand, 1958, pp. 617-629.
6. Johnston, R. A.: A methodological analysis of several revised forms of the Iowa picture interpretation test. *J. Pers., 25:*283-293. 1957.
7. Kagan, J.: The measurement of overt aggression from fantasy. *J. Abnorm. & Social Psychol., 52:*390-393. 1956.
8. Kagan, J.: The stability of TAT fantasy and stimulus ambiguity. *J. Consult. Psychol., 23*:266-271. 1959.
9. Kenny, D. T., and Bijou, S. W.: Ambiguity of pictures and extent of personality factors in fantasy responses. *J. Consult. Psychol., 17*:238-288. 1953.
10. Krumholtz, J. D., and Farquhar, W. W.: Reliability and validity on the n-Achievement test. *J. Consult. Psychol., 21*:226-229. 1957.
11. Lesser, G. S.: Conflict analysis of fantasy aggression. *J. Pers., 26*:29-41. 1958.
12. Lindzey, G., and Heinemann, Shirley H.: Thematic apperception test: Individual and group administration. *J. Pers., 24:*34-55. 1955.
13. Lindzey, G., and Herman, P. S.: Thematic Apperception Test: A note on reliability and situational validity. *J. Proj. Tech., 18:*36-42. 1955.
14. Morgan, H. H.: Measuring achievement motivation with picture interpretations. *J. Consult. Psychol., 17*:289-292. 1953.
15. Murray, E. J.: Conflict and repression during sleep deprivation. *J.*

Abnorm. & Social Psychol., *59*:95-101. 1959.

16. Stone, H.: The TAT aggressive content scale. *J. Proj. Tech.*, *20*:445-452. 1956.
17. Veroff, J.: Thematic apperception in a nationwide sample survey. In J. Kagan and G. S. Lesser (Eds.) *Contemporary Issues in Thematic Apperceptive Methods*. Springfield, Thomas, 1960.

A THEORETICAL AND RESEARCH REAPPRAISAL OF STIMULUS FACTORS IN THE TAT

Douglas T. Kenny, Ph.D.
University of British Columbia

ALTHOUGH the Thematic Apperception Test has been used extensively in clinical investigations and has been probed by a host of psychologists with varied orientations, we still stand a considerable distance away from understanding why and how it functions. I would like to mention at the outset, however, that this conference represents one step closer to that eventual day when the laws governing behavior to apperceptive techniques will be discovered.

It seems likely, too, that this day of enlightenment will be hastened when two primary problems are systematically studied. The first involves the critical relevance of the stimulus properties of the pictures in the determination of the thematic stories. The second general problem concerns the level of personality functioning reflected in the thematic apperceptive stories. In fact, these two problems are closely intertwined in the whole fabric of projective testing. A brief examination of the implications of a typical set of assumptions will bring into clear focus the interlacing of these two issues.

A frequently made assumption in clinical theory and testing is that ambiguous test stimuli will facilitate the expression of covert layers of personality functioning. Conversely, stimulus materials whose meaning is structured are thought to elicit behavior which reflects the overt aspects of personality. The theoretical and practical significance of this hypothesis of a positive relationship between ambiguity of stimuli and significant layer of personality is of paramount importance to the whole field of projective and psychometric measurement. Applied to the construction and use of thematic apperceptive techniques, one implication of this hypothesis is that a continuum of ambiguous picture stimuli would be indispensable to a comprehensive assessment of personality. The issues of the choice of the criterion in test validation, clinical inference from test behavior, and the organization of personality functioning are also at stake here.

In this connection, there are two pivotal questions: What is the relationship between the different layers or levels of personality functioning? What is the relationship between levels of personality functioning and stimuli in the social environment? There appears to be, at the present, no agreement between writers as to what level of personality functioning is tapped by thematic apperceptive techniques. If it is assumed that thematic techniques reveal unconscious or repressed material, then a curvilinear relationship between thematic content and overt behavior may be hypothesized. Other investigators, working within either a "hydraulic theory" or a "catharsis formulation" of thematic stories, may postulate an inverse relationship between these two variables. On the other hand, if it is assumed that conscious material is obtained from thematic techniques, a positive relationship between thematic content and behavior will be expected. However, all of these formulations are deficient in one important respect: the nature of the stimulus situation in which the criterion behavior is to be manifest is not specified. They also overlook the fact that apperceptive materials vary along a continuum of ambiguity. It seems reasonable to suppose that clinical inferences should vary depending upon the degree of ambiguity of the picture stimuli and the degree of ambiguity contained in the social environment. Thematic stories to highly ambiguous picture stimuli should provide more information about how a person would respond to an ambiguous social environment than would thematic stories to a well-structured set of pictures. Similarly, thematic stories to moderately well-structured stimuli should provide the most valid base for inferences on how an individual would respond to a moderately ambiguous social environment.

While other sets of assumptions than those I have cited could have been mentioned, these do indicate, however, that the problems of the stimulus properties of thematic apperceptive pictures and levels of personality functioning are interdependent. In the present paper an attempt is made to examine a new avenue of approach to the stimulus properties of thematic cards, particularly that of ambiguity, and to suggest a program of research designed to test some of the implications of this approach. Some of the ramifications of the model for personality functioning will also be discussed.

EVASION AND DELINQUENCY IN THE TREATMENT OF STIMULUS PROPERTIES

A persistent and elusive enigma of projective techniques has been how to treat conceptually the patterns of distal stimulation from testing materials. The problem has, of course, been recognized in various theoretical explications of thematic apperception. The relevant research literature on the stimulus properties for apperceptive fantasy techniques has been excellently reviewed by others (5, 31) and will, therefore, not be dealt with in this paper. Nevertheless, an examination of the theoretical and empirical literature should convince one that writers have been very lethargic in their efforts to develop a theoretical schema which deals adequately with the problem of the stimulus. I should hasten to point out, however, that McClelland (25) and Atkinson (1) have started to show some interest in the cue properties of thematic cards. More often than not, to date, the theoretically oriented person merely tips his hat to this perplexing problem and leaves it posthaste for the seemingly more fascinating and fruitful topic of personality interpretation of fantasy stories. I always react with some amazement to statements on the stimulus that do not go beyond saying that Watson's (41, p. 167) dictum ". . . given the response the stimuli can be predicted; given the stimuli the response can be predicted" is false. Of course it is false. Surely this was known by at least 1930 in psychology, if not at the time Watson wrote it. It seems to me that we should be able to say something more profound about the stimulus than simply make a negative assertion.

There are at least three historical reasons for the neglect and avoidance of stimulus variables in projective test research. First, the reluctance to develop a detailed analysis of the stimulus reflects the basic failure of most theoretical models in psychology to unravel the thorny problem of the stimulus. The well-known terminological and conceptual confusions about the stimulus contained in the theorizing of Guthrie (11) and Hull (13) are sufficient documentation of this point for psychology in general. Second, the relative paucity of rewarding measurement techniques to gauge the stimulus dimensions of thematic cards has prevented research from moving forward. Productive research on the stimulus awaits upon ingenious solution to the diverse mensurational problems. Thirdly, the aversion of most workers within the projective field mirrors their profound minimization of stimulus factors or situations in determining behavior. Generally speaking, the content analysis of fantasy stories is personality centered, with only a token recognition of the fact that the stimulus properties of the cards may have affected the stories. Any comprehensive theory of fantasy, which is linked to apperceptive fantasy techniques, must be able to incorporate the stimulus variable into it.

As a consequence of this general failure to come to grips with the stimulus problem, the present formulation of the relation between stimulus properties of thematic cards and thematic fantasies cannot be expected to be too precise or extensive. A margin of error in the model is also to be expectd because comprehensive principles of levels of personality functioning and thinking are not available in psychology. And yet, progress in science seems directly related to the willingness of scientists to hypothesize about the properties of concepts, Skinner notwithstanding. This is what I propose to do.

It should be acknowledged that this theoretical framework has its derivation from some of Piaget's (32) contemporary ideas, Kanfer's (17) and Bruner's (6) illuminating analysis of perception, and Bartlett's (2) notions on schema.

THE MODEL

Any experimentally aroused behavior, including fantasy production, may be viewed as a function of four main classes of variables: (a) changes in sensory input from the physical environment — comprising the test stimuli in the case of apperceptive fantasy techniques, (b) organismic or physiological, (c) psychological, including perceptual, learning, motivational and thought processes, and (d) methodological or experimental design features of a study. Under the latter variable, the social context of the test situation and serial position effects of thematic pictures would be subsumed. Probably no one would disagree with such a relatively neutral conceptualization, nor would they dispute the statement that very little is known about how these variables operate in thematic stories. Accordingly, theory is an indispensable guide through this muddy terrain of unknowns.

The theoretical model centers around the conception that *changes in sensory input are assimilated into a schema after a hypothetical process of differentiation or categorization of the stimulus has taken place.* This implies that picture stimuli never really elicit the storyteller's fantasies in their own right. Stimuli modify and maintain existing schema or reactivate previously established schema. Once a schema is activated by the differentiating reaction that occurs to the picture stimuli and the tester's instructions, instrumental story-telling behavior occurs that *accommodates* an individual to his environment. Within this model, perception of the picture stimuli is not passive reception, but is an active process of categorization or differentiation.

Some definitions of the concepts used in this model are in order. If you consider, as I do, that science does not demand closed or precise definitions of its terms in virgin areas of investigation, then do not expect sharply delineated meanings of these terms. I offer no apology for this possible fuzziness, other than stating my conviction that all scientific concepts are open-ended.

Assimilation refers to the process of incorporation of stimuli into a schema by differentiation or categorization. Within this framework, *perception* means the process of categorization whereby the subject identifies, labels, categorizes, or differentiates dimensions of a stimulus. The categorization may be conscious, preconscious, or unconscious. In the case of TAT protocols the categorization process is assumed to be primarily preconscious, that is, it is readily available in awareness. The categorizing systems are to be thought of as so many "analysers" which act as neural systems for identifying distal stimuli. When an analyser fires, only a limited amount of the total information in a stimulus will be passed on to the next stage, namely, the arousal of schematized ways of thinking and remembering. Mandler (24) and Postman (33) have stressed the importance of categorization reactions as mediators of learning. In the field of perception, Bruner (6), the Gibsons (9), and Kanfer (17) have emphasized their critical role. *Schema* refer to imaginative trains or sequences of thought. Schemata should not be thought of as so much "storage" in a digital computer, nor should they be thought of as "traces" in the central nervous system. Schemata are assumed to be under continuous revision, change and transformation, with new information added and old information altered. Our schematized ways of remembering and thinking are used to deal with new experiences, such as being requested to tell a TAT story. Schematic determination of TAT stories is more than the mechanical running off of memories organized into schematic patterns. The schematically remembered material will be reconstructed and organized into thought patterns so that the story behavior is somewhat accommodated to the total demands of the TAT testing situation. *Accommodation* refers to the instrumental adaptive behavior that is aroused by a schema. In other words, themata are the expression of schemata!

The foregoing skeleton outline of the theoretical schema presents only the main constructs of the system. It does not specify how the constructs are anchored to the four main classes of the previously mentioned variables. The main emphasis of the discussion will be on how the constructs of categorization and schema are related to sensory input from picture stimuli. At the same time, some discussion of methodological and psychological variables will be necessary.

THE CRITICAL ROLE OF CATEGORIZATION REACTIONS

We should not make the mistake of confusing the stimulus properties of thematic picture with the categorization (perceptual) reaction to it. The stimulus refers to changes in physical energy impinging on the eye when a picture is presented to a subject. The categorizing reaction is some perceptual activity evoked by the stimulus card. It is assumed that the availability of past experience as organized into schemata, motivation, set, and ability factors, are the four most important psychological variables determining the categorizing reaction.

When a thematic card is presented to a person, it is hypothesized that he attempts to identify, label, categorize, or differentiate certain of the stimulus dimensions of the picture. In short, he codes the stimulus input into some coding or categorizing system. "This picture presents a boy who is not interested in the violin," "The boy is thinking of success as a great violinist," "This girl wants to leave the farm," "They are in love," "The boy wishes to be a doctor" would all represent categorizing reactions. They are categorizing reactions because the stimulus input from a TAT card is assigned to categories or coding systems.

It will be immediately recognized that such statements go beyond the stimulus properties of the TAT cards. Perceptual reactions are always likely to go beyond environmental events because the latter are always referred to category systems. Of special interest in this connection is Weisskopf's (42) Transcendence Index which attempts to quantify the categorizing reactions that go beyond straight description when an individual is asked to describe what he sees in a TAT card. It is also interesting to note that our categorizing reactions refer to what Rosenzweig (35) calls *apperceptive* norms in contra-distinction to *thematic* norms. Apperceptive norms are stimulus-oriented in that they "pertain to the descriptive statements made by the subject about the stimulus materials presented to him" (35, pp. 476-477). Thematic norms, on the other hand, are subject-oriented and refer to the repetitive themata and needs contained in TAT stories. Unfortunately, the apperceptive norms for the TAT pictures provided by Rosenzweig and Fleming (36) were obtained from stories told to the TAT cards and not from card descriptions. If the categorization reactions are desired, then, rather than have subjects tell stories to picture stimuli, the subjects should be asked to describe what they see.

After the categorization reaction occurs, the sensory input, as categorized, is assumed to be assimilated into a schema; that is, into certain organized trains or sequences of thought. The resulting story is mediated by whatever the prevailing schema is. In this complex series of events, it is hypothesized that the categorizing reaction will be more highly correlated with the stimulus properties of the picture stimuli than will be the fantasy story. This assumption implies that the potency of learning experiences, set, and motivation to affect process constructs is greater in the case of schemata than in categorizing (perceptual) reactions. While the model's postulated relations between learning, set, and schemata are not the concern of this paper, I would like to mention one assumption about motivational effects upon schemata. The model assumes that schematized ideas will be disrupted if strong drive and unambiguous drive cues are present. Such a set of conditions is assumed to instigate anxiety which disrupts the organized schemata of an individual. Hence, these conditions should produce TAT stories which are disorganized, card-dominated, barren, and stereotyped. On the other hand, moderate drive states and intermediate drive cues should produce schemata which are drive-oriented. Accordingly, the TAT stories would be rich in drive content.

In order to determine which stimulus properties of a thematic card determine the categorizing reaction, it would be necessary to systematically manipulate the structural properties of the picture. If stimulus alteration failed to produce any shift in the categorizing reaction, such evidence would indicate that the critical stimulus dimensions correlated with perception have not been isolated. However, if the categorizing reaction were to change, such results would indicate that the critical stimulus dimensions controlling the categorizing reaction were isolated. According to our theorizing, if stimulus alterations fail to produce any change in the categorizing reaction, then no crucial changes in the thematic content of a story should ensue. On the other hand, if the stimulus changes are sufficient to trigger off different categorizing reactions, then it should follow that the thematic content of the story should also change in the direction of the schema associated with the categorizing reaction.

TESTABILITY AND SOME RESEARCH IMPLICATIONS

In this section the testability of the model will be discussed, along with further research implications.

Stimulus Ambiguity and Personality Revealingness. The hypothesis has long been held that there is a monotonic relationship between stimulus ambiguity and personality revealingness. Little is known, however, about the empirical status of such a belief. Before such a hypothesis can be tested, the elusive concepts of *stimulus ambiguity* and *personality* revealingness must be unambiguously defined! For purposes of clarification, two procedural avenues of defining stimulus ambiguity will be discussed, and an attempt will be made to show that only under certain special cases would the foregoing hypothesis be derived from our theoretical model.

One could define a scale of ascending stimulus ambiguity in terms of increasing physical impoverishment. This first approach will be viewed as defining the problem in terms of *physical ambiguity*. Impoverishment of the stimulus may be readily accomplished by several techniques, such as, reduction of time exposure, photographic blurring through reduced exposure, reduction of illumination level, random removal of stimuli, incomplete line tracings, and exposing the stimulus at different angular distances from a point of fixation. If one assumes that stimulus ambiguity is adequately defined in terms of physical impoverishment and that transcendence indices are adequate reflections of the amount of personality factors introduced, then the results of a series of experiments (42, 43, 44) indicate that the proposition under consideration is false. Within the present framework, however, such impoverishing methods would not ensure that stimulus ambiguity has been manipulated. While I do not wish to contend that such kinds of operations with thematic cards are either unjustifiable or do not produce interesting results, I would maintain that they do not ensure variations in ambiguity.

Stimuli, as stimuli, are never ambiguous. A stimulus refers to changes in physical energy impinging on a receptor. It does not make sense to talk of ambiguous physical stimuli. However, stimuli are ambiguous in perception when, and only when, they elicit different categorizing reactions within the same person at different times. Impoverishment of the stimulus would not necessarily ensure an increase in the number of categorizing reactions. In fact, their number might actually decrease under some conditions of stimulus impoverishment. Thus an adequate test of the hypothesis will necessitate thematic cards that elicit different categorizing reactions.

Accordingly, a second avenue of approach to ambiguity, and the one accepted here, is in terms of *perceptual or categorizing ambiguity*. This kind of ambiguity refers to a dispositional concept, and means "if a stimulus impinges on a receptor, it evokes different categorization reactions." In this approach, perceptual ambiguity is measured by recording the number of categorization reactions that a stimulus arouses. A good quantitative index of this ambiguity should take into account not only the number of alternative categorizations, but also the proportion of cases or individuals making any given categorization. The assumption behind such an index is that picture stimuli vary in at least two ways: (a) the number of stimuli available for different categorization reactions or perceptual reactions, and (b) the definiteness level of the stimuli to provoke a degree of perceptual response agreement.

Such an index is available from information theory, and its use in no way commits one to any of the assumptions of information theory. Assume, for example, that three different thematic cards, 1, 2, and 3, evoke four different categorization reactions, R_1, R_2, R_3, and R_4, and that the proportion of cases giving the four reactions is as follows:

	Thematic Cards		
Categorization	1	2	3
R_1	.96	.25	.50
R_2	.02	.25	.10
R_3	.01	.25	.20
R_4	.01	.25	.20

What thematic card is the most ambiguous? All three cards arouse the same number of different categorization reactions, indicating that the number of stimuli available for different perceptual reactions is the same. However, thematic card 1 is certainly more structured than the other two cards because the definiteness level of the stimuli in it provokes a degree of perceptual response agreement that is high. With respect to thematic cards 2 and 3, the former is probably more ambiguous than the latter because the definiteness level of its stimuli is not as high as card 3. The measure of uncertainty from information theory takes into account these two dimensions of picture stimuli. If we let *p(i)* indicate the proportion of cases in each of the categories, then $\hat{H}$, the measure of uncertainty, is

$$\hat{H} = -\Sigma p(i) \log_2 p(i)$$

for the case when the categorization alternatives are either equally alike or different. In the case of our artificial data, $\hat{H}$ is equal to .2557, 2.000 and 1,7510 for thematic cards 1, 2 and 3, respectively. It should be noted that as $\hat{H}$ increases, perceptual ambiguity increases.

A much simpler index, and one that gives similar results to the uncertainty measure, is

$$PA = 1 - \Sigma p(i)^2$$

where *p(i)* has the same meaning as before, and PA stands for perceptual ambiguity. Here, PA is equal to .08, .75 and .66 for thematic cards 1, 2 and 3, respectively.

Having defined a suitable index of ambiguity, let us see how our treatment of the problem can be extended to a method of obtaining the categorization reactions to picture stimuli. Research is under way on this method, but my comments have to be programmatic since I have no concrete data to present. The first phase of the research is to have subjects examine each TAT card for twenty seconds, and with the card before them, to describe what they see. The second step is like a critical incident study in that the card descriptions are assigned to critical categories that seem to best reflect the perceptual descriptions. The various critical categories are not formed *a priori,* but are empirically derived from the categorizing statements. It is proposed in the third phase of the research to provide a checklist of the main critical categories to subjects and have them check that category which they think best describes what they see in a given TAT card. The uncertainty measure will be applied to the data in order to provide a quantitative index of the ambiguity for each thematic card.

A sampling of some of the procedural problems that need to be investigated with this method are: optimal length of exposure of the TAT cards, the formulation of the critical categories to adequately reflect the categorizing reactions, the extent of agreement between independent judges in arriving at the same critical categories, and how many sentences are required of the subjects in order to obtain an adequate sample of the categorizing reactions. The changes in categorizing reactions that take place as a function of age, sex, personality, and cultural factors all need to be extensively studied before this proposed measure of perceptual ambiguity is fully understood. Indeed, these are all difficult problems to solve, but they should not be insurmountable.

Inasmuch as this new measure of ambiguity is somewhat different from methods used in previous studies (3, 4, 14, 15, 16, 18, 19, 20, 26, 30, 38), it seems appropriate at this time to compare the various procedures that have been employed to obtain picture stimuli that vary in degree of perceptual ambiguity. Studies of perceptual ambiguity have used three methods. In the *subjective consensus* method judges are usually asked to rank order the thematic cards on the basis of their ambiguity; this is the method used in the investigations of Bijou and Kenny, Kagan, Lawton, Murray, Murstein, and Scott. In some studies (16), the expert opinion of the experimenters has been relied upon to define the ambiguity properties of TAT cards. The main objection to the subjective consensus method is that it is deficient with respect to the problem of weighting the different categorization alternatives. In fact, the procedure ignores this problem. In the *normative* method, as employed by Berg and Polyot (3), a set of incompletely drawn stimulus pictures of everyday subjects or objects were shown to subjects who had to identify what the stimulus figures were. The normative index of a structured stimulus card was defined in terms of more than 50 per cent of the subjects correctly identifying the stimulus figure. All other stimulus cards were called ambiguous. The criticism of the previous method is also applicable here. In addition, the method is limited to picture stimuli of objects that can be either correctly or incorrectly recognized. In the *themata checklist or ranking* method subjects are asked to rank order a list of needs or goals that are thought to be portrayed in each thematic picture. An operational measure of ambiguity may be computed by obtaining "the average intercorrelation between the rankings of the same picture by all of the judges" (14, p. 625). If the average intercorrelation between the rankings of the needs for a picture is high, this would indicate that the picture is structured in meaning. A low average intercorrelation would identify an ambiguous picture. Two criticisms may be made of the themata ranking method. First, this method also fails to take into account the problem of weighting the proportion of subjects who give different categorization reactions. Second, the procedure of providing subjects with needs or goal concerns would seem to define the ambiguity of thematic cards in terms of themata, and not in terms of stimulus (perceptual) ambiguity. Since our new technique for defining ambiguity takes into account the weighting problem and relates the picture stimuli to perceptual reactions, it is thought to be more satisfactory than the previously employed methods. In any case, it would be most interesting to determine if the different procedures for scaling picture stimuli for ambiguity produce similar results.

This entire methodological discussion of ambiguity was a necessary detour before we could present our analysis of the widely accepted hypothesis of a positive relationship between stimulus ambiguity and personality revealingness. Our previous research (18, 4) indicated that a curvilinear relationship exists between the ambiguity of TAT cards and personality revealingness. In the Bijou and Kenny (4) study, three sets of TAT cards varying in degree of perceptual ambiguity were given to a group of male subjects. We defined ambiguity in terms of the estimated number of interpretations a group of judges thought would apply to each TAT card. Two clinical psychologists, utilizing a Q-sort method, judged the significance of the personality factors injected into the stories. The cards of medium ambiguity (TAT cards 4, 7 BM, 8 BM, 12 M, and 13 MF) revealed the most about personality factors. There were no differences between the least ambiguous cards (TAT cards 12 BG, 1, 2, 9 BM, and 17 BM) and the most ambiguous set (TAT cards 5, 15, 18 BM, 11 and 19). In the other study (18), it was shown that the cards of medium ambiguity had the highest transcendence indices. The fact that the hypothesis was not confirmed in these two studies may have been a consquence of several factors that are worth mentioning. First, the procedure of defining ambiguity left much to be desired. Second, the operational definition of personality revealingness used in these studies may be open to criticism.

Personality revealingness was defined in terms of the Q-sorts of two clinicians who sorted the separate stories of all the subjects in terms of how revealing they thought the stories. Some, (45) might object to this method on the grounds that it is clinically naive to ask judges to assess individual stories of a person for personality significance out of context of the total TAT protocol. It is quite true that this method will miss repetitive themes. To such a criticism I would like to make several comments. First, the correlation between the two judges was .68, indicating that the cues made use of by the clinicians were not entirely equivocal. Second, the obtained relationship seems meaningful in light of the findings of other investigators who have used our three sets of ambiguous cards. For example, Murstein (30) found a significant curvilinear relationship between our ordering of the TAT cards for ambiguity and the productivity of themes, as indicated by Eron's (8) normative study. Ullmann (40) has shown that clinicians make more frequent use of the TAT cards in the moderate ambiguity group than in the other two sets. Gurel and Ullmann (10) found that the intermediate group produced higher transcendence indices than the other two sets. Such findings permit some confidence in our procedures. Finally, this possible criticism will be investigated in future studies by having one set of clinicians judge all the stories of a subject to a set of cards of a specified level of ambiguity and another set of clinicians will assess the separate stories for revealingness. I suspect that both procedures will not be different in the results they provide.

I now wish to turn to a general discussion of the conditions under which the hypothesis of a positive relationship between ambiguity and revealingness may be expected to be valid or invalid. In order to focus our attention on the implications of our model for this hypothesis, three aspects of the problem will be discussed: (a) the nature of the stimulus dimensions of the cards, (b) whether global judgments of personality significance or separate dimensions of personality are being assessed, and (c) the drive level of the subjects.

Since the discriminatory reactions to the stimulus properties of thematic apperception cards are, in part, dependent upon stimulus generalization, and recognizing that everyday learning experiences are directed toward people, it seems reasonable to hypothesize that the lack of clarity in facial expressions and/or activities of the portrayed persons, the omission of humans or the presence of only one human in contrast to two humans in social interaction should produce increases in perceptual ambiguity. In terms of such criteria, card 19 of the TAT is highly ambiguous. The model makes the following prediction: as the non-social aspects of thematic cards are increased, personality revealingness should decrease. The experimental testing of this hypothesis, and the related one that ambiguity increases as the non-social aspects of the cards increase, should be a relatively straightforward one.

In terms of their stimulus complexity, two different kinds of thematic apperceptive tests should be distinguished. One kind is composed of pictures that evoke a wide variety of conflicts and drives. The TAT is the classic illustration of this type of fantasy test. The other kind involves pictures that have been scaled for a single problem or drive. The set of ten pictures constructed by Lesser (23) to measure aggressive fantasy would be an example of this second type of apperceptive test. In his cards, the number of figures was constant for all pictures, and the stimulus cues for drives, other than aggression, were minimized.

With the second type of apperceptive test, the pictures are usually scaled to insure an ordering of them in terms of the personality dimension being measured. That is, the cards vary along a continuum of ambiguity for a particular personality variable. If one were to score or Q-sort the stories told to the pictures for the personality variable measured by them, one would have to find a perfect inverse relationship between stimulus ambiguity and the personality variable score. If it were not perfect, this would indicate that there was a margin of error in the original scaling of the pictures. However, the finding of an inverse relationship would not invalidate the hypothesis of a positive relationship between ambiguity and revealingness because the results are attributable to the test construction procedures. Accordingly, personality revealingness for the second type of thematic apperception test would have to be defined in terms of some external criterion behavior. Thus, the set of cards that has the highest correlation with some criterion behavior would be regarded as the most revealing.

One interesting implication of the commonly accepted hypothesis of a positive relationship between ambiguity and revealingness is that the most ambiguous cards should provide the most fruitful stories for valid inferences to external criteria. On the other hand, our model would only predict a linear relationship between ambiguity and revealingness in the case of subjects with mild-to-moderate drives. A curvilinear or inverted U-shaped relationship is expected for subjects with strong drives. My conception is that, as picture stimuli become more drive-structured, anxiety will constrict the schemata of strong drive subjects and the richness of their stories should start to decrease.

In a broad way, experiments by Kagan (15), Murray (26), Stone (39), and Epstein and Smith (7) are relevant to these contrasting predictions. However, these studies do not permit one to make a decision between the alternative hypotheses because the exact stimulus properties of the thematic cards and the precise range of the drive level of the subjects are not clear. The study by Kagan showed that the picture most suggestive of aggression was more predictive of overt aggression than the least suggestive picture. In regard to drive strength, I may infer that the elementary school children serving as subjects had low-to-medium aggressive drives as compared to children who may have to be confined because of serious assaultive offenses. If this is the case, then ambiguous aggressive cards are less predictive of overt aggression than more structured aggressive cards. Such a finding is in keeping with our model's linear hypothesis for mild-to-medium drive subjects. In examining the effects of about 86 hours' sleep deprivation on TAT stories. Murray found that sleep-deprived subjects had significantly fewer sleep themes than control subjects on a high sleep suggestion card. There was no difference between the experimentals and controls on either a low or medium sleep suggestion card. Interestingly enough, the two groups did not differ for fatigue themes, tension ratings, or number of words on the sleep cards. Similarly, on a series of three TAT cards graded in terms of hostility, Murray found no difference between the two groups for hostility themes.

In general, then, Murray's experiment shows that strong-drive subjects, relative to low-drive subjects, manifest a constriction in the number of sleep themes to a well-structured sleep card, a finding consistent with our model prediction.

In testing predictions to the external criterion of arithmetic performance by way of achievement fantasy scores, Reitman and Atkinson (34) found that need-achievement scores based on achievement-related pictures did not predict the external criterion any better than need-achievement scores based on affiliation-related pictures. If the achievement-related pictures were only moderately ambiguous for the achievement drive and the drive level of the subjects was only low-to-medium, my model would have serious difficulty in handling such a finding. At any rate, the precise generality of the finding should be subjected to detailed empirical study. Such studies should have precise estimates of the ambiguity of the cards and the drive level of the subjects.

It should be noted that the Reitman and Atkinson finding is not in agreement with the work of Stone (39) who found that TAT cards with moderate "aggressive pull" (Cards 3 BM and 3 GF) produced the greatest discrimination between assaultive and non-assaultive prisoners. High "aggressive pull" pictures (Cards 13 MF, 18 GF, and 19 BM) were not as discriminatory. Undoubtedly, the drive level of Stone's subjects was considerably stronger than that of the subjects in the Reitman and Atkinson study. In addition, the studies differ in the drives measured and the criterion predicted. Stone was predicting from fantasy aggression to overt aggression. Reitman and Atkinson were predicting from fantasy achievement to arithmetic performance. It seems reasonable to interpret Stone's results as being in conformity with our model's predictions. To bring us full circle round, Epstein and Smith (7) showed that a picture with low-pull is a better predictor than either a high picture-pull card or moderate picture-pull cards. They found that their "hungry group, relative to the control group, gave more hunger-related responses to low picture-pull, fewer such responses to high picture-pull, and did not respond differentially to moderate picture-pull" (7, p. 383).

The authors interpreted their findings as an indication of inhibitory reactions in strong drive subjects to highly need-relevant stimuli. Their experiment raises several interesting and important methodological problems. First, it indicates a need for standardization of terms in this area of research. What one investigator may call a strong drive, another may call a moderate drive. Similarly, a well-structured card for one researcher may be a moderately ambiguous card for another. It should be noted, for example, that their hungry group had only been deprived of food for four hours. While the authors speak of this group as a strong drive group, I would call it a mild drive group. Until terminological differences between investigators are resolved and a methodology of defining ambiguity is standardized, it will be practically impossible to compare different studies. A second point about their experiment is that only one picture stimulus was used at each of the high and moderate picture-pull levels. I would suspect that any data based upon a single picture stimulus would be most unreliable. Consequently, their study bears replication in order to see if the same results occur. In light of these considerations, the Epstein and Smith findings are regarded as equivocal in terms of our theoretical model.

While these five studies call attention to the possible relation between ambiguity of picture stimuli and specific dimensions of personality, they are very inconclusive in their findings and do not provide crucial tests of our conceptual formulations. Further research must be conducted to resolve the apparent contradictions between these studies, and to clarify and extend the assumed relations between ambiguity and revealingness.

Relationships between Categorization and Story Content. For final purposes of exposition of the theoretical model, I wish to mention some additional implications of it.

I have assumed that categorization reactions to picture stimuli are assimilated into a schema which determines the story content. Hence, once the categorization reaction occurs, the picture stimuli should only play a minimal role in the determination of a particular thema. From such an assumption, it may be hypothesized that any procedure which arouses a categorization reaction similar to the one of a picture stimulus should produce the same kind of thema or story content as the picture stimulus. Two kinds of available evidence would seem to support the validity of this hypothesis. In the first place, it has been found that verbal descriptions of thematic apperception cards seem to evoke comparable kinds of story telling as the picture cards themselves. Lebo and Harrington (22) found that the emotional tone of the stories, the level of response, and common themes were very similar under visual and verbal presentation of the TAT cards. McClelland, Atkinson, Clark and Lowell (25) have reported similar results. It may be surmised that the verbal and visual presentation of the TAT cards aroused similar categorizations in the subjects.

Most of the findings from what I have called physical ambiguity studies provide the second line of support for the hypothesis. For example, the correlation between transcendence indices and personality revealingness for five-second and two-minute exposure time of TAT cards was .62 and .64, respectively (18). Such a finding indicates that the categorization reaction takes place at around five seconds, and that longer exposure of TAT cards does not radically alter the revealingness of the stories. It also supports Murray's (28) new way of exposing the TAT cards to patients. He now permits the subject to examine a picture for only twenty seconds and then it is removed.

A converse implication of the model is that procedures which change the categorization reaction to picture stimuli should produce changes in story content. The design for this kind of study could be essentially similar to the experiments that have shown transfer effects of verbal pre-training upon the learning of discriminative motor responses (12, 37). One or more experimental groups would be given verbal pre-training to picture stimuli and their subsequent stories would be compared to those of a control group which had no pre-training. For example, if two comparable sets of aggressive cards were constructed, one set could be used for the verbal pre-training. Subjects could be asked to describe the cards to the first set and specified kinds of categorizing reactions could be reinforced. It would have to be shown, of course, that the pre-training increased the number of categorization reactions relative to a control group whose categorizations were not reinforced. If the number increased in the pre-training, it would be predicted that the effects of this verbal pre-training would be to alter the story content.

SUMMARY

Historically, the stimulus properties of thematic apperceptive techniques have acted as a form of aversive stimulation to clinicians and theorists alike. To aversive stimuli, we usually respond with avoidance. It is probably not unfair to say that avoidance has been the commonest reaction to the problems posed by thematic stimuli. In this connection, I have emphasized not only the lack of research on stimulus dimensions of thematic apperceptive tests but also the inability of current conceptual models to satisfactorily account for the functions of thematic stimuli. In short, we have suffered from a form of functional blindness.

An attempt was made to improve upon this state of affairs by outlining a tentative conceptual model of the functions of picture stimuli. The model is not, of course, wholly original with me. The model centers around the notion that picture stimuli function as arousers of categorizing reactions. The categorizing reactions are assimilated into schemata and the fantasy story is the consequence of the schemata. In order to consider the testability of the model, it was primarily applied to the problem of the relation between ambiguity and personality revealingness. The relevant research literature was reviewed in terms of the derivations from the model, and it was concluded that the evidence to date lends some support to the model. A detailed analysis was also made of certain of the methodological problems involved in measuring ambiguity and personality revealingness.

REFERENCES

1. Atkinson, J. W.: (Ed.) *Motives in Fantasy, Action, and Society.* New York, Van Nostrand, 1958.
2. Bartlett, F. C.: *Remembering.* Cambridge, Cambridge Univ. Press, 1932.
3. Berg, J. and Polyot, C. J.: The influence of color on reactions to incomplete figures. *J. Consult. Psychol., 20*:9-15. 1956.
4. Bijou, S. W., and Kenny, D. T.: The ambiguity of TAT cards. *J. Consult. Psychol., 15*:203-209. 1951.
5. Birney, R. C.: Thematic content and the cue characteristics of pictures. In J. W. Atkinson (Ed.) *Motives in Fantasy, Action, and Society.* New York, Van Nostrand, 1958.
6. Bruner, J.: On perceptual readiness. *Psychol. Rev., 64*:123-152, 1957.
7. Epstein, S., and Smith, R.: Thematic apperception as a measure of the hunger drive. *J. Proj. Tech., 20:*372-384. 1956.
8. Eron, L. D.: A normative study of the Thematic Apperception Test. *Psychol. Monogr., 64*: No. 9 (Whole No. 315). 1950.
9. Gibson, J. J. and Gibson, Eleanor J.: Perceptual learning: differentiation or enrichment? *Psychol. Rev., 62*:32-41. 1957.
10. Gurel, L. and Ullmann, L. P.: Quantitative differences in response to TAT cards: the relationship between transcendence score and number of emotional words. *J. Proj. Tech., 22*:399-401. 1958.
11. Guthrie, E. R.: *The Psychology of Learning.* (Rev. Ed.) New York, Harper, 1952.
12. Hoffeld, D. R.: Transfer from verbal pre-training to motor performance as a function of response similarity and angle of movement. *J. Exp. Psychol., 54*:353-357. 1957.
13. Hull, C. L.: *Principles of Behavior.* New York, Appleton, 1943.
14. Jacobs, B.: A method for investigating the cue characteristics of pictures. In J. W. Atkinson (Ed.) *Motives in Fantasy, Action, and Society.* New York, Van Nostrand, 1958.
15. Kagan, J.: The measurement of overt aggression from fantasy. *J. Abnorm. & Social Psychol., 52:*390-393. 1956.
16. Kagan, J.: The stability of TAT fantasy and stimulus ambiguity. *J. Consult. Psychol., 23*:266-271. 1959.
17. Kanfer, F. H.: Perception: identification and instrumental activity. *Psychol. Rev., 63*:317-329. 1956.

18. Kenny, D. T.: Transcendence indices, extent of personality factors in fantasy responses, and the ambiguity of TAT cards. *J. Consult. Psychol., 18*:345-348. 1954.
19. Kenny, D. T., and Bijou, S. W.: Ambiguity of pictures and extent of personality factors in fantasy responses. *J. Consult. Psychol., 17*:283-288. 1953.
20. Lawton, M. P.: Stimulus structure as a determinant of the perceptual response. *J. Consult. Psychol., 20*:351-355. 1956.
21. Lazarus, R. S.: Ambiguity and non-ambiguity in projective testing. *J. Abnorm. Social Psychol., 48*:443-445. 1953.
22. Lebo, D., and Harrigan, Margaret: Visual and verbal presentation of TAT stimuli. *J. Consult, Psychol., 21*:339-342. 1957.
23. Lesser, G. S.: Application of Guttman's scaling method to aggressive fantasy in children. *Educ. Psychol. Measmt., 18*:543-551. 1958.
24. Mandler, G.: Response factors in human learning. *Psychol. Rev., 61*:235-244. 1954.
25. McClelland, D. C., Atkinson, J. W., Clark, R. A., and Lowell, E. L.: *The Achievement Motive*. New York, Appleton, 1953.
26. Murray, E. J.: Conflict and repression during sleep deprivation. *J. Abnorm. & Social Psychol., 59*:95-101. 1959.
27. Murray, H. A.: *Thematic Apperception Test*. Cambridge, Harvard Univ. Press, 1943.
28. Murray, H. A.: Uses of the Thematic Apperception Test. *Amer. J. Psychiat., 107*:557-581. 1951.
29. Murstein, B. I.: Nonprojective determinants of perception on the TAT. *J. Consult. Psychol., 22*:195-198. 1958.
30. Murstein, B. I.: The relationship of stimulus ambiguity on the TAT to productivity of themes. *J. Consult. Psychol., 22*:348. 1958.
31. Murstein, B. I.: A conceptual model of projective techniques applied to stimulus variations with thematic techniques. *J. Consult. Psychol., 23*:3-14. 1959.
32. Piaget, J.: *The Origins of Intelligence in Children*. New York, Internat. Univ. Press, 1952.
33. Postman, L. J.: The analysis of incidental learning. In J. J. Jenkins (Ed.) *Associative Processes in Verbal Behavior*. Univ. of Minnesota, 1955.
34. Reitman, W. R., and Atkinson, J. W.: Some methodological problems in the use of thematic apperceptive measures of human motives. In J. W. Atkinson (Ed.) *Motives in Fantasy, Action, and Society*. New York, Van Nostrand, 1958, pp. 664-683.
35. Rosenzweig, S.: Apperceptive norms for the Thematic Apperception

tion Test I. The problem of norms in projective methods. *J. Pers., 17*:475-482. 1949.

36. Rosenzweig, S., and Fleming, Edith E.: Apperceptive norms for the Thematic Apperception Test II. An empirical investigation. *J. Pers., 17*:483-503. 1949.
37. Rossman, I. L., and Goss, A. E.: The acquired distinctiveness of cues: The role of discriminative verbal responses in facilitating the acquisition of discriminative motor responses. *J. Exp. Psychol., 42*:173-182. 1951.
38. Scott, W. A.: The avoidance of threatening material in imaginative behavior. *J. Abnorm. & Social Psychol., 52*:338-436. 1956.
39. Stone, J.: The TAT aggressive content scale. *J. Proj. Tech., 20*:445-452. 1956.
40. Ullmann, L.: Productivity and the clinical use of TAT cards. *J. Proj. Tech., 21*:399-403. 1957.
41. Watson, J. B.: Psychology as the behaviorist views it. *Psychol. Rev., 20*:158-177. 1913.
42. Weisskopf, Edith A.: A transcendence index as a proposed measure in the TAT. *J. Psychol., 29*:379-390. 1950.
43. Weisskopf, Edith A.: An experimental study of the effect of brightness and ambiguity in projection in the Thematic Apperception Test. *J. Psychol., 29*:407-416. 1950.
44. Weisskopf, Edith A., and Lynn, D. B.: The effect of variations in ambiguity on projection in the Children's Apperception Test. *J. Consult. Psychol., 17*:67-70. 1953.
45. Wyatt, F., and Veroff, Joanne B.: Thematic apperception and fantasy tests. In D. Brower and L. E. Abt (Eds.) *Progress in Clinical Psychology*. Vol. 2. New York, Grune & Stratton, 1956.

DISCUSSION OF DR. KENNY'S PAPER

Paul H. Mussen, Ph.D.
Primary Discussant

Dr. Mussen: I should like to raise two issues. Dr. Kenny's paper outlined how to derive a measure of ambiguity, taking into account not only the number of different categorization reactions, but also the proportion of cases giving any particular categorization reaction. This bears on a very disturbing and confusing issue: statistical versus individual criteria for ambiguity. A statistical criterion, based on group data, seems to me to be very much a secondary concern, unless, of course, you are interested in stimuli as stimuli. The real concern is whether or not the stimulus is ambiguous to the *subject*. Thus, in Dr. Kenny's Table, 25 percent of his subjects make responses R_1 to Card 2, and this card is considered a highly ambiguous one. Actually, however, each individual making response R_1 or R_2 may not find the stimulus ambiguous. It may be a very clear, highly structured one as far as he is concerned, even though, in a group of people, different interpretations occur (and hence the stimulus is considered ambiguous from a statistical, or information theory point of view). In short, it seems that two types of ambiguity are confused. The same point was made earlier by Dr. Lesser in his discussion of Dr. Murstein's paper, but the confusion seems neatly illustrated in the Table in Dr. Kenny's paper.

I should also like to ask a very general question that bears upon the theoretical importance of Dr. Kenny's model. I can see the importance of "attention to the stimulus" as a technological and diagnostic (clinical) problem, but can it be conceptually linked to theory, and, more specifically, to a theory of human motivation?

Dr. Kenny: I think it can. I am trying to indicate that there is an interaction, for example, between certain properties of the card and drive level; what the resultant story will be; and how my proposed model is capable of making certain kinds of predictions.

Dr. Tomkins: While I think that Dr. Kenny's proposed model has important theoretical implications, what we must elaborate in conjunction with it is a theory about the relationship of the stimulus to the mediating processes. This is the big problem, and I would like to make the beginning of a suggestion about how this might work. It seems to me that what we need here is a theory of memory; that is, a theory of how information is retrieved when sensory input comes into the sensory channels. My assumption is that any organized final product of information, whether it pertains to a percept, an action, or a thought, is composed of a number of component messages, which are programmed in much the same way that a computer is programmed. Were the time available, I could illustrate this approach with examples from our research. But the general point is that, important as the stimulus is, we ought to move away from it, actually, into what is going on in the human being and how he organizes his information.

Dr. Kenny: I couldn't agree with you more. There are two problems that need to be studied systematically. One is how memories are recalled from stimulus input. But I think there is also another more crucial question, and I think Dr. Tomkins was implying it in his remarks: how are memory trains organized one on top of the other? I could outline here several studies on retroactive interference, where I have what I would call organized sequences of thoughts placed into a typical retroactive interference design. I am obtaining results which are very predictable in terms of what I think my model would predict.

Dr. Mussen: I should like to raise a question concerning the relationship between the two processes hypothesized in your model, the categorization process and the schemata process. You referred to the schema or schemata as a process or processes. It was my impression that once the categorization is done, the schema process automatically follows.

Dr. Kenny: They are sequential in the model I propose.

Dr. Mussen: This is what disturbs me. Once you have categorized the picture, there is nothing left to do; the schema simply follows.

Dr. Kenny: Yes, the stimulus is done as far the the picture is concerned, after he has categorized it.

Dr. Mussen: Then, what is the link between the category that results and the categorization process and the schemata?

Dr. Kenny: I think certain internal associations are built in between categorization processes and schemata processes, just in terms of the way we learn things in life; there are interconnections, inter-associations.

Dr. Tomkins: I don't think anyone will argue with that point, but there is quite a jump between that and the finished story. In other words, I have never said the sentence I am saying in the last five minutes before in my life; I am tailoring what I am saying to what you are saying. If I simply relied upon my past memory and schema I would be quite a stupid speaker.

Dr. Kenny: The schemata are there, and are fired, and then the individual accommodates himself to the environment. In other words, there will be certain changes, and this is all that I say.

Dr. Mussen: When I first read this, I made a kind of analogy — maybe a false one — between afferent and efferent nerves, and I could not get the two together. Categorization and the schemata seemed to be parts of the afferent system, but then the efferent connections are not apparent, because clearly you are not assuming only one link. There also has to be some linkage between the categorization and schema on the one hand, and the efferent process (that is, the story or fantasy that the *S* gives) on the other.

Dr. Kenny: I would accept this; the schema certainly has to be anchored in behavior.

Dr. Mussen: But it also manifests itself indirectly.

Dr. Kenny: This is where I tried to bring in the notion of accommodation.

Dr. Tomkins: If I understand you correctly, you are saying that after the schemata get retrieved, then there is a further process of transformation which you call *accommodation to the environment.* I would have called it something else, but that is trivial. But that seems to me to be a very critical part of the theory.

Dr. Kenny: Your understanding is correct, but it is probably not made explicit enough in my presentation.

Dr. Feshbach: There is another disturbing problem in this analysis of the relationship between categorization and schemata. The factors that influence the categorization reaction may be intimately related to the schemata reaction. I do see some distinction between them. But in social prejudice, for example, Allport has observed that the prejudiced individual selects a stimulus dimension, yet prejudice is part of the same schemata that will influence his subsequent reaction to the person. So it is not a one-way reaction in any simple sense; schemata feed back on the category reaction. While it is in some ways useful to make the distinction, it is not clear as to the direction of influence.

Dr. Kenny: In the main what you are saying is quite correct. That it is a two-way channel system and I have only worked out one channel at the present moment, I would accept.

Dr. Feshbach: I suppose the distinction between categorization reaction and schemata is a continuing thing. For example, a subject says, "The boy is thinking of success as a great violinist." The categorization of a boy and the reference to a violin seem reasonable categorizations. Thinking of success seems to me to be part of the schemata notion, and so it probably is somewhat of a continuing interacting process, and certain statements are difficult to assign to categorization or schemata.

Dr. Tomkins: Couldn't this aspect of your model be demonstrated experimentally in the following way? As you vary the kind of question you ask of a subject when you present him with a TAT card, his responses change. An individual complies with what you ask. You can ask him to do elementary operations, medium operations, or very complex ones with the same stimulus.

Dr. Kenny: The illustrations I provided are probably obtained from the simplest kind of operation, similar to that which you have just described.

EPILOGUE

For too many years the language and conceptualizations that surrounded projective tests have been divorced from the main corpus of psychological thinking. The conference included representatives from both areas and several points of contact and agreement were apparent throughout the four day meeting.

The application of Miller's approach-avoidance paradigm to thematic responses constitutes a powerful guide for the understanding of existing data and the invention of new instruments. Miller's model predicts that as the picture stimuli became more suggestive of goal related, conflictful behavior there should be a tendency for the goal related content to be inhibited by individuals with conflict in the area illustrated. It seems appropriate, therefore, to construct instruments that contain stimuli both ambiguous and nonambiguous for conflicted motives and assess differences in content to the two types of stimuli.

Theoretically, the high conflict person should show, to the nonambiguous pictures, a greater inhibition of the conflicted content and greater distortion of the stimulus than low conflict individuals. The pattern of behavior to ambiguous and nonambiguous stimuli could yield a sensitive index of conflict. The eventual construction of series of stimuli for various motive areas seems to be a reasonable task for the future.

Kenny's application of Piaget's notions of assimilation, accommodation, and schemata to the apperceptive response links thematic behavior with a theoretical network concerned with all intellective processes. The balance between assimilation and accommodation is an index of reality orientation and these ideas provide clues to understanding the psychic events that mediate the bizarre and autistic story.

The approach-avoidance model, the chained sequence of categorization and schemata, the possibility of scaling thematic stimuli — all of these suggestions direct our attention to the *stimulus.* Second only to the question of whether stories measure motives, the conference repeatedly stressed the role of the eliciting stimulus in the apperceptive interpretation. This return to the stimulus (Tomkins called it "the return of the repressed") promises to provide a greater predictive power to the apperceptive method.

Conferences are delicate affairs. Their success is measured in terms of the stimulation of new ideas and the cross-fertilization of information. This process depends on the group atmosphere and receptivity of each scientist to challenge and debate. The editors hope that this spirit, which we believe was present at the meeting, was captured in the edited remarks.

AUTHOR INDEX

SUBJECT INDEX

www.ingramcontent.com/pod-product-compliance
Ingram Content Group UK Ltd.
Pitfield, Milton Keynes, MK11 3LW, UK
UKHW041131071026
15587UKWH00009B/409

9 780837 188423